Lindsay Coleman is a film and television academic completing his doctorate at the University of Melbourne. The books he has contributed to include *The War Body on Screen*, *Taking South Park Seriously* and *Gilmore Girls and the Politics of Identity*. He has also served as Editor on the anthology *The Philosophy of Pornography*.

'It is commonly claimed that pornographic films haven't got convincing narratives. Normally, this is meant as a criticism, but others have responded that this misses the point – that pornographic films are not meant to act narratively. The current volume offers an alternative to both of these claims and examines the relationship between sex and storytelling in a range of different ways. Largely focused on contemporary cinematic representations of sexual acts, the volume includes contributions by an impressive range of names and should prove a provocative contribution to literature.'

Mark Jancovich, Professor of Film Studies, The University of East Anglia

SEX AND STORYTELLING IN MODERN CINEMA

EXPLICIT SEX, PERFORMANCE AND CINEMATIC TECHNIQUE

EDITOR: LINDSAY COLEMAN

I.B. TAURIS
LONDON · NEW YORK

Published in 2016 by
I.B.Tauris & Co. Ltd
London • New York
www.ibtauris.com

The right of Lindsay Coleman to be identified as the editor of this work has been asserted by him in accordance with the Copyright, Designs and Patents Act 1988.

Copyright Editorial Selection © 2016 Lindsay Coleman

Copyright Individual Chapters © 2016 David Andrews, Chelsea Birks, Lisa Coulthard, Barbara Creed, Taine Duncan, Torben Grodal, Jacob M. Held, Claire Hines, Beth Johnson, Sean Redmond, Deborah Walker-Morrison and Linda Ruth Williams

All rights reserved. Except for brief quotations in a review, this book, or any part thereof, may not be reproduced, stored in or introduced into a retrieval system, or transmitted, in any form or by any means, electronic, mechanical, photocopying, recording or otherwise, without the prior written permission of the publisher.

Every attempt has been made to gain permission for the use of the images in this book. Any omissions will be rectified in future editions.

References to websites were correct at the time of writing.

International Library of the Moving Image 19

ISBN: 978 1 78076 639 3 HB
978 1 78076 640 9 PB
eISBN: 978 0 85772 888 3

A full CIP record for this book is available from the British Library
A full CIP record is available from the Library of Congress

Library of Congress Catalog Card Number: available

Typeset by Freerange Book Design & Production Limited
Printed and bound in Great Britain by T.J. International, Padstow, Cornwall

Dedicated to my love Sarah and our little darling Audrey

Contents

	Contributors	ix
	Illustrations	xiii
	Acknowledgements	xvii
	Introduction	1
1	*Maîtresse*: Pornography, Ritual and the Question of the Animal *Barbara Creed*	9
2	What is and is not Porn: Sex, Narrative, and *Baise-moi* *Jacob M. Held*	25
3	Perverse Passions: Catherine Breillat's *Une vieille maîtresse* *Deborah Walker-Morrison*	49
4	Horrible Sex: The Sexual Relationship in New Extremism *Lisa Coulthard and Chelsea Birks*	71
5	*Shortbus*: Smart Cinema and Sexual Utopia *Linda Ruth Williams*	95
6	Becoming Animal in *Lust, Caution* *Sean Redmond*	119
7	Sex, Drugs and Rock and Roll: Analysing Aesthetics, Performance and Pleasure in *9 Songs* *Beth Johnson*	137
8	Tragedy of Hands: Rape in Gaspar Noé's *Irréversible* *David Andrews*	159

9	*Antichrist*, Explicit Sex, Anxiety, and Care Torben Grodal	179
10	Explicit Teen Sex and Utopian Problem-solving in *Ken Park* Claire Hines	195
11	Witness to the Pain: How Explicit Sex Scenes in Michael Rowe's *Leap Year* Demonstrate Vision Beyond Visibility Taine Duncan	217

Bibliography 233
Index 247

Contributors

David Andrews is an independent scholar who specializes in film genre. He is the author of *Theorizing Art Cinemas: Foreign, Cult, Avant-Garde, and Beyond* (University of Texas, 2013) and *Soft in the Middle: The Contemporary Softcore Feature in its Contexts* (Ohio State, 2006). Andrews is now working with Oxford University Press on a manuscript entitled *Rape-Revenge: Biocultural Investigations*. He lives in Chicago, Illinois (USA).

Chelsea Birks is a PhD student at the University of Glasgow. She wrote her MA thesis at the University of British Columbia on Jean-Luc Nancy and European new extremist cinema. Her research interests include film philosophy, contemporary French cinema and violence, and she was the co-editor (with Dana Keller) of issue 8.2 of *Cinephile* on the topic of contemporary extremism. She will be writing her dissertation on cinematic excess and Georges Bataille.

Lisa Coulthard is an associate professor of Film Studies at the University of British Columbia. Her research focuses on violence, cinematic extremism, and film theory. She is currently completing a book on sound and the films of Quentin Tarantino. Her recent publications include 'Haptic Aurality: Resonance, Listening and Michael Haneke', 'Dirty Sound: Noise in New Extremism', 'Interrogating the Obscene: Extremism and Michael Haneke', and 'Uncanny Horrors: Male Rape in Bruno Dumont's *Twentynine Palms*'.

Barbara Creed is Professor of Screen Studies in the School of Culture & Communication at the University of Melbourne. She is a member of the Australian Academy of the Humanities. Barbara has spoken and published widely in the area of film and visual cultures and more recently in animal studies. Her books include *The Monstrous-Feminine: Film, Feminism, Psychoanalysis*, *Phallic Panic: Film, Horror and the Primal Uncanny* and *Darwin's Screens: Evolutionary Aesthetics, Time and Sexual Display in the*

Cinema. She is currently carrying out research in two related areas: animals and the emotions and the cinema of human rights. She is Director of HRAE – 'Human Rights & Animal Ethics Research Network'.

Taine Duncan is an assistant professor of philosophy and director of the Gender Studies programme at the University of Central Arkansas. She works with critical theories of all kinds, from Rosi Braidotti to Jürgen Habermas to George Yancy. Her research focuses on solidarity and how to conceptualize emancipation beyond difference. Part of this research has included publications using art and culture to think through philosophical issues. Recent publications in this area include 'What Kind of Men are Larry and Jeff?' in *Curb Your Enthusiasm and Philosophy: Awaken the Social Assassin Within* (2012) and two forthcoming chapters: 'Of Mice and (Posthu)Man: Roald Dahl's The Witches and Ethics Beyond Humanism' in *Roald Dahl and Philosophy* (2014); and 'Utopic Futures of the "Other": Pornography and the Creative Imaginary' in *Pornography: An Interdisciplinary Survey* (forthcoming).

Torben Grodal is Professor Emeritus at the Department of Media, Cognition, and Communication at the University of Copenhagen. In addition to having written books and articles on literature he has authored *Moving Pictures. A New Theory of Genre, Feelings, and Emotions, Embodied Visions: Evolution, Emotion, Culture and Film*; an advanced introduction to film theory in Danish, *Filmoplevelse* and edited *Visual Authorship*. He has also published a series of articles on film, emotions, narrative theory, art films, video games and evolutionary film theory. He is currently working on a theoretical description of crime fiction and on a general theory on the relations between brain and narrative.

Jacob M. Held is Associate Professor of Philosophy in the Department of Philosophy and Religion at the University of Central Arkansas. His primary research interests focus on legal and political theory, nineteenth-century German philosophy, and applied ethics. In addition, he works extensively at the intersection of philosophy and popular culture, most recently editing, *Roald Dahl and Philosophy: A Little Nonsense Now and Then*.

Claire Hines is Senior Lecturer in Film and Television at Southampton Solent University, UK. She is co-author of *Fantasy* and co-editor of *Hard to Swallow: Hard-core Pornography on Screen*, and her research and publications focus on James Bond, men's magazines, and representations of gender and sexuality on screen.

Beth Johnson is a senior lecturer in Film, Television and Visual Theory at Keele University, UK. She is the author of various articles in journals such as *Angelaki* and *Screen* and her book chapters include 'Shortbus: Highbrow Hard-core' in *Hard to Swallow: Hard-core Pornography On Screen*, 'Sex, Psychoanalysis and Sublimation in Dexter' in *Investigating Dexter: Cutting Edge Television* (I.B.Tauris, 2010) and 'Realism, Real Sex and the Experimental Film: Mediating New Erotics in Georges Bataille's Story of the Eye' in *Realism and the Audiovisual Media*. Beth has recently co-edited a collection entitled *Television, Sex and Society: Analyzing Contemporary Representations* and has published a monograph on British television auteur Paul Abbott as part of The Television Series.

Sean Redmond is an associate professor of Media and Communication at Deakin University, Melbourne, Australia. He writes on stardom and celebrity, science fiction, screen aesthetics, and film authorship. He edits the journal *Celebrity Studies*, and his latest books, *Celebrity and the Media*, and *The Cinema of Takeshi Kitano: Flowering Blood*, were both published in 2013.

Deborah Walker-Morrison teaches French language, cinema and translation at the University of Auckland, New Zealand. Her research interests and publications are wide-ranging, including French and American film noir, the cinema of Alain Resnais, the translation and reception of indigenous Pacific film and literature, and gender and sexuality in contemporary French cinema. She has authored *Le style cinématographique d'Alain Resnais, de Hiroshima mon amour (1959) aux Herbes folles* (2009), and co-authored (with Alistair Rolls) *French and American Noir: Dark Crossings*.

Linda Ruth Williams is Professor of Film in the English Department at Southampton University, UK. She is the author of four books including *The Erotic Thriller in Contemporary Cinema* (2005) and *Sex in the Head: Visions of Femininity and Film in D.H. Lawrence* (1993), and is the editor of other titles including *Contemporary American Cinema* (co-edited with Michael Hammond, 2006). She has written widely on censorship, pornography, gender and culture in edited collections and journals including *Screen* and *Cinema Journal*, and has also written for the British Film Institute magazine *Sight and Sound*.

Illustrations

Figure 4.1. The cinematography of Denis' camera languishes over the textual details of skin in *Trouble Every Day*. © 2001, Canal +. — 79

Figure 8.1. In this frame capture, Marcus misbehaves at the party. He restrains Alex in an evocation of the rape sequence that viewers have already witnessed. © 2002, Nord-Quest Production & Studio Canal, © 2003, Lions Gate Home Entertainment (DVD). — 162

Figure 8.2. In this frame capture, Marcus reveals his dark side while in the taxi en route to the sex club The Rectum. © 2002, Nord-Quest Production & Studio Canal, © 2003, Lions Gate Home Entertainment. — 163

Figure 8.3. After blocking her exit with his hands, Le Tenia puts his knife to Alex's face in this frame capture. The change in camera angle reinforces the change in mood. © 2002, Nord-Quest Production & Studio Canal, © 2003, Lions Gate Home Entertainment. — 165

Figure 8.4. Throughout the lead-up to sodomy, Alex struggles to free her mouth from her rapist's grip. Notice the figure in the background of this frame capture; the figure soon retreats, signalling the pessimistic outlook of the film. © 2002, Nord-Quest Production & Studio Canal, © 2003, Lions Gate Home Entertainment. — 167

Figure 8.5. In this frame capture, Alex tries to use her hand to dislodge her rapist after he penetrates her. © 2002, Nord-Quest Production & Studio Canal, © 2003, Lions Gate Home Entertainment — 167

Figure 8.6. The third function of Alex's hands in the mise en scène of *Irréversible*: to signal trauma. Frame capture © 2002, Nord-Quest Production & Studio Canal, © 2003, Lions Gate Home Entertainment.   167

Figure 8.7. Hands as symbols and indices of trauma in *Irréversible*. Frame capture © 2002, Nord-Quest Production & Studio Canal, © 2003, Lions Gate Home Entertainment.   168

Figure 8.8. This frame capture presents what is perhaps the most poignant, shocking shot in the film: Alex's outstretched hand, which measures the extent of her pain. © 2002, Nord-Quest Production & Studio Canal, © 2003, Lions Gate Home Entertainment.   168

Figure 8.9. Hands signalling orgasmic connection in an iconic art film: a still from *Les amants*.   170

Figure 8.10. Close-ups of the heroine's hands in erotic imagery from Alain Resnais's *Hiroshima mon amour*.   170

Figure 8.11. Historically, faces have been used to show female sexual pleasure in art films, with hands being secondary. Here is a shot of Hedy Lamarr in *Ekstase / Ecstasy*.   171

Figure 8.12. Because a wide variety of postwar art films had used hands as sexual symbols, hands could also be used to indicate pleasure or pain in rape scenes. In this frame capture from Lynch's *Wild at Heart*, a film in which the hand is an important sign of sexual pleasure, the heroine's orgasmic hand is used to indicate the 'semi-consensual' trajectory of a psychosexual conflict with a coercive male. © 1990 PolyGram Entertainment, Propaganda Films, © 2004 MGM Entertainment (DVD).   172

Figure 8.13. This frame capture depicts the hand-to-hand struggles of rape during the non-consensual portion of the semi-consensual scene in Peckinpah's *Straw Dogs*. © 1971 ABC Pictures, © 2004 MGM Home Entertainment (DVD).   173

ILLUSTRATIONS   xv

Figure 8.14. Frame capture of struggle becoming the hand-to-hand embraces of coerced consent in *Straw Dogs*. © 1971 ABC Pictures, © 2004 MGM Home Entertainment.   173

Figure 8.15. From there, the heroine's face is used to indicate her sexual pleasure in the semi-consensual rape scene of *Straw Dogs*, with her hands becoming marginal to the mise en scène. Frame capture, © 1971 ABC Pictures, © 2004 MGM Home Entertainment.   174

Figure 8.16. After viewers have seen the rape, Alex's hands become ironic symbols of an event that hasn't happened yet in the plot, due to the reverse structure. In this frame capture, she attempts to dance with Pierre at the party. © 2002, Nord-Quest Production & Studio Canal, © 2003, Lions Gate Home Entertainment.   175

Figure 9.1. In this picture from *Antichrist*, the intercourse between 'He' and 'She' is foiled by a mythological frame. Thereby their intercourse becomes abstract and anonymous, a symbolic manifestation of the human condition. © 2009, Christian Geisnaes.   183

Figure 10.1. In the foreground, Shawn performs oral sex on Rhonda. In the background, framed photographs and trophies are on display. © 2002, Busy Bee, Marathon / Cinea, Kasander Film Company, Lou Yi Inc. © 2003, CP Digital.   201

Figure 10.2. 'Good girl' Peaches teases Curtis tied-up. © 2002, Busy Bee, Marathon / Cinea, Kasander Film Company, Lou Yi Inc. © 2003, CP Digital.   202

Figure 10.3. Real-time urination adds to the animalistic behaviour of Claude's father. © 2002, Busy Bee, Marathon / Cinea, Kasander Film Company, Lou Yi Inc. © 2003, CP Digital.   203

Figure 10.4. Claude appears angelic when he is observed sleeping by his father. © 2002, Busy Bee, Marathon / Cinea, Kasander Film Company, Lou Yi Inc. © 2003, CP Digital.   211

Acknowledgements

There are many, many people to thank for this book. Big thanks go to my honours year lecturer Felicity Colman. Her tutorials on Breillat's *Romance* were a big inspiration. Similarly, I would like to thank those responsible for banning *Baise-moi* in Australia for their actions. For a film to pass the censor, be released, then be pulled from theatres after screening for weeks is loopy and enraging. And inspiring. My conversations with many film-makers on the subject of techniques used to express sexuality and passion in the cinematic language were also fascinating and illuminating. To that end I would like to thank cinematographers Rodrigo Prieto, Uta Briesewitz, and the film composers Carter Burwell and Jan Kaczmarek. The contributors to this book are its true stars. They are, to a man/woman, exceptional scholars and intellectuals and my interactions with them have made this project incredibly fulfilling for me. Thank you. Most of all I want thank my lovely partner Sarah and our little delight Audrey. This was my first real book and there were many ups and downs to be sure. Thank you to my two best gals.

Introduction

Sex in film is an evergreen topic. Whether implied or explicit, sexual content almost always provokes both critical consternation and wonderment. Even as the template seems set for what makes for the most effective balance of sexual content and narrative in cinema – the one enhancing the other – a new film will be released which pushes the boundaries yet further. Here are some examples of what have been branded as sexually confronting films from the past few years. In Lars von Trier's *Nymphomaniac* (2013) the genitals of copulating pornographic actors were digitally grafted onto those of mainstream actors simulating sex (Lanxon, 2013). The teen comedy *Wetlands* (David Wnendt, 2013) features actors engaging in actual group masturbation, then ejaculating over a pizza. *Stranger by the Lake* (Alain Guiraudie, 2013) unusually features inserts of ejaculation in the context of a consensual homosexual sex scene in which both participants are nude. *Beauty* (Oliver Hermanus, 2011) features similar all-nude scenes of simulated group homosexual sex between men well into middle age. Here is a review for *Wetlands* which crystallizes the bafflement and disgust certain critics experience in the face of such confrontational material:

> The toilet-rubbing scene is one of the two moments in *Wetlands* that made me queasy. The other involves an ensemble of men ejaculating on a pizza (one of Helen's many grotty fantasies). This is when I walked out of the theater. I'm pretty desensitized when it comes to most shock, but when something as gross as this gets inside my head, I can't handle it. (Whale, 2014)

A less emotive response, but equally cautionary, may be found in the following caveat offered in a review of *Beauty*:

> The subject matter is difficult, even confronting, but DoP Jamie Ramsay's wide-angled lensing, maintaining a cool distance from what it observes as

much as François does, brings to this film its own austere, aching beauty. (Bitel, 2012)

The statement is an appeal to the viewer to overcome their spontaneous resistance to the subject matter, a surprising appeal given the universal story *Beauty* represents, one of a man struggling with self-hatred. These responses, while found within positive reviews, are notable for their hesitancy, for the sense that the reviewers are struggling to find their critical bearings in relation to this explicit sexual content.

Upon closer inspection, however, this 'confrontational' sexual content contains a variety of technological, narrative and aesthetic revelations. In the case of *Nymphomaniac* von Trier highjacks not the imagery of pornography per se, but a portion of this said imagery only – the portion which, arguably, makes it truly pornographic. And yet, von Trier radically recontextualizes this imagery, grafting the engorged genitals of a porn performer to the well-known face and body of *Transformers* star Shia LaBeouf. *Wetlands* utilizes an expressly pornographic scenario to highlight the ungovernable libido and fantasy life of its teen *female* lead character. When the pizza masturbation scene is presented, it is arguably pornographic due to its inclusion of genuine erections and ejaculations. But beyond this it is also a fantasy originating from Helen (Carla Juri), the film's protagonist. In conventional narratives, this attractive young woman would be the subject of male fantasies, now the pornographic scenario originates from her desires and imaginative perspective. *Stranger by the Lake* not only features explicit homosexual sex, itself a relative rarity in narrative cinema, but also fuses it to a narrative obsessed with the universal themes of murder, survival, lust and loneliness, atypical imagery blending with a noirish tale complete with its own male version of a femme fatale, the killer Michel (Christophe Paou). *Beauty* atypically offers an explicit glimpse of not middle-aged flesh paired with youthful flesh in lustful trysts, a Hollywood gimmick common to dozens of films, but the heavy guts and hairy backs of middle-aged men engaging in passionate embraces with one another. Sex thus persists in pushing the boundaries of what we can see, hear, and indeed feel, in experiencing narrative cinema, and in so doing creates a visual record of sexual experience every bit as startling as any CGI wonder of the modern cinema age.

Many academics agree that the depiction of sex might insidiously impact both the narrative which surrounds it and the sensibilities of the viewer. An academic who has worked extensively on the subjects of both sexuality and sex on screen, Linda Williams, in the conclusion to her major work on the subject, *Screening Sex*, sees the depiction of sexuality in fact becoming integrated into the sensual / sexual nature of the viewer themselves:

> After more than a century of screening sex, perhaps the most important lesson I would like to draw from the last stage of this impressionistic chronicle is that the very act of screening has become an intimate part of our sexuality. The point therefore should not be to discover that screening sex brings us so much closer, spatially or temporally, to 'real sex.' Rather, it should be to discover that viewers and now users, have become habituated to these new forms of mimetic play with, and through, screens. (2008: 325)

Sex on screen is effectively now as much a part of a screen narrative as it might be a part of the audience's sense of its own real-world stimulation. Sex, on screen, time and again stirs viewers. In doing so it also becomes a part of our list of everyday turn-ons, a part of our sexual fantasies. Narratives which feature sex thus become a part of our daily sensations, our daily needs. These needs, beyond their obvious relevance to our sexuality, exist to enhance the chance of our survival in a hostile world.

Film academic Torben Grodal, who is a contributor to this volume, goes to some lengths to clarify how in fact all narratives serve a greater function to enhance our evolutionary capabilities.

> Pleasure is an inbuilt go-mechanism aimed at motivating fitness-enhancing activities, just as pain is an inbuilt fitness-enhancing avoidance-and-stop-mechanism. There is therefore no evolutionary reason for thinking that romance novels that articulate mating fantasies, pleasurable go-scenarios, should in principle be more or less fitness enhancing than stop-enhancing tragedies that cause pain by depicting failure and death, or that even glorify heroic suffering or martyrdom. (2008: 194)

Narratives featuring sex, even permutations of sex and death, connect to audiences on a rudimentary level. They offer up scenarios which, in their barest details, present guidelines for success, gratify the audience's urges to see, in the form of a story, their own hopes to reproduce, survive and thrive.

The purpose of this book is to explore the insidious manner in which cinema does, in fact, utilize sex to address the audience's understanding of its own basic, survival needs, its complementary desire to thrive, as well as explicate the manner in which the sex we watch in films in turn becomes a part of our own sexual make-up. This book will explain how, rather than being pornographic, explicit sex can be an essential element of storytelling in narrative cinema. It aids characterization; highlights themes; provides events which develop plot. The book will attempt to detail, through the fundamentals of cinema, the shot by shot, moment by moment manner in which explicit, even actual, sex can be an essential component of a dramatically powerful narrative. It is aided in its impact by effective, nuanced performances and incisive directorial techniques. This anthology will offer detailed analysis of how choices are made in the presentation of explicit sex from these two perspectives, performance and technique. Film is, in many respects, intrinsically suited to the depiction of sex as both Linda Williams and film theorist Christian Metz note, in its unique blend of provocation and nuance:

> The way the cinema, with its wandering framings (wandering like the look, like the caress), finds the means to reveal space has something to do with a kind of permanent undressing, a generalised strip-tease, a less direct but more perfected strip-tease, since it also makes it possible to dress space again, to remove from view what it has previously shown, to *take back* as well as to retain. (Metz, 1982: 77)

This book also maintains a fascination with the manner in which sex avails itself to the demands of narratives, all the while integrating with our experience of our own sensual nature. There is similarly a focus on the manner in which cinematic explicit sex seems to engage with the tropes and conventions of pornography while at the same moment reconstituting itself in the manner which Metz describes.

The chapters in this book cover a wide range of films, from the seventies through to the present day. They vary from the comedic, *Shortbus* (John Cameron Mitchell, 2006), to the entirely dramatic, *Antichrist* (Lars von Trier, 2009). All utilize actual or explicit simulated sex to tell their stories. Barbara Creed explores some of the earliest uses of non-simulated sex acts in a mainstream narrative film in her chapter on Barbet Schroeder's *Maîtresse* (1976). Intriguingly, this film features scenes in which much of the sexuality on display takes the form of actual, unsimulated sadomasochism, while the congress enjoyed by the film's young lovers is simulated and non-explicit. Remarkably, Creed explores how the symbolic presence of animals in the film provides a paradigm in which these real sex acts may be absorbed. Jacob Held's chapter jumps forward by around 25 years to the 2000 film *Baise-moi* (Virginie Despentes and Coralie Trinh Thi), a mainstream release which utilized pornographic actresses, directors from a pornographic film background, and a story which in turn featured plentiful real sex to tell a story which, as Held ably proves, is not in fact pornographic. Deborah Walker-Morrison engages in not only a detailed analysis of Catherine Breillat's masterpiece *The Last Mistress* (2007), but equally credits the film's source material, the nineteenth-century novel *Une vieille maîtresse* by Jules Amédée Barbey d'Aurevilly for the singularity of its depiction of erotic love. Walker-Morrison explores in detail the specific manner in which the book's sensuality transitions to a cinematic depiction. In doing thus she traces the manner in which the experience of sex in the filmic medium is unique when compared with others, and in turn a reflection of the multivalent impact which both Metz and Williams note as unique to film sex. In these early chapters, the focus is on what might be construed as foundational aspects / questions related to explicit sex. Early explicit sex in narrative cinema, the perennial question as to what constitutes pornography, and the link between the erotic in literature and the erotic in film.

In the following two chapters the manner in which explicit sexual content is integrated into contemporary film genres is explored. Lisa Coulthard and Chelsea Birks peer behind the explicit couplings of *Twentynine Palms* (Bruno Dumont, 2002), *Trouble Every Day* (Claire Denis, 2001) and *Antichrist* and see the masculine insecurity at their hearts. They contextualize the use of sex in these films within the broader aesthetic goals of the New Extremism, a movement dedicated to the abject and an obsessive attachment to the body. Linda Ruth Williams, in her exploration of the surprising sex comedy *Shortbus*, delivers a startling and incisive chapter which traces this film's interest with voyeurism and surveillance all the way back to Hitchcock's *Rear Window* (1954). As Birks and Coulthard align the predilections of *Antichrist* and *Trouble Every Day* with the New Extremism, Linda Ruth Williams similarly notes that *Shortbus* aligns well with the trend of 'Smart Cinema'. This is significant in that it affirms the possibility that explicit sex might align not only with unexpected genres such as comedy, as found in *Shortbus*, but also a school of cinema noted for its wit and cerebral qualities. Sean Redmond locates within *Lust, Caution* (Ang Lee, 2007) an existential ache in the lovers, one which is best expressed through sex, but still remains unsatiated. In turn he locates this complex play of desire and satiation within the purview of a wider trend towards haptic cinema, effectively an elaboration on many of the ideas explored in relation to New Extremism. This haptic cinema expresses the possibility of the experience of imagery within one's body, the sensations of sensual desire at once manifested on the screen and, through various forms of mediation, within the viewer. This is essentially an advancement on ideas promoted in the two previous chapters.

Both Beth Johnson's chapter on *9 Songs* (Michael Winterbottom, 2004) and David Andrews' on *Irréversible* (Gaspar Noé, 2003) are entirely preoccupied with the twin components of the actors' performance and the film-makers' cinematic technique. Perhaps only in *9 Songs* could a 'money shot' – the image of an erect phallus ejaculating in front of a female face – not seem a money shot, rather some new, distinct, tastefully cinematic means of capturing the male orgasm. This doubleness is explored in some detail in Beth Johnson's chapter on the film. It is also an exploration of what Metz describes as the 'strip-tease' quality of film, one in which that which might be pornographic is reconstituted before the viewer's eyes. Andrews' chapter, like Johnson's, is expressly concerned with technique. Like Creed's it also approaches explicit sexuality from a somewhat unconventional angle, the main sexual activity found in the film an extended rape scene. While not consensual it still represents a form of sexual desire and content and David Andrews' chapter breaks down the directorial choices made by auteur Gaspar Noé in his epic depiction of rape in the notorious *Irréversible*, a series of choices remarkably mirrored by Sam Peckinpah's in *Straw Dogs* (1971), a similarly infamous film released 30 years previously.

The final three chapters of the book are not expressly related but each address the future relevance of explicit sex in film storytelling. Torben Grodal reduces the ambiguities of Lars von Trier's *Antichrist* to an innovative physiological study of arousal. True to his claims that basic evolutionary needs are found at the heart of narratives the essential bodily response of arousal is proven as a prime constituent of *Antichrist*, and an opportune conceptual vehicle to comprehend its otherwise opaque narrative. Evolutionary drivers may be found within narrative, and in turn the cinematic techniques used to express said narrative. Claire Hines goes to considerable lengths in her chapter on Larry Clark and Ed Lachman's *Ken Park* (2002) to trace a series of links between Clark's famed work as a photographer of American youth and drug culture and the unique eye he brings to the plight of the abused teens in this disturbing lost gem. Clark's work represents a far larger project, the possibility that explicit content may, in its ubiquity, come to represent far more than mere biological function, or obscenity. Take away the explicit sexuality from Clark's photographic and cinematic work and there is little left to be transferred thematically. His oeuvre, as explored by Hines, represents sexuality at its most insidious, an essential means of the artist communicating their message. In this book's final chapter Taine Duncan sees in Michael Rowe's explicit and ambiguous *Leap Year* (2010) the heroine's struggle to define her racial, emotional and sexual identity all at once in her many erotic encounters. Here, in the final chapter, the exploration of explicit content leads to a realization, on Duncan's part, that sex, and sex in cinema, is the essential medium for the heroine's establishing her selfhood, struggling with in turn a profound ambivalence on the subject of her own life and death. This final chapter represents a strong case for the notion that narratives concerned with sex are likewise ultimately concerned with what Grodal titles 'fitness-enhancing activities', the mixture of emotional and physical pleasure and pain a guide for audiences as to their own strategies for evolutionary survival.

In its entirety this book represents not a definitive statement on the subject of explicit sex in narrative film, but rather a medium for the continuation of a vital debate. Explicit sex will always be a component of the cinema. This volume represents an addition to a field of research which will continue to evolve so long as film-makers wish to explore sexuality. The diversity of this expression is mirrored in the range of contributors presented, and in turn the wide range of research and opinions they represent. This diversity will hopefully continue to inspire yet more passionate debate on the subject of sex and storytelling.

Chapter 1

Maîtresse

Pornography, Ritual and the Question of the Animal

Barbara Creed

Barbet Schroeder's *Maîtresse* (1976) is a love story that also offers a confronting study of sadomasochistic practices in scenes that are both simulated and actual. An acclaimed art-house film, *Maîtresse* pioneered the narrative and stylistic strategy of interweaving fiction and documentary in what many regard as a pornographic film. It stars Gérard Depardieu as Olivier, a petty thief who breaks into an underground S/M dungeon owned by a professional dominatrix, Ariane, played by Bulle Olgier. The two commence a relationship, which is played out against a background of Ariane's sadistic practices, performed in a secret parlour situated beneath her chic Parisian apartment and eventually, the couple fall in love. Schroeder uses a professional maîtresse to film the demanding scenes of intense flagellation and nailing, and real-life masochists, wearing masks, to perform as her slaves. Schroeder presents confronting S/M practices in order to explore directly questions about the extremes of human behaviour, the importance of ritual in everyday life and the relationship between human and animal. The film achieves this by interweaving three tiers of experience into a complex narrative: 'normal' human love and perverse sexual behaviour in the everyday world; consensual sadomasochistic ritual practices in the dungeon; and the cruel slaughtering of animals for human consumption at the local abattoir which, like the S/M dungeon, is hidden in an ordinary suburb. In an interview, Schroeder stated that the masochism, which is enacted in the dungeon below, is mirrored in the love relationship between Ariane and Olivier that takes place in the world above. He felt that the masochism in the film should be seen as a 'creative' force (Stein, 1977: 342). As it explores its complex subject matter, *Maîtresse* generates contradictory effects for the viewer, ranging from the erotic to the unpleasurable and even unbearable. When the film was first submitted to the British Board of Film Classification (BBFC) in 1976, the Board concluded that the film was not suitable for classification. *Maîtresse* was finally released uncut to the public in 2003.

Although *Maîtresse* was considered pornographic by some, its focus on sadomasochistic sex meant that not all viewers would have found it sexually arousing, which according to Lynne Segal is the intended aim of most pornography. 'Traditionally defined as sexually explicit, and therefore obscene [pornography refers to] words or images intended to provoke sexual excitement' (Segal, 1993: 207). There are no scenes of explicit heterosexual sex in the 'real' world between two people involving penetration – actual or simulated – in which the sexual organs are on display. The filming of the love scenes between Olivier and Ariane is relatively modest. Although theirs is a heterosexual love story, graphic depictions of the sex act between Olivier and Ariane are not essential to the development of the heterosexual narrative or love story which is focused on themes of trust and betrayal. The scenes of masochism played out in the dungeon, however, are essential to the overall development of the heterosexual love story in that they symbolize the power play enacted between the couple that is both emotional and sexual. In other words, the sadomasochistic (S/M) scenes which take place in the dungeon below potentially signify a repressed dimension to the love story above.

Completed in 1976, over two decades before the new wave of erotic mainstream pornographic films began to appear in the late 1990s, *Maîtresse* was very much a forerunner of this movement, which was championed by directors from various countries – such as Lars von Trier, Larry Clark, Virginie Despentes and Catherine Breillet who have all made films with sexually explicit content. The new wave was characterized by a series of developments: the emergence of female directors who set out to explore films about explicit sex from a woman's perspective; the representation of scenes of actual as distinct from simulated sex in a number of these films; scenes of explicit sex that were not gratuitous but crucial to the development of the narrative; and an exploration of sexual and ethical issues specific to the era. In their study, *The New Pornographies: Explicit Sex in Recent French Fiction and Film*, Victoria Best and Martin Crowley set out to establish why narratives about the representation of explicit sex became so dominant internationally in *fin de siecle* culture of the twenty-first century. They argue that one of the key aspects of this new movement is a desire to make transparent the sexual issues and anxieties of the era. Produced two decades earlier, Maîtresse similarly explores sexual anxieties of the age through a pornographic aesthetic.

Maîtresse examines the role of dominance and submission in actual relationships with specific reference to male masochism as well as the constructed and hence fragile nature of dominant heterosexual role-playing. It also exposes the dark underside of so-called civilized societies. Maîtresse achieves these aims through a focus on explicit sex. The film insists on the narrative importance of depicting actual S/M sex acts between the Maîtresse and her male customers. It also uses actual devotees of S/M sex rather than professional actors engaged in simulated sex acts. Further, as mentioned, there are no images of erect penises or scenes of heterosexual coitus, masturbation or anal sex that characterized other films of the late 1990s which was part of the radical innovation of sexual representation in art cinema. There is however one scene which portrays the female genitals, as a female masochist kneels in order to receive a heavy beating on the buttocks. Maîtresse was not the first art-house film to represent confronting scenes of S/M sexual desire and to use well-know actors to star in the key roles. Earlier films included Louis Bunuel's *Belle de Jour* (1967), Lilian Cavani's, *The Night Porter* (1974), and Just Jaeckin's *The Story of O* (1975). However it was the first to combine documentary and enacted footage in order to depict actual scenes of sadomasochistic sex. In its focus on sexual issues and the relationship between representation, realism and reality, Maîtresse both anticipates the future emergence of art-house pornography of the late 1990s, while also remaining somewhat of an 'outsider' even today, specifically because of its emphasis on male masochism and its alignment with the death drive.

One of Schroeder's most remarkable achievements is the way in which he integrates the film's three worlds (dungeon/household/abattoir) into the overall narrative as well as integrating his professional and non-professional cast. The film's integrated narrative was a factor that the BBFC gave for deciding not to release the film – the Board was concerned that cuts might ruin the overall atmosphere and meaning of the film. How does Schroeder represent the film's scenes of explicit S/M sex? How do they relate to the relationship, which evolves between the couple, and the scene of abject cruelty at the abattoirs? What is the film's attitude to emotions and feelings such as masochism, sadism, and cruelty? What responses does the film seek to elicit from its audience?

Schroeder's representation of the S/M scenes is direct and confronting. Olivier arrives from the provinces and takes a job, with his friend Mario, selling encyclopaedias door to door. They are not well received. One irate man yells 'Bugger your arts!' Mario is easily rebuffed but Olivier wants to gain entry into people's apartments, to see what's 'behind people's walls'. His wish is soon granted when a distressed young woman invites them inside. She will buy all of their books if they can fix her plumbing and stop the bath from overflowing. She tells them not to worry about letting the people below know about water seeping into their apartment because the owner is away at the Riviera. She will write to her. The two thieves return and break into the downstairs apartment. Puzzled, they find nothing of clear value – only leather costumes, masks, handcuffs, a noose, chains, a baby's bottle and very long stiletto shoes. 'All junk!' Mario says in disgust. Disappointment suddenly turns to shock, when Olivier stumbles across a naked man, wearing a dog collar and lipstick, locked in a cage. Opening a door, they encounter a large Doberman guard dog, which holds them at bay.

Next a retractable ladder descends into the room and a woman dressed in an elegant black frock and black stilettos slowly descends into the darkened space. 'Careful he is trained to kill!' she warns them. 'Ah, you again!' she exclaims. The dog snarls. 'Texas is jumpy tonight,' she explains making it clear they should not attempt to move. It is the pretty blonde woman from upstairs. In contrast to their previous encounter, she is completely in control of the situation. 'Well aren't you ashamed!' she exclaims as she spies the sack of stolen goods. The doorbell rings. She presses a buzzer and the retractable ladder, which looks like a large skeletal insect, folds silently back up into the ceiling. Within seconds she expertly handcuffs them to a heater rail. 'Sorry, but I can't trust you!' She opens the door to a good-looking well-dressed man. As she ushers him into the next room, he looks back intently at the two men. The couple disappear into another room. Next, the stunned duo hear the sounds of a whip. The woman suddenly reappears. She offers Olivier 200 francs for three minutes work. He agrees and follows her into the darkened room.

Silently Olivier watches a scenario of sadomasochistic rituals unfold. Schroeder has carefully arranged this scene so that we can observe Olivier's responses. To the left of the screen we observe Olivier as he watches the couple. To the right of the screen we see the S/M scenario through images reflected back via mirrors. The dominatrix reclines in a chair as the anonymous man licks her long, phallic stilettos. She inserts the heel of her shoe into his mouth for him to suck. The room is dark, its marble surfaces shiny and hard. She whips the man, who is wearing a collar and a corset, and orders him onto his knees then mounts him as if he were a horse. Handing Olivier the whip, she pulls Olivier towards them and unbuttons his fly. 'Piss in is face!' she commands. Apart from a fleeting smile, Olivier shows no other emotions. She unexpectedly kisses Olivier as he urinates in the man's face. As suddenly as it started, the ritual is over. Ariane chats to the man, gives him a red robe and asks him if he is still going to Barcelona. What is most striking about the entire scene is its domestic and banal atmosphere. He departs. Olivier hands her back the whip; she pays him his wages. Instead of leaving, Olivier invites her out to dinner. Clearly attracted to her petty thief, she agrees.

Olivier's earlier voyeuristic wish to see what is behind people's walls has been fulfilled in an unexpected manner. He has a curious, probing mind: Ariane is similarly curious but her interest is in the taboo sexual desires of her male masochists. Ariane later describes her work as creating 'scenes', that is, sex to her is not unlike a stage performance in which she is the director and the participants are actors. The ritualistic nature of sadomasochistic practices is evident from its reliance on set pieces, costumes and related paraphernalia – scenarios of debasement, flagellation, urination, nailing and equipment such as handcuffs, whips, stilettos, racks and cages. These set the stage for the enactment of the masochist's specific fantasies of degradation and punishment. The mise en scène of the dungeon (dark lighting, mirrors, implements of torture, costumes) is crucial to the enactment of the sexual scenarios. According to Elliott Stein: 'Like the best cinema, S & M is about *mise-en-scène*' (Stein, 2004: 2). The dungeon has a cold and clinical exterior: it is decorated with dark marble, mirrors and reflective surface, which reinforce the film's philosophical inquiry into the unconscious desires of its performers. Is it possible to see the 'self' in the subject's own reflection or is the self only revealed though laying bare the individual's innermost desires? When Olivier first enters the dungeon and watches the scene being enacted before him, it is not clear at first if he is looking directly at the scene or though the reflections in a mirror. This confusion of boundaries, which is central to the atmosphere of the dungeon, gradually begins to dominate the world above where Olivier and Ariane play out their own version of the S/M scenarios taking place below.

Schroeder invited Néstore Almendros (*Nadine*, *The Last Metro*, *Days of Heaven*) one of the cinema's great cinematographers, to film *Maîtresse*. Distance is crucial to the filming. Schroeder explained in interview that if the camera is located too far from the scene being filmed then it appears as if the film is avoiding its confronting subject matter: if the camera is too close it can look as if the director is trying to manipulate the spectator by playing to a voyeuristic gaze (Stein, 1977: 56). In the main, Schroeder does not use close-up shots, which would direct the viewer's gaze, but rather films from a carefully controlled middle-distance. When he does employ a close-up, for instance of the penis in the nailing scene, the combination of distance and proximity serves to destabilize the look. The mise en scène of the dungeon (dark, mysterious reflective surfaces) contrasts with that of the upstairs apartment (natural light, open windows, domestic settings) in furthering the heterosexual love story where the couple are guided by spontaneous outbursts of feeling as distinct from the pre-arranged scenes of dominance and submission in the dungeon. By filming both worlds with the same detachment, Schroeder carefully interweaves the two realms, one becoming a mirror image of the other – although the masochistic games of the lovers are by comparison less rehearsed and not marked by sadistic ritual.

The third world is that of the abattoir. After their first evening out together, Ariane and Olivier watch the sunrise over the city. On hearing the clock tower chime the stroke of five, Olivier tells Ariane that this is 'the hour that they kill horses'. He once worked in an abattoir but left as soon as he became accustomed, or desensitized, to the slaughter of the animals. In a particularly confronting scene Olivier visits the abattoirs which like Ariane's dungeon is hidden amongst human dwellings in a lovely neighbourhood. Olivier appears to be identifying with Ariane's masochists to the point where this is beginning to make him feel vulnerable as if he were one of the doomed horses. Schroeder also intertwines this world with that of the dungeon, through repeated references to horses in the dungeon. In contrast to the S/M scenarios, the scene at the abattoirs is not about masochism but about the plight of the victim – in this case the butchered animals. There is also a sense of repetition and of mundanity that characterizes the activities at the slaughterhouse. To what extent are the male masochists in *Maîtresse* victims in the way the horses are victims?

Sadomasochistic practices are consensual. The masochist pays the dominatrix to carry out his or her personal desires. In a sense the masochist appears to be helpless, a total victim, but he is actually in complete control. At one point Ariane says that she is the 'slave – just fulfilling their wishes'. He desires to be humiliated, hurt, punished and debased. He also desires the experience of surrendering completely to the will of another – a dominating woman often dressed in leather and bearing instruments of torture. A number of these acts – spanking, crawling on all fours, suckling – suggests that the encounter is based on infantile experiences when the child was powerless before the authority of the mother. Regardless of the origins of masochistic desire, the important factor is that now it is the adult male who is in control of a variety of scenarios in which he performs a role of abject helplessness. These scenarios have the potential to invoke both pleasure and disgust on the part of the viewer. It is not that the masochist is only able to derive pleasure from encounters of this kind. As Ariane says to Olivier – some of her customers have wives and children and live 'perfectly normal' lives at home.

The most confronting encounter which takes place in Ariane's dungeon involves a scenario of nailing. In interview, Schroeder explained that he was determined to convey the fact that he was not making a 'dirty documentary', that there was a 'spiritual dimension'. 'But how, through the image, do you make the spectator feel that ritual and the beauty that's in the head of the character at that time [...] how to communicate something essentially non-cinematographic?' (Stein, 1977: 57). Schroeder links ritual to beauty – possibly in the way intended by Georges Bataille. He refers to his directorial debut, *More* (1969), a film about heroin addiction in which he set out to represent the non-cinematographic; here he drew on the place and location of the filming. In *More*, 'it came across because it was shot in a real paradise and the sensuality of the surroundings helped to visualize this idea' (Stein, 1977: 57). In *Maîtresse*, Schroeder uses the ritualized nature of the S/M scenarios to represent the 'paradise' being experienced by the masochists as they submit willingly to pain and humiliation.

This is particularly relevant to the scene in which one of the men submits to the professional maîtresse, playing Ariane, who hammers his penis to a wooden plank with nails and pins. The nailing scenario is heavily ritualistic: the man wears a leather mask and long jacket and sits in a chair with his arms strapped to its sides with his naked genitals resting on a board fixed to the seat. 'Ariane' prepares him for the ritual. She adjusts various leather straps and then expertly nails long pins through the skin of his penis to the board underneath. He moans in response to the pain. Next she pushes long pins through his nipples, telling him his 'punishment is half-an-hour in the dark'. She turns off the light, leaving him groaning quietly to himself in the dark. Almost all reviews of the film select this scene, described by one as this 'notorious scene', as the one, which represents the extremities of pain. This scene however has a spiritual dimension. Such intense agony would cause the individual to lose awareness of himself, his ego, and his bodily boundaries as the pain engulfed his entire being. The connections to Christianity are clear; Christianity teaches that it is necessary to suffer to enter paradise. The universal motif of this message is the image of the wounded and bleeding Christ nailed to a cross. Two of the female saints, Catherine of Siena and Theresa of Avila wrote about their own experiences of ecstasy. 'Both, along with others, wrote of ecstasy in intensely physical terms, using imagery that would now seem more in line with representations of sexuality, particularly masochism' (Maitland, 1993: 78).

The general definition of masochism is the experience of sexual pleasure that is derived from pain. Some argue that masochism works through fantasies in which death signifies the main sexual event. Various objects in the dungeon such as the instruments of torture and the noose indicate that the threat of death is ever present. Tina Papoulis explains that this is 'a death which is always about to occur but is always kept at a distance, anticipated. The central feature of the scenario is suspense, waiting, deferred fulfilment of desire' (Papoulias, 1993: 165). This may help to explain why the masochists in the film are left alone in cages, chained to walls, nailed to boards – awaiting the return of their mistress as they anticipate their next punishment, which signifies another step towards a death that never arrives.

Schroeder's discussion of the film's spiritual dimension recalls the writings of Georges Bataille the French intellectual, former surrealist, essayist and author who influenced several generations of intellectuals including Julia Kristeva, Jacques Derrida and Michel Foucault. Elizabeth Young describes him as 'a high priest of the perverse' who sought to bring about a 'primal confrontation with the self' (Young, 1993: 24).

Briefly, his philosophical and religious writings investigate our loss of 'intimacy'; that is, a sacred state, pure animal existence. Human self-consciousness dooms us to treat nature and ourselves as instruments and objects; we are imprisoned by rationalism and the process of production and cannot attain the unfettered boundary-less state of being 'like water in water'. We may glimpse it – this is the link to his erotic novels – 'through violent excess and debauchery' (Young, 1993: 24).

The erotic is connected to violence – particularly violence done to the body. Violent excess results in the erosion of boundaries and the privileging of formlessness, which Bataille wrote about in his short article, 'Informe'. His theory of *informe* was intended as an attack on the human organization of the world into neat and definable categories.

Formlessness 'serves to bring things down in the world' and do away with traditional concepts of structure by affirming, 'On the other hand ... that the universe resembles nothing and is only formless' (Bataille, 1929: 382). According to Rob Weatherill, 'Bataille lived the death drive' (2013: 1). He was fascinated by images and accounts of individuals who had experienced the extremes of torture such as being flayed alive or dismembered. He felt that as they suffered their expressions seemed to 'resemble those of mystics in states of ecstasy' (ibid.).

> What so impressed Bataille was the juxtaposition of divine ecstasy and extreme horror. What followed was his lifelong search for the 'sacred' beyond the enlightenment of the civilized world. (Ibid.)

Death is what matters most.

> The flesh is cursed, because the body is tied inexorably to its own decay and death. There is no sexual liberation (as in the sex manuals which promote an idealized sexuality) but rather a black erotics, where the orgasm is the shattering moment of nothing, linked to the final death which it anticipates and rehearses. (Ibid.: 2)

In his writings on the slaughterhouse at La Villette, Paris, Bataille focused on masses of abject blood and matter. He saw slaughterhouses as transforming 'death from something sacred to the technical' (Noys, 2000: 24). Eli Lotar's photographs to which Bataille refers display rows of dismembered animal legs and hooves propped up against a wall. Schroeder's decision to film actual scenes of masochism alongside documentary footage from an abattoir contrasts the enacted 'sacrifice' of the human, who really sacrifices nothing, alongside the actual sacrifice of the animal who is forced to sacrifice its life, that is, everything.

Confused and feeling that he is losing control of his life, Olivier visits the abattoirs. Here in a documentary sequence, he watches the slaughter of a horse. The horse is hung upside down on hooks. In an eerie moment, the horse's legs move involuntarily as it begins to gallop. The image of the horse's legs moving, as if it were galloping, are strangely lyrical – even uncanny. It is as if the horse were still alive, enjoying freedom of movement, life and pleasure in its own body of which it has already been divested. Shortly afterwards Olivier visits a butcher's shop where he buys horsemeat, which he takes back to the apartment where he cooks and eats it. In an interview Barbet Schroeder said of this scene:

> He chose to identify with the victim by watching this slaughter and then going to a butcher and buying a horsemeat steak and eating it. It was a kind of primitive, unconscious ritual. I interpreted it as an attempt to shock himself into a renewed awareness of his humanity: eating the horsemeat was a way of embracing the cruel side of human nature.
> (Smith, 1995:12)

The slaughterhouse represents a complex and contradictory space. It raises more questions than it answers. Animals are abandoned and treated as objects by a system that is methodical and murderous; it is here that Olivier comes to shock himself into an awareness of himself, to embark on a 'primitive unconscious ritual'. The abattoir scene is in stark contrast to those in the dungeon where the men choose instead to be in darkness, with their bodies tied, chained and impaled. They choose cruelty. The horse however has not chosen its own death. Trustingly, it allows itself to be led into a stall by its executioner. One heavy blow to the head and it falls to the ground. This is the death that the men pursue – up to a point. In stating that consuming the horsemeat offered Olivier a way of 'embracing the cruel side of human nature', Schroeder does offer an ethical viewpoint on human nature.

Olivier identifies with the horse not just through the consumption of its flesh but also presumably throughout its ordeal – when it is alive in the yard, the moment of its death, the scene of its involuntary movements. Through his personal experiences in the dungeon and the slaughterhouse, Olivier awakens his own capacity for sadism, masochism and cruelty. The project of *Maîtresse* appears to be to do just that – to bring about a confrontation between Olivier and his repressed emotions. At the commencement of the narrative, Olivier is very much the tough guy. He throws his friend down the stairs, tells Ariane he could kill her, sadistically attacks one of her customers. By the end he is a different person. He identifies with the animal, incorporating its flesh into himself in a personal ritual.

The abattoir scenes also recall Georges Franju's poetic documentary *Blood of Beasts* (1949) which depicts with clinical precision the slaughter of animals for human consumption. Franju located the abattoir in a suburb seemingly indifferent to such hidden cruelty. It has been argued that Franju was comparing the activities within the abattoir with those of the Nazis during World War II. They too practised extreme cruelty within concentration camps located near towns and cities. The inhabitants similarly said that they had no idea of what was taking place.

The moment of the horse's death, and its subsequent involuntary movements, is of particular interest in that it is probably the most unrehearsed moment in the film – a moment of complete realism. While the scenes of flagellation and nailing in the dungeon are actual scenes, the participants are nonetheless conscious of being filmed. There is room for artifice, for performance. In his essay on bullfighting, Andre Bazin wrote about the capacity of the cinema to capture the moment of death – for human and animal. This is the moment in which something changes irreversibly. 'The representation of a real death is also an obscenity, no longer a moral one, as in love, but metaphysical' (Bazin, 2003: 30).

That Schroeder wants the audience to draw close parallels between these two worlds – slaughterhouse and dungeon – is made clear by his repeated reference to 'becoming animal' in the dungeon. On at least two occasions Ariane, as *Maîtresse*, rides her slaves as if they were horses. Perhaps, in the performance they think themselves to be horses. They have become the animal that is an intricate part of the human – the animal that anthropocentric discourses deny. The men wear a saddle and bridle. She carries a crop and guides them around the room. The first occurs during the early scene of urination when she orders the 'horse' onto all fours while she mounts him. Ariane is very much queen of her domain, and in complete control – a strong, sexualized woman. The body language of the dominatrix has been described as comparable to the posturing of dominant animals. Ariane and the male masochists both perform the animal and also become the animal. In another scene, a man behaves as if he were a horse. Schroeder commented on this in an interview. He explains that during the filming a strange thing occurred. For the fantasy to work:

> The man had to believe he was a horse [...] His itinerary was to pace around. It was a real *mise-en-scène*. But instead of following this itinerary, the 'horse' obeyed Bulle's wrong order and went in the direction she was indicating to him with the reins. He behaved like a horse rather than a man playing a role. (Stein, 1977: 56)

These are not wild animals – rather animals domesticated and subjected to human domination. Given that the masochists who appear in the dungeon are actual practitioners it is reasonable to conclude that the pleasure they express, in being subjected to a regime of harsh discipline, punishment and pain is real. Olivier however holds himself back from his own masochistic desires. Earlier he secretly entered the dungeon and subjected one of the customers to a brutal attack. Eating the flesh of a horse, with whom he identified as victim helped him to re-experience his humanity and his capacity for suffering.

Schroder represents a number of carefully scripted scenes in which Olivier and Ariane together open themselves up to their sadomasochistic desires. The film does not attempt to present value judgements on any of the behaviours it depicts – apart from the scene in the abattoirs. The S/M scenarios are also represented as rituals – fantasies of desire in which the trappings of fantasy, the specific details of the mise en scène, are of crucial importance. In both the motifs of death and incorporation are central. The masochists ritually confront death at the hands of the dominatrix as well as incorporation in that she dominates their every movement, their every desire. At times she finds their demands overwhelming. After one harrowing scenario of piercings and punishments in the dungeon, she rushes up the ladder, gasping for air, at the point of collapse. 'I can't give what they want anymore' she cries. For a moment she senses that there are limits to the extent to which she can fulfil their desires. In general, however, she remains firmly in control – both above and below ground.

Throughout *Maîtresse*, Schroeder interweaves the events in the dungeon with those above ground to demonstrate that extreme forms of human behaviour in the end foreshadow what takes place in the so-called 'normal' world, which almost always attempts to disassociate itself from any erosion of so-called civilized forms of behaviour. These scenes of sexual extremes are not presented as interruptions to the narrative but as a key part of the overall narrative. This appears to be a central feature of the way in which so-called pornographic images and scenes function in mainstream art-house narratives. In contrast to hard-core pornography, which consists primarily of the repetition of sexual scenes, art-house cinema such as *Maîtresse* utilizes representations of extreme sexuality in order to comment on the dark side of human nature. This is the main reason why such films are so confronting – not because of the images of erect penises or S/M practices but because these films draw on sexuality to comment on the ethical anxieties of the era.

Throughout the narrative, Schroeder depicts Olivier as confused about his own sexuality and innermost desires. From the moment he agrees to participate in the S/M sexual scenario with Ariane's client, he attempts to dominate her. While in the dungeon he obeys her, symbolically handing back her whip. However, when they return to her apartment after their first date, he grabs her. 'I could kill you now if I wanted to. It's simple. One squeeze and you are dead.' Instead he lifts her into his arms, kisses her and takes her to bed. The next day they embark on an outing in the countryside. After a tussle in the car, he insists on taking the driver's seat. After lunch at a country restaurant, she takes the driver's seat. 'I am in control. The biggest don't always win.' She tells him she must visit a friend who lives in a chateau in the country. The chateau turns out to be a variation on Ariane's dungeon. The servants, are actually masochists enacting fantasies of humiliation. Ariane harshly criticizes the butler for not cleaning to her satisfaction. In the drawing room, a woman is bent over, her naked buttocks on display. Olivier is invited to smack her, which he does without hesitation until red welts cover her skin.

One of the most telling episodes takes place immediately after the scene where Ariane nails the man's penis to a board. The lovers enact an S/M scene in the streets. Olivier pretends he is trying to pick her up. 'Please listen Mademoiselle. We could go for a drive.' He follows her down a side street. 'I'm not going to eat you although I wouldn't mind.' He grabs her bottom. 'Leave me alone, I'm married. I'll call the police.' The performance is semi-serious and appears largely spontaneous. Eventually he wields a knife to 'force' her into a bungalow situated in a courtyard. Knife in hand he pulls up her dress to reveal her bare bottom. The camera moves outside into the courtyard. We hear Ariane's cries and moans. Then unexpectedly we hear the sounds of a horse whinnying. Do these animal cries come from Olivier? In the subsequent scene when Olivier eats horse flesh, he also neighs like a horse as if he were becoming the animal he is consuming. When they emerge from the bungalow, and the owner confronts them, Olivier says to her: 'She's my wife. She's an exhibitionist. She like dustbins. She likes to fuck in the muck!' 'You are criminals. You're mad!' the old lady replies.

Although the couple explore their own sadomasochistic desires, the difference between their sexual role-playing in daylight and the S/M scenarios which take place in the darkened cellar are marked – the former represent the extremes of sexual fantasies, involving actual pain, whereas the latter are milder versions which are enacted for fun, some pain but mainly pleasure. However, Olivier's identification with the doomed horse at the abattoir and by implication the male masochists who become horses in the dungeon, indicate that his normally dominant posturing is giving way to a more complex sense of himself in which he is prepared to explore his own masochism. This is made clear in the final scene when the couple drive once again into the countryside. Here masochism invokes the spectre of death.

Schroeder says that he intended this scene to represent the 'extreme of the couple's relationship'. Olivier and Ariane drive the car together with Ariane sitting astride Olivier while both grip the steering wheel. At first both are in control – then each one takes their hands on and off the wheel as they begin to enjoy sex. As he brings her to orgasm, they lose interest in steering the car. They narrowly miss colliding with several other cars on the road. Eventually, the car rolls over coming to rest amid vegetation at the edge of the forest. The couple face death, but fate decrees that they only receive minor wounds. They wander off into the forest, laughing at their lucky escape and leaving the wrecked car behind them. Perhaps they are also leaving behind their former lives for something more complex and dangerous. To Schroeder this is a moment of equality – equality in masochism and in death: 'there's an equal dose of masochism in each of them. It's because of their pleasure that each may take the other into death' (Stein, 1977: 57). Schroeder has said: '*Maîtresse* stages a kind of negotiation between the urge to control and the need for submission and surrender.' Schroeder describes this as a 'happy ending' (Smith, 1995: 12). Some argue that masochism works through fantasies in which death signifies the main sexual event. Papoulias explains that this is 'a death which is always about to occur but is always kept at a distance, anticipated. The central feature of the scenario is suspense, waiting, deferred fulfilment of desire' (Papoulias, 1993: 165). Orgasm may bring a 'little death' but Olivier and Ariane share a fantasy of sexual pleasure aligned with the anticipation of actual death.

When the film was first submitted to the British Board of Film Classification in 1976, the Board members concluded that there was no possible way that the film could be cut in order to win an X rating. They agreed that *Maîtresse* had 'merit' and noted: 'Because we felt the film to be a responsible treatment of a difficult theme, we suggested the possibility of cuts but did say that for a national certificate these would have to be extensive' (BBFC, 2012: 3). The Board recommended that the distributors of *Maîtresse* should seek local certificates, for private cinema clubs, which they were awarded in some instances. When the film was resubmitted by a new distributor in 1980, after changes in the legislation, the Board agreed to release *Maîtresse* with cuts in just three scenes. These were the scene of the woman's genitals on display as she is bent over and beaten, the scene of the man's penis nailed to a board and the scene of needles probing a man's genitals followed by flagellation. The Board's earlier objection to the screening of the scene of slaughter at the abattoir was no longer an issue. The Board commented: 'The film remains a serious study of an extreme form of human sexuality [...] It never exploits its sensational material but we never thought it did' (BBFC, 2012: 3). When asked why it took so long for the film to be released, even with cuts, the Board replied that they and the public had changed more than they realized. *Maîtresse* was finally released uncut to the public in 2003. *Maîtresse* is exceptional in that the BBFC openly acknowledged that the sadomasochistic scenes in the film were crucial to the development of its narrative, and exploration of its themes, and not simply there for the voyeuristic entertainment of the viewer.

It is somewhat ironic that the film which was a forerunner of things to come, in relation to gender roles, was not released uncut until 2003, a number of years after the new wave of erotic films appeared in the 90s. Schroeder's film certainly anticipated a more dominant role for women, and passive role for men, in the new erotic films. Perhaps this is also a reason why the Board felt the public were not yet ready to see *Maîtresse*. Schroeder himself has drawn attention to this.

> Surveys showed that women were much less shocked or disturbed by *Maîtresse* than men were. Women don't identify with the men in the film and they like the fact that this woman is completely free and holds her own life in her hands. But I've really seen panic in some men because somewhere inside they see that it could be themselves on the screen. (Stein, 1977: 417)

Two other sexually explicit films of the period similarly explored themes of female sexual empowerment – these were *Emmanuelle* (1974) and *The Night Porter* (1974). Interestingly, the film version of *The Story of O* (1975), a study of female masochism, changes the ending of the novel so that the heroine asserts control over her male lover when she brands him with a cigarette that leaves the letter 'o' burnt into his skin. *Maîtresse*, however, presents the most confronting study of female sexual power – a power that was not to be fully explored again until the release of Catherine Breillat's *Romance* in 1999. Pornographic art-house films such as *Maîtresse* are not designed specifically for the spectator's pleasure. *Maîtresse* both elicits contradictory responses from its audience while also exploring the sexual and ethical issues of the era including the abuse of animals.

Chapter 2

WHAT IS AND IS NOT PORN

SEX, NARRATIVE, AND *BAISE-MOI*

JACOB M. HELD

In a book on sex and storytelling there has to be a chapter that deals with how to define pornography. Such a discussion should focus on the defining characteristics of pornography; its essence and what distinguishes it from other genres of film. But defining pornography is difficult. In order to define it properly, one must begin from the history of the concept, and doing so requires one interrogate previous, failed attempts at defining the pornographic. In addition, one must grapple with the fact that current definitions are often motivated not by a search for truth or understanding, but regulation and control. But defining pornography should be about the aesthetics of porn as an art form, and for this essay specifically as a genre of film, not a moral, legal, or political exercise. In this regard, when I ask 'What is porn?' I am offering a query about what differentiates porn from other film genres. What is it about a specific presentation of sex in film that makes it pornographic? Is the mere presence of explicit sex in a film sufficient to warrant classifying it as pornographic? Is explicit sex even a necessary element of the pornographic? By interrogating these and similar questions I hope to garner important insights into the nature of pornography as a film genre as well as develop a clearer understanding of the role of sex in narrative cinema.

The first half of this chapter will be devoted to defining pornography. The second half will seek to prove the first by applying this new definition to contemporary presentations of sex in narrative film focusing on *Baise-moi* (Virginie Despentes and Coralie Trinh Thi, 2000). The primary claim of this chapter is that pornography, as a genre, is marked not by explicit sex, arousal, or visual penetration, but rather by a lack of narrative strength such that the film becomes a mere delivery system for the spectacle of sex presented as a spectacle alone beyond any further meaning. In pornographic films the sex is present for the sex's sake alone, whereas in non-pornographic narrative films that include explicit sex (simulated or non-simulated), the sex fulfils a diegetic role. In a pornographic film, the spectacle of sex is the *sine qua non* of the film. In non-pornographic, albeit sexually explicit narrative cinema, the sex is part and parcel to the narrative and enhances it in such a way that its absence would detract from and leave incomplete the narrative.

DEFINING PORNOGRAPHY: PART ONE

One thing seems to connect the myriad and diverse historical definitions of pornography; they are motivated by a desire to regulate material deemed obscene, filthy, dangerous, or otherwise undesirable under a particular conception of sex and sexuality. Defining pornography has historically been about regulating the discourse on sexuality. As one scholar notes, 'If people were not trying to pass laws against pornography, a definition might not be so crucial [...] Whoever controls the definition [...] will determine which words and images the law will suppress. They will decide the framework of future debate over pornography' (McElroy, 1995: 41). In this regard, the issues surrounding pornography often get conflated with issues surrounding the obscene, where obscenity is the legal term connoting sexually explicit materials of limited or no redeeming value. These various definitions are often normatively loaded; they are laden with evaluative terms such as 'prurient', 'degrading', or 'subordination'. This pattern has led some to claim that classifying a work as 'pornographic' is not a discovery or mere act of definition, but an argument (Kendrick, 1996: 31). In the legal instance of obscenity in the US it is an argument about what type of discourse on sexuality is permissible, meritorious, and so protected by the First Amendment.

One of the first federal laws restricting obscene material in the US was the Comstock Act, 17 Stat. 598 (1873). This act restricted the trade, possession, manufacture, and distribution of 'obscene' materials and materials of an 'immoral nature' including information on contraception and abortion. Then in *Roth v. United States*, 354 U.S. 476 (1957) the Supreme Court revisited the issue and Justice William Brennan (1906-97) offered the following definition of obscenity: 'The standard for obscenity

[...] is whether, to the average person, applying contemporary community standards, the dominant theme of the material, taken as a whole, appeals to prurient interest' (Brennan, 1957: 477). Brennan's intention was to offer a definition that was neither too broad nor too narrow. The problem is that any definition of 'obscene' creates the class of utterances it picks out; it is a value judgement. Only after the criteria of evaluation has been enunciated and applied can 'obscene' be determined. And the motivation to determine 'obscene' is to decry a kind of presentation of sex as without merit or undeserving of public expression or dissemination. Thus, the evaluation of the justices determines how broad 'obscene' will be insofar as it is their interpretations of 'prurience' or related concepts that determine the scope of the obscene. Brennan's definition is thus as broad or narrow as the aesthetic/moral judgements of the justices applying it.

The problems *Roth* created were numerous. One of the most common was the fact that the justices had to assess each 'obscene' work to see if it was truly obscene. For each doubtful work, the court had to determine whether it had 'redeeming social importance'. The court held that to be classified as obscene materials must be 'utterly without redeeming social importance' so in adjudicating these cases they had to determine what value, if any, these works possessed. But is anything without any redeeming social importance? As one justice remarked, 'Redeeming to whom? Importance to whom?' (Douglas, 1966: 490). Obviously people value works others might deem obscene, they produce, distribute, and/or consume them. Frustrated over the topic in general and the court's inability to develop a precise definition of obscenity, one justice famously declared with respect to hard-core pornography, 'I know it when I see it' (Stewart, 1964: 197).

In 1973 the court revisited the issue of obscenity in a pair of rulings, *Miller v. California*, 413 U.S. 15 (1973) and *Paris Adult Theatre I v. Slayton*, 413 U.S. 49 (1973), and offered new guidelines for the determination of obscenity. The new guidelines consisted of three criteria: a) whether 'the average person, applying contemporary standards' would find that the work, taken as a whole, appeals to the prurient interest; b) whether the work depicts or describes, in a patently offensive way, sexual conduct specifically defined by the applicable state law; and c) whether the work, taken as a whole, lacks serious literary, artistic, political, or scientific value.

This new standard, far from solving the previous problems, exacerbated them by expanding the scope of 'obscenity'. This new standard rejected the notion that a work must be utterly without redeeming social importance and instead merely required that the work lack 'serious' value. Given the problematic nature of determining the value of a literary, artistic, political, or scientific work this new criteria, just as the old, demanded that judges function as art critics. Justice Antonin Scalia once responded to these criteria by stating:

> [I]n my view it is quite impossible to come to an objective assessment of (at least) literary or artistic value [...] Since ratiocination has little to do with esthetics [sic], the fabled 'reasonable man' is of little help in the inquiry, and would have to be replaced with, perhaps, the 'man of tolerably good taste' – a description that betrays the lack of an ascertainable standard. (Scalia, 1987: 504-5)

The problem with this approach to obscene material is that it affords the law the power to regulate the public discourse on sex and sexuality according to the idiosyncratic normative judgments of a handful of justices. It is at root a political assessment of the value of certain presentations of sexual material that although not coextensive with pornography, includes only instances of pornography. Not all porn is obscene, but all obscene material is porn. Thus, as a definition of obscenity, or pornography, it is not a descriptive account of what porn is, but rather an assessment of what presentations of sex ought to be accessible to the public.

Another legal history revolves not around the value of pornography or obscene material, but around whether pornography itself is a form of discrimination against women. Two of the most vocal proponents of this view are Catharine MacKinnon and Andrea Dworkin (1946-2005). MacKinnon and Dworkin's basic claim is that pornography 'eroticizes hierarchy, it sexualizes inequality [...] It institutionalizes the sexuality of male supremacy, fusing the eroticization of dominance and submission with the social construction of male and female' (MacKinnon, 1995: 59-60). As a practice, pornography reinforces a hierarchy of inequality and perpetuates a culture that excuses and rationalizes sexual aggression and male dominance. Some have made the additional claim that pornography is discriminatory insofar as it presents as authoritative a ranking of women as inferior (Langton, 2009).

In 1983, MacKinnon and Dworkin drafted an amendment to the Minneapolis Civil Rights ordinance that would construe pornography as discrimination. Then in 1984 the Indianapolis City and County Council adopted a similar law. It was subsequently challenged in court and ruled unconstitutional by the Seventh Circuit Court of Appeals. The ordinance in question contained prohibitions on trafficking pornography, coercing others into performances, and forcing porn on anyone. In order to be applied, the ordinance needed a working definition of pornography. Pornography was defined as:

> The graphic sexually explicit subordination of women, whether in pictures or in words, that also includes one or more of the following: (1) women are presented as sexual objects who enjoy pain or humiliation; or (2) women are presented as sexual objects who experience sexual pleasure in being raped; or (3) women are presented as sexual objects tied up or cut up or mutilated or bruised or physically hurt, or as dismembered or truncated or fragmented or severed into body parts; or (4) women are presented as being penetrated by objects or animals; or (5) women are presented in scenarios of degradation, injury abasement, torture, shown as filthy or inferior, bleeding, bruised, or hurt in a context that makes these conditions sexual; or (6) women are presented as sexual objects for domination, conquest, violation, exploitation, possession, or use, or through postures or positions of servility or submission or display. (*American Booksellers Association, Inc. v. William H. Hudnut, Mayor, City of Indianapolis*, 771 F.2d 323, 324 (7th Circuit, 1985))

Wendy McElroy notes that this is not a definition, but a conclusion (1995: 46-8). As with obscenity laws in general, the most problematic element of this law is the use of evaluative criteria. Consider the definition of pornography as 'the graphic sexually explicit subordination of women'. This criterion is fraught with the same interpretative problems from which previous obscenity laws suffered. Who determines if a representation is 'subordinating?' Whether or not a depiction represents an inappropriate power relation is very much open to debate, aside from the contentious claim itself that presenting such relationships is itself discriminatory. One's conclusion regarding these matters will ultimately rest on one's view of sexuality and interpersonal relationships. To illustrate the problem this standard raises consider MacKinnon and Dworkin's own view on the matter. Dworkin once claimed, 'It's very hard to look at a picture of a woman's body and not see it with the perception that her body is being exploited' (Dworkin, 1994: 23). It is not a stretch to conclude that the definition above if interpreted in light of Dworkin's own perceptions of female sexuality would determine all sexually explicit, and perhaps all, depictions of women to be pornographic. Likewise, 'MacKinnon has condemned pornography specifically because it shows that women "desire to be fucked." [...] MacKinnon also echoes Dworkin's thesis that women who believe they voluntarily engage in, and enjoy, heterosexual sex are victims of "false consciousness"' (Strossen, 2000: 111). What anti-porn definitions show is not what porn is, but how the anti-porn activist views sexuality. 'Such descriptions are normative, or biased. They embody the viewer's reactions, and their desire to condemn pornography' (McElroy, 1995: 43). But sex can have many meanings beyond what one viewer or critic may ascribe. These definitions are motivated by a desire to promote one view of sex over another. As such these definitions are unhelpful in understanding what porn is. But the purpose of a definition is to describe a phenomenon, not evaluate it.

The problem of normatively loaded definitions is highlighted again in the case of trying to distinguish pornography from erotica. Gloria Steinem recommends understanding erotica as 'mutually pleasurable' or sexual expression among equals, whereas pornography is 'violence, dominance, and conquest' (Steinem, 1995: 31). Porn is about domination and objectification, erotica is about mutuality. And what is the point of the distinction: to vindicate erotica while condemning pornography. If the purpose was not to condemn porn it would be hard to find a reason to make the distinction at all. Both erotica and pornography may contain explicit sex, both may arouse. They seem to be identical except that some find the presentation of sex and sexuality in porn abhorrent whereas the sex in erotica is appropriate, it is acceptable. This distinction is only relevant if the point of classification is to implicitly evaluate what is being classified.

The problem we face, therefore, is that all definitions seem to begin from the idea that the presentation of sex is itself problematic. But the definition thus begins from a sexual ethic, from a prejudicial view that only certain kinds of sex are worth viewing or merit being rendered visible. These definitions are, therefore, mere traces of social norms. Thus, we do not learn about sex in narrative film through these definitions. Instead, we learn about how society views sex and sexuality and how it reacts to transgressive or alternative presentations of sex. A new definition of porn as non-normative would begin from the idea that sex is a fact of the human condition, deserves to be represented, and then interrogate how that occurs in art, specifically film.

DEFINING PORNOGRAPHY: PART TWO

Many seemingly non-evaluative definitions of 'pornography' have been offered. Etymologically, many point to the origins of the word: 'Porno' meaning prostitution, and 'graphos' meaning 'writing about or description of' (Steinem, 1995: 31; Kendrick, 1996: 1). Some make a lot of hay out of the word's etymological formation or its literal meaning, but little is gained from this exercise. The meaning has changed over time as the material it was meant to denote and the societies in which that material was located have evolved. Then there are myriad contemporary definitions, which David Andrews (2012) has helpfully compiled: 'the explicit depiction or representation of human beings engaged in sexual activity'; 'a certain content, explicitly sexual representation, with a certain intention, sexual arousal'; 'flagrant erotic display designed to excite the spectator, reader, or listener'; and 'the presentation in verbal or visual signs of human sexual organs in a condition of stimulation'. Other suggested definitions include McElroy's 'Pornography is the explicit artistic depiction of men and/or women as sexual beings' (McElroy, 1995: 51) and Linda Williams' definition of film pornography as 'the visual (and sometimes aural) representation of living, moving bodies engaged in explicit, usually unfaked, sexual acts with the primary intent of arousing viewers' (Williams, 1999: 30). Andrews also highlights the various problems with these definitions, for example, reliance on concepts like 'explicit' or 'arousal'. 'Explicit' is itself insufferably vague and often hetero-normative; usually implying penetration whether penile-vaginal, -anal, or -oral. But the fact that we distinguish between soft-core and hard-core pornography where the differentia between the two is the presence or absence of the meat or beaver shot seems to indicate that the inclusion of 'explicit' leaves out members of the pornography family. If soft-core pornography is pornography then 'explicit' is an unhelpful and, in fact, inaccurate differentia. A definition of porn must be applicable to all forms of pornography, and some forms are not 'explicit'. One might define 'explicit' by removing penetration as a necessary element of explicit sex and thus include soft-core presentations of sex and sexual themes under traditional definitions of pornography. But at that point the word 'explicit' would lose any meaning since it would effectively be reduced to mean any presentations of sexual themes, and hence all presentation of sex would become pornographic, even the innocuous love scenes present in mainstream films.

There are additional problems surrounding 'arousal' as a criterion. Predicating a definition of a thing on the intent of the author or the reaction of the consumer, as does the inclusion of the criterion 'arousal' in a definition of pornography speaks not to the essence of the thing but elements external and non-essential to the nature of the object. But a definition must refer to the essence of the thing. Viewer response does not determine or affect the nature of the thing being experienced or defined. For example, Gustave Courbet's *L'Origine du Monde* (1866) does not become pornographic because one is aroused by tightly framed beaver shots. It is what it is in terms of art regardless of the response it elicits from the viewer. Likewise, it does not become pornographic merely because it is 'explicit' under any rendering of that term.

Defining an object is ultimately about looking at a collection of entities and finding a family resemblance that seems essential to those items, an essence that both accounts for why they are the way they are as well as how to differentiate them from other things that might otherwise be related to them. In order to find such a definition, we should begin by looking at recognizable, incontestable examples of porn and asking: 'What is the family resemblance between all these things we call "porn?"' Justice Potter Stewart (1915–85) was basically correct; when it comes to pornography we tend to know it when we see it. But what do we know?

We can begin with obvious, incontestable examples, and then abstract essential characteristics they share. If we look at uncontested, paradigmatic examples of porn, from the golden age classics such as *Deep Throat* (Gerard Damiano, 1972), *Behind the Green Door* (James Mitchell and Arthur Mitchell, 1972), *Taboo* (Kirdy Stevens, 1980), *The Opening of Misty Beethoven* (Radley Metzger, 1976), to the oeuvre of 1980s porn icons such as Ron Jeremy or Christy Canyon, to the work of 90s stars such as Jill Kelly, Kaitlyn Ashley, and most notably Jenna Jameson, all the way to contemporary pornography and the work of burgeoning stars like Bree Olsen, James Deen, or Jesse Jane, the protagonist in the venerable *Pirates* (Joone, 2005), we do see commonalities. Some claim that the genre can be marked by the essential presence of the money shot (Williams, 1999: 121), or perhaps a more inclusive list of standard shots including not only the money shot, but the meat and beaver shots, close-up penetration and medical grade photography of female genitalia (Johnson, 1993: 31). Porn as a genre seems to be denoted by the presence of a hyper-visuality of the sex act with framing and blocking orchestrated to maximize visibility and verify male pleasure through the presence of the cumshot, that is, the 'very functioning' and 'hydraulics of sex' (Williams, 2008: 5). Yet to frame the genre so narrowly would be to exclude other films such as soft-core classics like *Emmanuelle* (Just Jaeckin, 1974), *Lady Chatterley's Lover* (Jaeckin, 1981) and the recent work being done by Candida Royalle and Femme Pictures where the absence of hard-core pornographic conventions is the norm and in fact the raison d-être for these 'female friendly' productions. There is a clear difference between the conventions of mainstream hard-core pornography and the conventions of soft-core pornography, such as the avoidance of the money shot, full body coverage as opposed to just a focus on penetration, as well as a focus on the context of the sex act (Johnson, 1993: 39). This difference needs to be acknowledged while still recognizing all of these forms of pornography to be pornography properly so called. One ought to look at all these representatives and ask whether there is a commonality that would justify categorizing them all under the umbrella of 'pornography'.

What I propose is looking not at what type of sex is present or how it is shot, but rather the role it plays in the narrative structure of the film. The commonality that quickly becomes apparent is that pornography seems to be sex scenes loosely connected, if at all, by a narrative. It is not the presence of explicit sex that makes a film pornographic, it is not whether one sees the money shot, it is not about the visual presentation of sex, but instead it is about the role the sex plays in supporting or furthering the narrative of the film.

Consider what some take to be the best that porn has to offer, namely, the pinnacle moments from the golden age of porn, *Deep Throat*, or Linda William's favourite film to interrogate, *The Opening of Misty Beethoven*. These films are taken to be classics, the ideal towards which all aspire. Yet even with all the ink spilled trying to deconstruct them, we still call these films 'porn'. Why? Because at the end of the day, regardless of how much one wants to read into the narrative, the plot, or the characters, they are simply fuck films. The idea that in retrospect, and out of a sense of nostalgia for the now existent mythos of an era of libertine, free sex often associated with the 1970s and early 80s they get elevated to a status among actual narrative film is interesting, and problematic (Paasonen and Saarenmaa, 2007: 23–5), but it does not make them narrative films. Consider *Deep Throat*. The plot is banal at best: a woman's clitoris is located in the back of her throat, so in order to achieve an orgasm she must perform 'deep throat' oral sex. Attempts to defend the plot or legitimate *Deep Throat* as an interrogation into gender norms are doomed to failure. Can one honestly claim that *Deep Throat* is about the gender binary and the opposition being posed 'as pure anatomical difference, with the resolution coming through the right number with the "right" man, though in fact the fellatio "solution" really works *for the male*' (Williams, 2008: 139). Even being generous and granting that the plot is not worse than most contemporary action or horror films, the place of the sex is questionable. What role does the sex play in the film? Is it a commentary on female pleasure? No. The story would move as well without the sex as it does with it. So what is the role of the sex? Consider screen time. In *Deep Throat*, roughly 60 per cent of the screen time is hard-core sex scenes, leaving merely 24 minutes of film to the narrative, five of which are opening credits. The narrative becomes peripheral to the spectacle of sex. Or rather, the narrative is an excuse to present sex on film. Legally, the narrative allowed the film-makers to skirt the legal definition of obscenity by providing a modicum of artistic merit and thus provided an excuse for presenting sex on film (Schaefer, 2002: 3–4). But the sex is the *sine qua non* of *Deep Throat*, not the narrative. This is evidenced by the fact that *Deep Throat*, just as its contemporaries, was often aired without published air times and people would enter and exit the movie theatre in which it was being played without regard to the start or end times (Lehman, 2006: 4–5). There was no recognized narrative element and once video became popular the facade of narrative integrity dissolved entirely. These films were meant to be delivery systems for the spectacle of sex, even if after the fact one might interpret them as being more than they were. These films isolate the sex and allow it to dominate the film (Krzywinska, 2006: 222). In fact, after the advent of home video the boom in compilation videos illuminates exactly what pornographic film is about, it is all about the sexual number, not the narrative (Lehman, 2006: 9). Although Williams claims that porn is more akin to musicals than other film genres the analogy is weak (2008: 124). In pornography one can create compilation videos and films that sell as well or better than their narrative counterparts, whereas in musicals the integrity of the whole is fundamental to the integrity of the work. In musicals the musical number occupies significantly less screen time than the narrative. The narrative could survive as a film in its own right without the music, but the music demonstrates its value through its unique relation to the narrative of the film of which it is a part. In porn this is not the case. In *Deep Throat* a viewer can get the same meaning and content from watching Linda Lovelace fellate Harry Reams in a clip as he can seeing it in the context of the film as a whole, and removing a specific act of fellatio does not detract from the narrative. The sex in porn is superfluous to the narrative, or rather the narrative is superfluous to the presentation of the sex, and the time devoted to sex versus narrative, as well as the stock positioning and presentation of sex indicates as much. 'The fantastic fictional premise of the film is a pretext for the presentation of sexual "spectacle"' (Crabbe, 1988: 54). To put it simply, people watch their favourite porn stars, not their favourite porn movies.

Are we any closer to a definition of pornography? First, a good definition should be value neutral, it should not include assessments of sex and sexuality or vague references to things such as explicit sex, nor should it reference non-essential characteristics like arousal, and most importantly it must be functional: it should capture pornography and exclude most non-pornographic material. Any definition will be at some points inaccurate and should be tentative. After all, we are trying to classify something which is at root ephemeral and ever-changing, a genre of film, and genres are a constant work of negotiation (Esch and Mayer, 2007: 101). But even more to the point, definitions themselves are negotiations. As noted above, many previous definitions of pornography carried within themselves implicit evaluations of sex. Laying bare the implicit normativity of several of these definitions showed that far from merely describing a phenomenon, these definitions isolated the pornographic according to evaluative criteria aside from simple aesthetic judgements. These definitions were found lacking because they failed to capture objects that ought to fall under the umbrella of 'porn'. But it would be hubris to believe that a new definition will avoid any possible future pitfall. Just as our present understanding of sex and sexuality, as well as our shifting expectations about permissible topics of discourse, have rendered previous definitions inaccurate or untenable, so too may any newly offered definition be rendered obsolete in the future. Definitions seek to isolate essential characteristics of phenomena, but what is accepted as essential is determined by the metaphysical and epistemological presuppositions of particular discourses and so any definition is to some extent prejudiced by the episteme in which is it placed. This is not to say that definitions are relative such that all proffered definitions are equally as valuable. Some definitions are better than others at picking out phenomena and offering us an understanding and interpretation of our world. Rather, it is to recognize that any definition we offer is necessarily and inevitably a reflection of our present episteme, and so needs to be taken as tentative insofar as our regime of knowledge is itself contingent. Any proffered definition will focus on apparent substantive generalities and commonalities but we ought not to expect too much from it. But one commonality between apparent members of the porn family seems obvious, porn is non-narrative (Johnson, 1993: 33). This is not to say that porn lacks a narrative. All pornographic films, excepting compilations, have some narrative element, no matter how weak or superficial. Often it is some comedic ploy. Most recently the trend is to parody mainstream film narratives, examples such as *Spider-Man XXX: A Porn Parody* (Axel Braun, 2011) and *The Dark Knight XXX: A Porn Parody* (Braun, 2012) to *Star Wars XXX: A Porn Parody* (Braun, 2012) come to mind. What it means to call porn non-narrative is to say that the narrative of a porn film is not overly concerned with causal chains and coherent character developments. 'All in all, porn films consist of sexual scenes that are not necessarily tied together by narrative' (Paasonen and Saarenmaa, 2007: 30). Instead, the presentation of sex is the motive, the *sine qua non* of the film and the narrative elements are just excuses for the placement of stock sex scenes which include all the standard shots, framing, blocking, and conventions of mainstream hard-core pornography. Most of these numbers take a considerable amount of screen time over and above narrative development often occupying over 60 or 70 per cent of the film, with five or ten minutes of narrative interposed between 20–30-minute sex scenes. These scenes follow a similar patterning regardless of the narrative of the film. One begins often with female to male oral, moves to penetration, doggy-style, cowboy, reverse cowboy, missionary (rarely), anal, and always ends with a cumshot, usually across the woman's face. The interchangeability of these scenes among films speaks to their stock nature and lack of narrative content. A definition can, therefore, begin from an intuition accepted by most, the primary focus of porn is sex (Zuromskis, 2007: 4). I propose the following definition of pornography (focusing on porn as a genre of film specifically): 'Pornographic film is film wherein the *sine qua non* of the film is the presentation of the spectacle of sex. That is, the presence of sex in pornography exists without any necessary connection to or reliance upon the narrative of the film and the narrative of the film is not necessarily enhanced or driven by the presence of the spectacle of sex.'[1] This definition could be broadened out to all media of art from the plastic arts to print, but I am choosing to focus on film.

The definition above has several strengths over competitors and seems to capture something both true and illuminating about pornography. First, this definition avoids the assessments found in the Supreme Court's definition of obscenity, assessments about merit, offensiveness, and legitimate versus illegitimate (i.e. prurient) interests.

The court's use of the SLAPS (Serious Literary, Artistic, Political or Scientific) criterion implies that sex itself is not meritorious on its own, but must be justified with reference to some other supervening value, such as artistic expression, or scientific knowledge. But why is sex itself, even as a spectacle, not meritorious or worthy of visual presentation? The same fault can be found with their use of 'prurience' as a way of differentiating obscene from non-obscene material. The implication that a juvenile attitude betrays lack of merit would equally discredit the majority of non-sexual popular culture. Again, the court's criterion betrays an implicit normativity, an evaluation of particular expressions of sex and sexuality as inappropriate or off limits. Secondly, the definition offered above claims that the essence of pornography, the reason it exists is to present sex as a spectacle. The sex is presented outside of the context of any narrative element of the film. Although such films may have narrative components they are inessential to the purpose of the film and in fact threaten to distract from it. Ron Jeremy has noted you cannot act too well or be too funny in porn. 'Porn is about the sex, not the punch lines [...] you're not trying to distract from the action' (Jeremy, 2007: 168). Likewise, when the actors perform their characters well, as in *The Dark Knight XXX*, the performances detract from the spectacle of sex. Does anyone want to see an imitation of Heath Ledger's Joker, even a good one, fuck Batgirl (Penny Pax)? If someone wants to see Penny Pax have sex, they will most assuredly be turned off by Brendon Miller's performance. They want to see the spectacle of Penny Pax getting penetrated in every way imaginable, not Miller's acting skills. If a consumer wants to watch a good movie they do not rent *The Dark Knight XXX*. They rent it for the sex. Here again the above definition shows its strength. It offers a criterion by which one can evaluate pornographic films. All pornographic films are not bad films. They may be bad by the criteria used to evaluate narrative films, but as films whose purpose is to present the spectacle of sex, some can be better than others. One need only ask has the film presented the best possible, most spectacular sex?

Another way to understand the same point is to consider the role of the sex in the film. The fact that stock shots and techniques permeate porn films, that the same positions, framing, positioning, and blocking occurs regardless of the theme or narrative should indicate what the purpose of the sex is, and that it is not to further or deepen the narrative elements of the film. Rather, it is to present the spectacle of sex in the way the viewer has come to expect. This also explains why film declined with the rise of VHS, and why starlets, not directors or screenwriters, drive the consumption of a film.

This definition also captures hard-core and soft-core porn; it covers all forms from feminist and female friendly to the most extreme. It captures porn with or without money shots, that do or do not arouse. But most importantly this definition guarantees that the mere presence of sex in a film, even explicit, titillating sex is not enough to relegate a film to the pornographic. This is its ultimate strength. Whether one agrees or not, classifying a film as pornographic is to condemn it to the dustbin of film history. But there are films that contain explicit sex, both simulated and real, which merit respect as narrative films. These are films in which the sex means something, it adds to or even becomes the narrative. Sex as spectacle is not morally evaluative but descriptively accurate, and using this as an essential differentia allows us to appreciate better how sex can function in a narratively driven film without making the film about the sex act itself. So the proposed definition does not presume that sex is inherently pornographic, it rather asks for the context. Is the sex a spectacle, is the film a fuck film, or is the sex a constitutive narrative element in the way music, violence, or other diegetic conventions might be? We accept horror, violence, or comedy as legitimate topics for discussion and exploration, and as legitimate performances. We see them as part and parcel to the human condition and laud films that interrogate these themes well. Sex is an equally valuable component to our lives and so it too ought to be explored in film without the film then being branded as 'pornographic' and ruled unfit for decent society. Porn has always been about the sex. And that does not make it good or bad, it merely denotes its essence. But the fact that pornography is all about sex should not lead to the conclusion that any film with sex is pornographic, and one can truly appreciate the difference if one considers a film like *Baise-moi*.

BAISE-MOI

Baise-moi is representative of a recent trend in European, primarily French art-house cinema where sex is not simulated but real. So how ought one to classify *Baise-moi*? Is it pornographic? Finding an answer is problematized by the use of porn actresses, Karen Bach (Lancaume) (1973–2005) and Rafaella Anderson, as well as it having been co-directed by a hard-core porn veteran, Coralie Trihn Thi. Yet, ostensibly this film is not pornographic insofar as the sex is not the purpose of the film.

Instead, the sex amplifies various themes in much the same way the violence does. So although the film includes real sex, uses porn actresses, and is co-directed by a porn director it is not pornographic according to the definition offered above.

Baise-moi is primarily a noir film in the rape-revenge tradition of the genre. It has even been referred to by Linda Williams as 'Thelma and Louise Get Laid' (Williams, 2001: 28). Insofar as it focuses on female subjectivity in response to phallocentrism expressed through violent irruptions of female desire/anger/angst, plus sex, this is accurate. However, what *Baise-moi* adds comes by way of the sex, not so much the presence of the act itself, but the absence of the traditional phallocentric representations of explicit sex; close-up penetration shots, shows of female orgasmic pleasure, and finally the ubiquitous presence of ejaculate, the money shot. The sex is framed differently than in porn, (Krzywinska, 2006: 13) and this raises the question, 'Why?' If mainstream porn can be standardized since the purpose of the film is to present sex as mere spectacle, then it would seem that avoiding these conventions is purposive, and suggests that the sex cannot be reduced to spectacle but is purposively integrated into and forms an element of the narrative itself. Below I will illustrate how the sex in *Baise-moi* furthers the narrative and underscores various philosophical themes present in the film. Whereas some might maintain that *Baise-moi* blurs the distinction between pornographic and non-pornographic film (MacKenzie, 2002: 316) I maintain it emphasizes the distinction by demonstrating clearly that sex itself does not define porn, and in fact sex can be presented substantively on film as one of many diegetic elements in cinema.

In order to fully appreciate the role of sex in *Baise-moi* we must begin from a staple concept in psychoanalytic and feminist film theory, the idea of the gaze. Laura Mulvey maintains that film is shot from the perspective of the male gaze, by which she means that the point of view of the camera is meant to reinforce the dominance of the male over the female and thus reinforce a phallocentric worldview. Arguably, the male gaze does so through representing female characters as submissive or non-autonomous, passive objects to be used by their male counterparts on the screen. 'Women are simultaneously looked at and displayed, with their appearance coded for strong visual and erotic impact' (Mulvey, 1975: 11). Thus the female is shot in order to accentuate her form, her body as an object for appreciation or consumption, but as an agent she is minimized in her active and assertive capacities (Carroll, 1996: 263). Mulvey's theory has received a great deal of attention, and due to its influence a great deal of criticism. Most criticism expresses scepticism regarding Mulvey's focus on a monolithic meaning to the text of a film and singular overarching metanarrative that reduces all film to the phallocentric gaze (Carroll, 1996: 265; Hammett, 2003: 245). However, the idea that the gaze objectifies or dominates that upon which it gazes remains influential. 'In most cases, the gaze is used to help explain the hierarchical power relations between two or more groups or, alternatively, between a group and an "object"' (Manlove, 2007: 84). In pornography this is obvious, especially insofar as the female body is fragmented and blocked so as to be nothing more than the presentation of breasts, vagina, ass, or backdrop to the money shot. The lack of narrative only seeks to emphasize the woman's lack of agency. She is reduced to animality, pure sexual desire incapable of rational or human interaction beyond sex. In fact, recent studies seem to indicate that in the mind of the viewer, women in mainstream pornography get reduced to base animalistic, desirous creatures. '[O]bjectification might not lead to perceptions of women as inanimate objects but as different kinds of humans – ones that are capable of feeling but not thinking' (Valdesolo, 2011). The dissection or fragmentation, and subsequent objectification of the female form drives the conventions behind shooting mainstream, heterosexual hard-core pornography; conventions such as framing so as to show only close-up penetration shots, or fragmented views of the female anatomy as opposed to full body coverage. These standardized conventions are why sex scenes among porn films are interchangeable. These are the conventions against which *Baise-moi* ought to be appreciated. The actresses and directors of *Baise-moi* know these conventions; they are masters of the pornographic gaze. So how they respond to it, how they choose to use or subvert the male/pornographic gaze is instructive as one interprets the meaning of the sex in *Baise-moi*.

Simply put, the gaze in *Baise-moi* is purposefully not male, or rather; it is often a purposively frustrated male gaze. The gaze in *Baise-moi* is not possessive, not about the objectification of the female form, and it is through the rejection of standard porn conventions for shooting real sex that this rejection becomes most evident. The viewer is left wanting what is before their eyes, but not being made visible to them. It remains hidden and so the gaze is frustrated. Here is the transgression of *Baise-moi*, real sex is presented for the camera yet the gaze is frustrated leaving the viewer to wonder why real sex was necessary at all if it was not to be a spectacle. And that is the point, the meaning of the sex in *Baise-moi*.

The most powerful scene in *Baise-moi* is the rape scene. Mere minutes into the film we witness the rape of Manu and her friend by local thugs. Manu's friend is raped on the hood of a car, which is by far the most viscerally difficult aspect of the rape scene for the viewer. While being raped she is beaten so one is witnessing her bleeding while being violently penetrated, a penetration that is real, adding significantly to the unease of the viewer. Although the violence may be simulated the sex cannot be denied and so as she struggles against her fictive rape she is truly penetrated by her assailant. Manu, on the other hand, depicts a different aspect of the rape, the internal distancing victims often experience, locating themselves outside of their own bodies, dissociating themselves from the event as a defence mechanism against the total violation of the rape. In an attempt to inoculate herself from the total possession that the rapist seeks Manu distances herself from the rape in an attempt to diminish its significance.

While Manu is raped she seems almost resigned to the act. As one assailant remarks, 'It's like fucking a zombie.' The rapist ceases because Manu is clearly not accepting his pleasure, she denies his ability to give it to her. She rejects and thereby diminishes his power by refusing to allow herself to be possessed by him. She does not respond, because she rejects the value of sex as the patriarchal possession of her being. She later claims, 'I keep nothing precious in my cunt for those jerks.' Just as you do not leave anything valuable in your car in the projects because someone is bound to break in, you leave nothing precious in your cunt. 'It's just a bit of cock,' and she does not 'give a shit about their scummy dicks.'

Manu's cunt is not constitutive of who she is, her value or her place in the world. Likewise, all they inflicted on her was a 'bit of cock'. Men cannot harm her since she has nothing of value in her cunt, but also because they only have a 'bit of cock' to wield against her. In this exchange one might think Laura Mulvey has found confirmation of her thesis that women pose a castration threat to men in film (Mulvey, 1975: 6–7). Manu castrates her rapists and men in general by claiming that the worst violation that can be perpetrated against her or any woman is not that bad because the worst a man can offer is a 'bit of cock'. The rapist and the man's power is denied and so he is rendered impotent. The blocking of the scene reinforces the point. If the gaze of the camera is meant to be male, here one would expect it to show the penetration and violence close-up to reinforce the male possession of the female form. However, in this scene the blocking moves from the point of view of Manu's friend being violated to a wide, panoramic view shooting downward. Here the framing does not afford one a view of the details. This framing diminishes the significance of the event through distance in the same way Manu emotionally distances herself from the rape in an attempt to diminish its emotional significance. The male gaze of objectification and possession is thus acknowledged at the beginning and purposefully rejected by denying the viewer what he expects, violence and sex in a rape scene. Instead, the viewer is offered a detached view of the event, one that ends anti-climactically, especially for a sex scene. There is no money shot, no proof of male pleasure or signifiers of female pleasure. Here the viewer is treated to the transgressive element of *Baise-moi*, sex will continually be proffered, and the viewer, being familiar with the conventions for shooting sex and perhaps even familiar with the actresses, will expect the standard, pornographic/male gaze. Yet traditional pornographic conventions will be conspicuously absent, and so the viewer will be frustrated, internally demanding greater visibility. It is this internal demand that the viewer himself must face. He is demanding ownership of the female form, he is asserting the legitimacy of the male gaze's claim over the female form, and this demand will leave a trace back to the viewer causing him to reflect on what was expected, why it was expected, and in so doing force him to confront his desire. In this way, *Baise-moi* mocks the male gaze and the machismo evinced by it through its overt denial of porn conventions, its purposive rejection of objectifying and possessive shots of Nadine and Manu's bodies, and its calling the viewer to account for his desire to enforce the male gaze. 'Mockery as a narrative strategy is an interesting phenomenon, as it appears capable of expressing a coherent, if not controlling, female gaze as well as effecting a fissure in the representation of power itself' (Gamman, 1989: 17). In *Baise-moi*, the camera mocks the male, that is, the pornographic gaze that seeks to possess, consume, use, abuse, and dispose of the female body.

Manu and Nadine are a castration threat to men. They kill those that seek to objectify women and deprive them of their autonomy (Fayard, 2006: 72), from men that randomly proposition them in the street to those that demand they fulfil his sexual fantasy and thus attempt to co-opt female pleasure for male use. 'The heroines in *Baise-moi* eliminate almost every male that crosses their path, using guns, one of the most overdetermined signifiers of socialized masculinity, as weapons of female agency' (Franco, 2004: 3). Consider the incident with the stranger in the hotel room, an incident that ends with Manu and Nadine declaring themselves the 'condom dickhead killers'. Why do they kill this hapless, horny moron? He picks them up and wants to have sex with them, but he first wants to wear a condom. Manu is clear, you do not pick up a strange, dangerous woman, a femme fatale, and then try to render the encounter safe through the use of a condom. His attempt to be safe is his attempt to exercise control. But Manu is in control of her sexuality and in fact she demonstrates as much by performing fellatio to the point where she vomits all over him. He screams at her for being a 'filthy little cunt', and is subsequently murdered. Male pleasure is not the purpose, the *telos* or goal, of female sexuality; it can be rejected as demonstrated by Manu's fellatio-induced vomiting.

In pornography, the male gaze defines female desire and writes lesbianism in a way that conforms to male desire. Yet in *Baise-moi* porn veterans choose to conspicuously avoid representations of lesbian desire thereby denying the hegemony of the male gaze over the female body. Ironically, absence speaks more loudly than presence in a film notorious for its inclusion of real, explicit sex. Consider the hotel scene wherein the viewer is proffered a pseudo-intimate moment between Nadine and Manu. The scene seems to fulfil the need of any porn film for an obligatory lesbian scene. As Nadine and Manu dance together, they touch. They flirt with each other and the camera. But as they dance they never go beyond the occasional touch or flirtatious glance. The viewer expects a kiss. The viewer knows what to expect. These women will give themselves to each other, not for their pleasure, but for the pleasure of the viewer. Yet the viewer is left wanting. The viewer's desire seeks the fruition of the standard lesbian sex scene, constructed and performed for heterosexual men. The viewer expects it; this is a film with porn stars, by a porn director, including real sex. Yet, the viewer is denied, his expectations frustrated, his demands rejected. Nadine and Manu do not dance for him or his pleasure. This denial of the male gaze is obtrusive insofar as the camera is acknowledged, and the viewer's desire, his gaze, overtly rejected. It is as if Nadine and Manu have caught the voyeur looking and following the trace back ask, 'Did you want to see us fuck?' while simultaneously closing the blinds. There is not merely a rejection of the gaze, but chastisement of the one who gazes; he is guilty of seeking what is not his to seek, to possess what is not his to possess. 'The path of the gaze [...] betrays the subject using it [...] The return of the gaze [...] threatens to destroy a subject's object *a*' (Manlove, 2007: 99). This reversal of the gaze destroys not only the viewer's claim to ownership of the female form but also comprises a denial of what he desires, his object *a*. The guilt inflicted through the chastisement destroys the conditions for the possibility of the viewer obtaining his desire, the possession of the female form. Nadine and Manu do not just reject his desire, they destroy the possibility of it, as if to claim it is illegitimate.

In another instance that demonstrates the rejection of the male gaze we have the example of Nadine kicking a sex partner out of her and Manu's hotel room when he suggests it would be 'hot' to see them together. Even though Nadine had already had sex with him while Manu had sex with his friend in the bed adjacent this suggestion gets him shown the door. Through his simple request he indicates his desire to own or co-opt Manu and Nadine's pleasure and their bodies for his own use, his own heterosexual, male, lesbian fantasy. There are also non-sexual, violent performances that underscore the same themes, such as the mass killing in the libertine club.

In the libertine club Nadine and Manu kill everyone. The killing of the men is obvious, they are representative of patriarchy. And the killing of the last man on all fours by shooting him through the rectum is self-explanatory. The gun as phallus penetrates him, owns and dominates him, thus figuratively castrating him while asserting Nadine and Manu's power. They have inverted classic power relations; the female becomes assertive and dominant, and the male becomes passive and dominated. But why kill all the women? The women in the libertine club are complicit in their own oppression, and reinforce a phallocentric, male hegemonic order. Instead of seeing libertine women as liberated sexually, these libertines are instead understood to have merely interpolated the male ideal of the woman as passive recipient of male pleasure and are therefore complicit in their own subjugation. They are not liberated, they merely accept their role as passive, they are victims of a false-consciousness, and so their acquiescence in this patriarchal order reproduces it while simultaneously giving it the appearance of legitimacy; women enjoy being used by men, it is their nature to be objects for male pleasure, and in fact they enjoy it. So these women are as guilty as any chauvinist male, and in fact their participation is even more insidious, so they deserve killing.

In both the hotel scene where Nadine ejects her partner from the room for suggesting that he would like to watch Manu and Nadine have sex, and in the libertine club where the women as well as the men are executed the filming of non-simulated sex serves the same purpose. In the hotel room, the camera has already witnessed Manu and Nadine have sex. In fact, it is one of the longer sex scenes in the film. But it is shot from a distance, and the pornographic gaze fails to capture the anticipated shots; the beaver shot, the meat shot, the close-up penetration, and most notably the money shot. The gaze is frustrated and demands more from a scene in which real sex is present. The gaze demands what Nadine's partner demands, something 'hot', something pornographic, that is, the spectacle of sex. But the gaze is denied just like Nadine's partner. In the libertine club, the gaze captures the libertine women in classic pornographic fashion. They are being used by men, and they are enjoying it. We see these anonymous libertines acting out the classic pornographic fantasy, women used for male pleasure, and enjoying every moment of it. They are what the viewer expects in a pornographic film, and for this they are murdered.

The sex in *Baise-moi* is essential to the narrative and underscores the themes of the film and thus its absence would detract significantly from the film. *Baise-moi* is filmed under the assumption that the viewer is an expert of the male/pornographic gaze. That he is familiar with porn conventions, that he has fully internalized this gaze and its expectations such that when they are absent the lack is noticeable. When this lack is felt by the viewer, his frustration places a demand on the film, a demand to show what is being held back, to render visible what he is owed, what he deserves, what is his to see, namely, the female form being dominated by men. This frustration forces the reflective viewer to hold himself to account for making such demands and so interrogate the male/pornographic gaze itself. In so doing, the male gaze is questioned, its authority disputed. By presenting sex in a way that frustrates the male/pornographic gaze *Baise-moi* holds that very gaze accountable and so the sex in *Baise-moi* is an essential moment in its act of transgression against phallocentrism. In *Baise-moi*, the themes of the film are not simply presented but manifest through the self-conscious shirking of porn conventions; a fact that justifies classifying *Baise-moi* as non-pornographic and emphasizes that sex may serve a legitimate diegetic role in film. To emphasize and reinforce this point it might be helpful to look at an obscure mainstream pornographic film with the same basic theme as *Baise-moi*, *Savage Fury* (Mark Carriere, 1985).

Baise-moi follows a simple plot: rape victims respond to misogyny and alienation through violence, violence directed mostly at symbols of misogyny, men. In *Savage Fury*, we have a hard-core analogue to *Baise-moi*. As the film opens, we see Christy Canyon and her friends sleeping in their dorm at Central State University. Almost immediately the dorm is ransacked by rambunctious young men who proceed to rape the women. The rape scene occurs for roughly 35 minutes where we are treated to all the usual porn conventions *ad nauseam*. The viewer is then fast-forwarded one year later where the women plan, for one minute of screen time, to seduce and 'waste' their attackers. The remainder of the film is a 45-minute montage of standard porn footage, the seduction element of the rape victims' trap, followed by a three-minute shooting spree where the naked, post-coitus rape victims machine gun their attackers. Here we have the same themes as *Baise-moi*; rape and vengeance. Yet there is a marked difference between the two films. Whereas in *Baise-moi* the sex adds to, reinforces, and in fact becomes a narrative element, in *Savage Fury* it is the standard spectacle. It adds nothing to the narrative, and in fact could be stock sex scenes from any of Christy Canyon's pornographic features. Someone wanting to see Christy Canyon have sex would enjoy the film. Someone wanting a dialogue on rape, violence, and gender would not. Likewise, someone wanting to see Karen Bach have sex would not be satisfied with *Baise-moi*, even though she has sex in it. They would be better served watching *The Panty Thief* (Alain Payet, 1999). Sex is not the *sine qua non* of *Baise-moi*. Sex alone does not make a film pornographic; it is all about context and the diegetic role of sex in the film.

CONCLUSION

Defining 'pornography' is important for several reasons. First, any definition should be accurate, and current definitions of pornography are sorely lacking. They are either too broad due to the vagueness of terms such as 'explicit', or they are too narrow as a result of being loaded with evaluative terms predicated on normative conceptions of appropriate depictions of sex or sexuality. These later definitions do not serve to differentiate porn from non-porn as a simple definitional exercise or in order that we might more precisely use our words, instead they are utilized by particular regimes of knowledge to delimit our discourse over sex and sexuality and render some presentations illegitimate. Historically defining a film as 'pornographic' designated it as illegitimate, an inappropriate presentation of sex and in so doing reinforced the idea that sex itself was taboo for 'legitimate' film-makers. But film is an invaluable element of contemporary discourse, and insofar as sex is a fundamental element of the human condition it should be a legitimate topic for film. In addition, sex itself can be a powerful diegetic element in film, as *Baise-moi* illustrates.

The new definition offered above is valuable for various reasons. First, it is simply more accurate than previous definitions. It picks out all and only porn, at least at first blush. The fact that things that previously would have been considered porn under earlier definitions but under this definition are not, such as *Baise-moi*, is illustrative of fundamental issues that need to be addressed and that previous definitions glossed over or ignored. As a non-evaluative, non-normative definition, the new definition does not disparage pornography or relegate it to a lesser status among other films, it merely designates porn as different from non-porn insofar as porn is concerned with sex as a spectacle. The assessment of porn as good or bad as a genre is left to the viewer, not prejudiced from the outset. Thus porn is not stigmatized essentially by its own definition. This new definition also allows sex as a diegetic element to be integrated and accepted in mainstream film as a legitimate topic and fully justified. The mere presence of sex does not relegate a film to the pornographic along with the stigma commonly, if unfortunately, appended to pornographic films. Sex is thereby recognized as a legitimate topic of discussion, something currently lacking in film, as the debates surrounding *Baise-moi* demonstrate. Legitimate discourse is thus broadened to include sex. And given the important role sex and sexuality play in our lives, from questions about personal identity, gender, and politics, to interpersonal relationships it is needful that film be able to openly and freely discuss this topic without being classified as somehow 'less than'. Through an interrogation of previous definitions of pornography and an analysis of *Baise-moi* we have been able to lay bare the strictures of our current discourse on pornography, specifically pornographic film, and by laying bare and disassembling the implicit normative assessments and evaluations therein craft a new definition that marks a better understanding of the role of sex in film as well as open up our discourse to be more welcoming to topics dealing with sex and sexuality.

NOTE

1 'Sex' in this case must be defined broadly and without hetero-normative assumptions so as to include not simply penile-vaginal intercourse as well as other forms of penetration such as anal or oral, but also non-penetrative presentations of sexuality where a presentation of sexuality is taken to be the presentation of the other as an object for sexual consumption. Such a broad definition would thus include non-penetrative examples of pornography such as BDSM and lactation porn as well as soft-core pornography such as *Playboy* magazine. In fact, a lot of things would hereby become pornographic. But given that this definition is not an evaluation of an artwork's merit or value,

classifying it as porn is merely stating that its content is sex and its context is the spectacle of sex itself. How one chooses to evaluate the art work, or sex itself, is up to the individual.

Chapter 3

PERVERSE PASSIONS

CATHERINE BREILLAT'S
UNE VIEILLE MAÎTRESSE

DEBORAH WALKER-MORRISON

> Love scenes are the beauty of the world. The most absolute moments in our entire existence. Why shouldn't filmmakers be allowed to show them? ... Why shouldn't they be 'watchable'? Catherine Breillat (2007)

INTRODUCTION

'Penniless dandy forsakes marriage to young, beautiful, adoring heiress for ageing, ugly courtesan.' Such might read the storyline of *Une vieille maîtresse*, literally 'An Old Mistress'. Adapting Barbey d'Aurevilly's nineteenth-century tale of a scandalously unlikely, 12-year affair, (*The Last*) *Mistress* occupies a singular position within Breillat's most singular oeuvre. This chapter examines Breillat's perversely faithful adaptation of her perverse source text, as both a continuation and an interruption of her previous work on perverse gender (non-) relationships.

Emma Wilson claims that in Breillat's *Romance* (1999): 'the co-ordinates of female sexuality are remapped across the territory of her (Marie's) body' (2001: 145). Wilson describes how Breillat films the body of her heroine (Caroline Ducey) in a series of graphically illustrated sexual (mis-)adventures in order to expose the ways that patriarchal society codes active feminine desire as shameful. Not until *Mistress* however, will Breillat's sexual remapping chart the victorious trajectory of a feminine subjectivity unmarked by such patriarchal projections of shame. Less controversial and more lyrical in its representation of sex than her previous films, *Mistress* is unique in its staging of a mutual passion, within which both partners are both subjects and the alternately adored and detested objects of each other's desire.

As we shall see, the sometimes spectacular, often coldly clinical, almost surgical approach to filming sex of Breillat's previous films is here replaced by a burning attention to sexual intimacy. Bending and extending previous Breillat scholarship, this chapter will centre its discussion of *Mistress* around close readings of the film's five sex scenes and their visual and narrative ramifications, arguing that the strikingly different mise en scène of desire in this film restages and interrupts misogynous discourses of romantic love (Coulthard, 2010) which have ever been the target of Breillat's uncompromisingly investigative eye. In a radical rewriting of the Madonna / whore power dynamics and male sexual conquest of the patriarchal order, the reciprocal, haptic gaze of Breillat's camera proposes a perversely violent intimacy marked by female agentic subjectivity and gender inversion which, I propose, also demands 'acknowledgement' (Rushton, 2010) and 'demarginalizes' masculinity (Russell-Watts, 2010).

Her erotics are removed from the social sphere, 'unfold(ing) in emotional bell jars almost entirely insulated from the concerns of the mundane world' (Wilson, 2001: 147). And yet, Breillat's work simultaneously asserts a sustained opposition to the socio-cultural violence of patriarchal structures that would construct women in certain ways in order to contain and constrain them. Her cinema also proposes that woman is underdetermined and uncontainable by culture, in a radical rethinking of sexuality and gendered ways of being and opposes to these, an unruly feminine bodily-ness that pre-exists and exceeds the social. Also implicitly posited in Breillat to subtend the social order: the war of the sexes based on a male tendency to seek sexual conquest as opposed to a more holistic female need for sustained intimacy. The double bind of sexual relations is amplified via the codes of romantic, courtly love. Women must at once be resistant and compliant to male sexual demands and yet, within the Romantic tradition, their compliance also signals their destruction as both subjects and as objects of desire: since one cannot desire what one already possesses, slaked romantic desire descends inevitably into disgust (Coulthard, 2010). The root of the problem is in the non-mutuality, non-reciprocity of gendered power relations which gives men the exclusive right to sexual agency. For example, in eighteenth- and nineteenth-century France (and for Breillat, still today), male libertinage is superficially, officially frowned upon but unofficially admired while its female victims are 'compromised', branded as whores and then discarded. Breillat rightly deplores this perverse double standard (in all her films) and here uses d'Aurevilly's archteypically 'unruly fatale' (Walker, 2007) to redress this most human imbalance of power.

Breillat's 'comeback', made just over a year after a debilitating stroke, *Mistress* was her first (and, to date, only) film to be nominated for the supreme award (*Palme d'Or*) at Cannes (2007). As might be expected given the avant garde anti-entertainment reputation of its director, box office returns in France were modest, attracting slightly fewer than 100,000 spectators, putting it just below the top third of films released in theatres that year. Despite being passed over for the *Palme*, *Mistress* was critically well received, both at home[1] and abroad, Breillat surprising and impressing critics with her superbly cast, masterfully staged erotic recreation of this nineteenth-century tale of impossibly enduring passion.

PERVERSE ADAPTATION

On the surface, *Mistress* is a close, 'faithful' adaptation. Not just the main storyline but practically every scene and every line of dialogue are taken from Barbey's largely autobiographical, male-narrated novel. Notorious libertine Ryno de Marigny has won the heart and hand of the pure and beautiful Hermangarde, flower of the Parisian aristocracy, adored granddaughter of the Marquise de Flers. When his continuing ten-year affair with an older woman, the scandalous courtesan, Vellini, threatens to put an end to the marriage, Ryno recounts their affair to the Marquise, in a long flashback. Convinced of the depth and sincerity of Ryno's love for Hermangarde, the Marquise consents to the marriage and to Ryno's desire to remove himself and his young bride from the temptations of Paris. But when his old mistress follows Ryno to the Marquise's coastal fortress chateau, the ten-year-old passion is reignited, to his pregnant wife's despair.

That Breillat herself is largely a faithful mistress to her source text is clearly a measure of its closeness to her own controversial thematic concerns: love as battle versus love as conquest; passion versus social convention; demonic sexuality versus chaste attachment; animal magnetism versus classical beauty. Barbey also employs gender inversion: Ryno has a feminine side; Vellini is masculine. Breillat's affinity for the novel and its author (she had wanted to adapt it for many years before the project was realized) is thus, in a sense, unsurprising. Nonetheless,

Breillat's declared cross-gender identification with this scandalous nineteenth-century dandy whose work had been as much the object of censorship and prudish opprobrium as her own, obeys a perverse logic which, I will argue, subtly subverts the novel and enriches the film. Breillat's reappropriation of Barbey's male narrator and protagonist transforms the story from one of demonic sexual possession to one of enduring, violent intimacy. Superficially faithful, Breillat departs from the novel in essential ways. I am not thinking primarily of the much more frank, explicit representations of sex, Breillat's trademark. For sex in *Mistress* is less graphic than in her other work, less raw than what critics have come to expect from this pioneering exponent of cinematic excess, which the French call *le cinéma du corps*, the cinema of the body (Palmer, 2011). Both in terms of adapting Barbey and in relation to her own previous approach to filming sex, what Breillat leaves out or adds is as significant as what she includes. As we shall see, seemingly small shifts in emphasis and setting redraw Aurevilly's perverse love triangle along the lines of her own, differently perverse thematics.

PERVERSITY VERSUS PERVERSION

Before going further, let me outline precisely what I mean by perverse. Firstly, I want to distinguish between perversity and perversion. Perversity transcends the social by exposing the perversion inherent in the social. Sex, desire, passion, love, are always already perverse in Breillat, first and foremost because of the perverse Madonna / whore power dynamics of patriarchal order; the myriad contradictory constraints it places on feminine desire (Taubin, 2008: 28). In *Romance*, for example, Marie's desire is seen as shameful by the stranger who offers to pay her for sex before raping her and calling her a slut: men may legitimately desire anonymous sex while women who do so will be labelled as dirty, perverse, legitimizing their victimization. In the same film, the perverse pleasure Marie derives from bondage demands to be read as her working through of the emotional bondage she experiences in her relationship with her boyfriend, Paul, whose lack of desire for her is a denial of her sexual agency. Rather than a perversion, bondage is perversely liberating.

For Breillat, perversion, in its neurotic transgression of social codes, remains trapped within the social (Breillat and Clouzot, 2004: 173). Perversion is therefore linked to shame and indignity: viz the pornographic image circulated at the costume dinner in *Mistress*, which sees Ryno's first failed attempts to seduce Vellini. The boxed miniature, briefly glimpsed as in a voyeuristic primal scene, reveals an elegantly dressed couple before a drawing room mirror, man standing behind the woman, her skirts lifted to reveal her naked buttocks, while the man penetrates her (anally?). An index of polite society's sexual tastes, men smirk lewdly, displaying the bored interest of the jaded libertine, while the most innocent, demure looking women (The Queen of Spades, played by Caroline Ducey (Marie in *Romance*)) appear the most 'moved'. Breillat's invention, the image appears to gesture intertextually to several of her previous films figuring anal rape (*Parfait Amour, Romance, Fat Girl*) or penetration (*Anatomy of Hell*) (Keesey, 2009: 140, 43). The presence of Amira Cassar (here playing an opera singer) particularly evokes the latter film. Cassar's brief disinterested glance, reminiscent of one infamous scene in *Anatomy* in which the Man (Rocco Ziffredi) impales her with a garden fork, seems to say: 'Been there, done that ... wasn't impressed the first time.' As for Vellini, she passes the image on without even deigning to open the (Pandora's?) box. For Breillat and her heroine, eroticism is not erotica, even less is it pornography. The relegation of sex to the domain of the shameful and dirty, impersonal, i.e. pornography, this, for Breillat, is the true meaning of perversion.

Following Barbey, Breillat perversely destabilizes socially reinforced gender differences by amplifying and blending gender archetypes and gendered inversion in her protagonists: Ryno combines 'masculine' strength and courage with 'feminine' beauty and vulnerability; Vellini is a social and sexual rebel, an androgynous demon whose sexualized form she appropriates. For the costume party, (Breillat's reinvention of Barbey's dinner) she comes dressed as the Devil. Dialogues insist on the masculine gender: not some lowly she-devil she is the Devil himself, because 'I hate everything feminine. Except in young men, of course.' Vellini's gender perversity is Breillat's visualization of Barbey, whose text insists repeatedly on the gender inversion between his lovers and who compares Vellini (in the dinner scene) to a demon, a devilish temptress.

> She possessed true seductiveness, of the kind one imagines only in a demon. She had a demon's slim, sexless torso, a demon's dark, fiery features and a singularly impressive ugliness, bold and sombre – the only worthy substitute for lost beauty on the face of a Fallen Archangel. (278)

But Breillat's gender inversion, her refusal of patriarchal constructions of (masculinity as conquest) and femininity as girlish submissiveness is also part and parcel of a game of seduction: Vellini's low-cut demon gown reveals Argento's voluptuous breasts and slim waist. Unlike Barbey's flat-chested, sallow-skinned heroine, Breillat's visual reinvention of Vellini's gender-ambiguity reveals her singular femininity.

The protagonists are perverse in the sense that their adulterous desire is not simply transgressive of socio-sexual codes, its force impels them to act against their own best interests, their rational judgement, their own happiness even (Vignoles, 2011: 50). Vellini abandoned a doting husband who provided material security, Ryno destroyed the 'perfect' marriage. But Breillat goes even further than this, revealing the perversity subtending romantic discourse as linked to the internal contradictions inherent within the dynamics of human desire: the dissociation between love and lust; the all-consuming nature of desire, and its simultaneous impermanence. It is the perversely impermanent, illusory nature of romantic love, which, at the moment of conquest, falls into shame, boredom, disgust, that constitutes the central lie of conventional love relationships for Breillat. The impermanence of romance can only be overcome, enduring passion and intimacy can only be achieved by the incessant movement of an ever-changing balance of power.

This is why *Mistress* reveals its central passion as a paroxystic battlefield marked by violence and perversity, Eros and Thanatos, *odi et amo*. As Ryno and Vellini both declare: 'Nous nous sommes plus haïs qu'aimés.' They both attract and repel one another.

EMOTION IN MOTION

Mae West once said 'Sex is emotion in motion'. Even at rest, Argento's Vellini displays an electric potential for movement, described by Barbey as feline indolence, which can transform without warning into predatory motion. Every move she makes, every breath she takes is about sex and Breillat and Argento make sure we'll be watching.

The first sex scene between the two begins less than ten minutes into the film. It follows the visit of the conniving Marquis de Prony, close friend of the Marquise de Flers, come to gauge Vellini's reaction to his news of her lover's impending marriage to the most formidable of rivals, the fair Mlle Hermangarde de Polastron. Athough Vellini has been introduced verbally as an ageing courtesan, the old mistress of the film's French title (she is '36, time to make way for youth'), our first image of Argento defies the less than flattering description.

Barbey's Vellini is an improbable sex symbol, described at length as small and skinny, wrinkled, almost haggard. Her ugliness is partly culturally informed: olive skinned, she has visible facial hair, conjuring up visions of an ageing, flat-chested Frieda Karlo. Her androgynous silhouette is accentuated by her suave, accented contralto voice. While Asia Argento's Vellini shares her literary character's dark, unconventional beauty and husky accent, she is full breasted and more voluptuously feminine. Vellini's attractiveness is described in the novel as arising from the way she carries herself, 'something in the way she moves', one might say: an exotic infixability, a vitally mobile integrity. Breillat, for whom ugliness equates to social prohibitions on feminine sexual agency, picks up on this and uses Argento's off-beat, rock and roll, *Scarlet Diva* persona to take it to superb new heights.

The novel describes her as *une maîtresse serail*. An entire harem in a single body. Argento's quick-silver performance and Breillat's mise en scène and uniquely creative costuming encapsulate perfectly this unfixability, rendering her character as 'a chimera of bewildering multiplicity' (Romney, 2008: 35). When we first see her, Breillat stages Vellini reclining on her divan, as a proud, defiantly languid courtesan. Costuming, pose and framing is evocative of nineteenth-century painting, combining Goya's *Maja Vestida* (via costuming) with the impudent sensuality of Manet's *Olympia* (via a bunch of large red flowers worn over her left ear) (Brevik-Zender, 2012: 11). The tiger skin rug which is the central, decidedly unfeminine feature of the room, colours her stillness as feline repose. The ensuing conversation with the Vicomte is filmed as a shot reverse shot, verbal duel. Rising like the serpent she wears as a bracelet to confront her enemy as he delivers the cruel blow (Marigny is marrying for love, a younger woman of unsurpassed beauty), Vellini declares that it will do nothing to end things between them: 'Between Mr. Marigny and myself, there can be no ending.' Throughout the encounter, she appears indifferent, retaining her composure until the Vicomte's departure. But when Marigny arrives, Breillat cuts suddenly to a mid shot of Vellini, lying supine on the tiger skin, her tearful face covered by a lace handkerchief, breast heaving, quietly moaning: her superbly feigned disinterest has evaporated. Marigny's power over her at this point is underlined by their respective positions: she has been literally knocked to the floor by the news of his marriage and he enters the frame boots first, as if he might trample her further. Yet he is gentle, caring, quickly kneels beside her: draws her up onto his knee, tenderly consoles her, in an intimate two-shot MCU (medium close-up). There is a delicate closeness to the scene: younger than Vellini by six years, it is Ryno who plays a quasi parental role here. The dialogues underline the singularity of their attachment, its defiance of social codes. Ryno: 'What do people know of you and me.' Vellini: 'Exactly, they don't understand a thing.'

Sudden cut to Breillat's first sex scene: a single, 15-second shot high angle MCU two-shot as they fuck on Vellini's tiger skin. Ryno's naked head and shoulders fill most of the shot but his face and features are not visible: emotionally, he is barely present. Instead, Breillat shows us Vellini's desperate, animal pleasure. She remains clothed, still clutching the tear-soaked handkerchief, her face framed next to that of the tiger, its wild, predatory eyes now a lifeless trophy. In her consummate performance of the blending of physical pleasure and emotional pain, both visually and aurally, Argento dominates the frame. As Amy Taubin notes, 'Vellini's orgasms punctuate the narrative the way big arias punctuate a good opera. They arrest the narrative completely and yet they are the reason for the narrative's existence. Argento is the Maria Callas of orgasms – her formal control over the expression of passion is peerless' (2008: 29).

In framing the virtuoso performance of her star, Breillat shows comparable mastery. Moreover, in this film as in no other, the unpredictable pace of her editing is crucial to the representation of desire: she wields the cut like a sabre, like Vellini's Spanish *cuchillo* (dagger). Sudden, violent, we are taken by surprise, stormed, seduced. The suddenness of the cut also translates the socially incomprehensible dimension and physical intensity of their relationship. In terms of narrative construction, Breillat's elliptical, shock editing, which takes us from a tender conversation straight to furious sex, mirrors the way the story (a 12-year love affair between a younger, more beautiful man and older less beautiful woman) flouts the rules of courtly romance, which depends on the long, slow build-up and deferral of desire (Coulthard, 2010).

The scene ends with another shock cut. From Vellini's orgasm to a MS (mid shot) of the virginal Hermangarde, dressed in bare shouldered white, demurely bent over a piece of embroidery ... waiting silently, immobile, for a fiancé who will not come ... The camera moves into a CU to reveal her lovelorn, tear-filled eyes. There follows a lengthy conversation (the first of several, between the Marquise and her closest friend, the Comtesse d'Artelles) on the rules of courtly romantic love, which require that a woman 'never give a man the certainty of conquest'. To keep a man, a woman must feign a certain level of disinterest, a stratagem of which Hermangarde will be incapable. 'In love the first to suffer has lost. She is already bound hand and foot.' The discourse and rules of engagement of romance, the Herculean task women face in winning and keeping the perfidious hearts of men ever in search of new conquests, are an oft repeated leitmotif. And while Ryno's parting words to Vellini in the previous scene indicate that she has lost the battle of romance to the ultimate conquest (the perfect bride), Breillat's editing, which contrasts Vellini's fierce sensual pleasure with Hermangarde's cold beauty, begs to differ.

After Marigny's departure, Barbey's furious heroine hurls a medallion of Marigny into the fire. Instead, Breillat has her Vellini stare pensively into her mirror, gazing at her ageing features, framed by an ebony statuette of what looks to be an exotic African Cupid. Enter her beautiful young maid, Oliva, who consoles her mistress with a tender lover's kiss that is clearly not the first. Framing the two women's embrace in the mirror, far from the narcissism and/or split subjectivity that such a scene might easily connote, Breillat instead underscores Vellini's integrity, her defiant lucidity: unafraid to look herself in the face, her features express pain but not defeat. Adding a bisexual dimension to her protagonist (there is no such suggestion in Barbey) also highlights Vellini's sensous, 'polymorphously perverse' sexuality. Douglas Keesey (2010a: 6) reads the blonde Oliva as a double for Hermangarde, and the scene as serving to create a sensual link between the two rivals. Keesey reads the film as suggesting that Vellini and Hermangarde are joined by their love for Ryno, making them, in a perversely symbolic sense, sisters, as Anais and Helena in *Fat Girl*. However, in my view, Breillat's juxtaposition of the darkly defiant, sensuous Vellini with Hermangarde's cold blonde compliance, repeated again and again throughout the film, highlights not their similarity, but their difference and the unbridgeable distance of their rivalry.

LOVE AND WAR

The ten-year affair is retold by Ryno to the Marquise de Flers, as a long flashback which constitutes half the duration of the film. In the frame scenes, Breillat's use of shot reverse shot, with unusually tight framing on Fu'ad Ait Attou, accentuate the feminine beauty of his green eyes and full lips, captivating the viewer as he does the old Marquise. Although Vellini is the force that drives the narrative, the narrational point of view is Ryno's in this section of the film and Fu'ad's performance makes the character's sexual magnetism essential to the unfolding of the sexual drama. The mutuality of their relationship is mirrored in Breillat's organization of visual POV (point of view camera) and spectatorial allegiance, which oscillates between one and the other. While he is the narrating subject of the flashback, within these sequences he is more often than not the object of Vellini's vengeful then adoring gaze. Camera and dialogues underline the violent mutuality of the love affair announced by the dialogues: 'I was her victim for ten years. We were both each other's victims. Simultaneously or one after the other.'

Escaping from the vaguely disgusted boredom of a previous sexual conquest with a married woman, Ryno chances on a friend who describes the latest object of his romantic attentions. A Malagaise, illegitimate daughter of an Italian countess and a Spanish toreador, an exotic ex-street worker now married to a wealthy old English gentleman. As chance would have it, she passes by. Ryno is unimpressed: 'Surely you're not English enough or old enough to fall for such an ugly mutt. It would be pure vice.' Cut to a reverse CU of Vellini licking a sorbet like a hungry feline, her sombre, Carmen-like features framed by a black mantilla as she throws Ryno a look of pure hatred, which a reverse CU of Ryno reveals to have had the effect of a Cupid's arrow. Cut back to Vellini whose defiant smile announces her impending revenge as she repeatedly rebuffs Ryno's attempts to woo her. Here as elsewhere, in this sexualized battle of the gaze, Breillat gives her the last look and the last laugh.

The scene demonstrates the importance of the gaze to the dynamics of sexual desire, particularly in terms of its cinematic representation. The power of the gaze derives from the centrality of vision to human interaction, since it provides the primary initial means for humans to assess another human's emotional disposition, sexual attractiveness and availability, in what theorist Torben Grodal aptly describes as 'the battlefield of consent' (1997: 104). The metaphor illuminates desire as a power struggle, the power to wield the gaze equates to the power to realize one's sexual desires. Of course the problem for women is that to be a beautiful object of the desiring male gaze too often entails objectification in a general sense, entailing subjection and loss of subjectivity. Hermangarde epitomizes this beauty trap. Conversely, in a violent reclaiming of the gaze, Vellini interrupts such objectification. As with other femmes fatales, she is what one might term an agentic object: rather than be subjected to or simply offer herself up to the masculine gaze, she captures it (Walker, 2007: 16). Ryno, as Byronic hero and *homme fatal*, employs a not dissimilar strategy: rather than simply an admiring or dominating gaze, his power over women emerges from his beauty and sexual charm, which enables him to capture and monopolize their gaze.

From the moment Ryno and Vellini meet to the moment they become lovers, their interactions are like a perverse, blood smattered foreplay, the non-linear (flashback) plot investing every subsequent scene between the two with a potentially violent, sexual tension. Their courtship is a duel, a *corrida* in which each in turn plays the toreador (remember Vellini is a toreador's daughter) and the *toro*, provoking the other to riposte. This section of the narrative is a perverse variation on the courtly script of deferred desire: the inaccessibility of the pure, cold lady replaced by Vellini's fatale-like hot-cold, sensuous cruelty; the romantic suitor's adoring submissiveness replaced by Ryno's tenacious impudence, which ends inevitably, in a duel with her husband. The outrageous Vellini attends, dressed in Dietrich-like drag, complete with tails and rakishly angled top hat. The real duel is between the two. Ryno: 'If the toreador's daughter is thirsty for blood, let her see it flow.' Vellini: 'I hope my husband kills you today.' He almost does.

FROM PERVERSE TO PURE

The couple's 'first' actual sexual encounter occurs with Ryno still convalescent, after months between life and death. Introduced almost as a dream sequence, Breillat's camera insists on Vellini's fierce tenderness as she leans over his naked body, bloodied bandage still visible, blowing onto his face, brushing his skin with her heart shaped kiss curl that is also 'cheekily' evocative of a pair of plump buttocks. The sequence insists on ambiguity (Argento's leaning body is positioned as a potential vampire, her arms and angular shoulders resembling bat's wings) and gender-inversed intersubjectivity: the moment Vellini declares her surrender, their positions switch and Ryno goes from masculine pursuer to feminized slave. The first image we are shown of Vellini was that of an odalisque. Now it is he who is filmed willingly in this position: combining the iconography of crucified Christ and adored, sexualized object of Vellini's adoring gaze.

The following (two-shot) montage sequence of their lovemaking further insists on her agency and his sensual acceptance: 'we see a woman as sexual subject enjoying a man's body without his thinking himself demeaned or objectified as mere flesh' (Keesey, 2010a: 12). Filmed in soft focus and softly lit, the scene is intensely tender, insisting on all five senses: Vellini caresses Ryno's supine body, licking, smelling his underarms and pubic hair, declaring huskily, not 'I love you', but 'I love the odor of love'.

The experience is beyond the haptic: inviting a synaesthesic engagement that pulls us into the image (Williams, 2008: 20), allowing us to 'feel' the sex without the need to film actual intercourse or genitalia. The move away from a hard-core visual approach to sex is surprising for a film-maker who had built a reputation on an uncompromising frankness in filming non-simulated sex and genital close-ups. Moreover, soft-core filming of 'vanilla sex' runs contrary to general trends in erotic cinema. Gary Needham (2009) documents recent shifts to greater aestheticization and eroticization of extraordinarily beautiful photogenic male bodies, particularly through greater proximity in terms of framing and a focus on full frontal nudity. Close framing of the penis, especially in queer cinema, Needham argues, institutes a haptic gaze through which vision invites touch, interrupting the more distanced, voyeuristic scopophilia of mainstream film (2009: 145). That the haptic close framing of the penis should be largely confined to pornography and queer cinema is highly revealing of documented differences in male and female desire. Breillat's cinema confirms that because, generally speaking, female desire is more dependent on emotion, close-framing of genitalia is unnecessary for the construction of a haptic, erotic gaze. Graphic imaging of male and female genitalia (*Romance, Fat Girl, Sex is Comedy, Anatomy*) is generally associated with a de-eroticized, dispassionate or investigative gaze: the aptly titled *Anatomy of Hell* being the prime case in point. Thus, charges of pornography are misguided: Breillat's previous forays into X-rated hard core are philosophical rather than erotic, prompting the viewer to think about sex as a set of problems rather than aiming at arousal.

In this author's view, her mise en scène of sex in *Mistress* does construct a haptic, multisensory gaze, precisely because the focus is on the intense, transcendent, whole body emotion of the lovers. And it is emotion which renders sex transcendent, which enables the raw desire of flesh to touch the sublime. Sex in *Mistress* erases the duality between mind and body, heart and soul that is the subject of so much of Breillat's work, especially *Romance*. Vellini shamelessly and effortlessly achieves Marie's quest to reconcile heart and (w)hole (Beugnet, 2007: 47).

EROS AND THANATOS

Vellini and Ryno's 'honeymoon' period (which lasts several years) is interrupted by a sudden, tragic jump to the death of the couple's daughter. Breillat's transferral of the novel's Italian pastoral paradise setting to the barren beauty of the Algerian desert lends the episode an abstract quality, a surreal symbolism: the couple's love cannot be lived within the confines of society (Keesey 2010a: 12).

The film renders the child's short life and sudden death in three shots, lasting barely 15 seconds in total. The all too brief family idyll is rendered in a first MLS (medium long shot) as the couple bathe her; cut to a ten-second MS as the child sits in the sand, innocently unaware as a scorpion approaches. Cut to an extreme long shot of the desert hut, the death signified by Vellini's howling, off-screen scream. One is reminded here of the anguished cry of Elle in Resnais and Duras' *Hiroshima mon amour* flashback (after she returns home, having lost her lover and had her head shaved for sleeping with the enemy) which Duras explains as signifying a child's cry for her mother. Breillat reframes the reverse of the same, wild, primal cry as a mother's anguish for the death of her child, echoed by the howling of the desert wind.

In the novel, Barbey compares Vellini's maternity to that of a wild animal: she gives birth outdoors and her fiercely sensual love for her daughter is compared to that of a lioness. Breillat transfers this metaphor of birth to one of primal grief, demonstrating, yet again, that woman is underdetermined and uncontainable by culture. Maternity, the most singular difference between the sexes in humans, although central to the patriarchal order, is figured through Vellini as a purely instinctual process.

Cut to Vellini clinging to her dead child after five days; cut to her funeral pyre against a mountainous sand dune as Ryno struggles to keep the still screaming mother from joining her child. Cut back to a speechless Ryno in the Marquise's drawing room, lips quivering as he recalls, but has difficulty verbalizing the disturbing details of the following scene. Cut back to an MCU of Ryno's turbaned head as he lies in the sand, Vellini's head barely in shot, her hands tightening around his throat, sobbing more quietly now. Cut to an MLS which reveals the two naked, Vellini straddling Ryno, the pyre still burning, only feet away against a skyless expanse of sand. Cut to a low angle MCU, her full breasts heaving into and out of shot against an expanse of sky, as she thrusts desperately into a powerless Ryno, ejected from the frame. Sex here is filmed as a natural extension of Vellini's anguished cry, her visceral response to the loss of her child. Cut back to the Marquise's drawing room as Ryno struggles to tell how following the death, 'this thing, was no longer love but a never-ending fury. A kind of barbarous rape. ... But I had to let her do it. Even if I felt only self disgust.' Apart from the death of the child and

Vellini's desperate grief, the details of the entire sequence are Breillat's invention. Her relocation of the setting, surreal mise en scène, and use of (Ryno's) voice-over utterly blurs the line between sex, violence and death. Ryno's narration underlines the perverse love-hate nature of their sexual relationship following the loss of their child. Breillat suggests that (like the male protagonists in all her films) Ryno sadly misinterprets feminine desire: his narration tells of his disgust at what he sees as maternal perversion. But what Breillat shows us is no rape. Vellini's moans of grief morphing into desperate orgasm demand to be read as a doomed attempt to reassert life and love in the face of death (Keesey, 2010a: 13). What is demonic and perverse in terms of the social world (and religion is a central pillar of the social world), for Breillat, equates to the sacred. If sex in *Mistress* is every bit as inseparable from death as it is in her previous work (Brinkema, 2006), it is because desire, as the supreme manifestation of the life force seeks to counter death. Contra Freud's linking of Eros and Thanatos in the death drive, organic and inorganic systems cannot be assimilated. Unlike the latter, living organisms do not strive to return to a state of entropy, which would be a perversion; life is precisely a battle against entropy (Armengou, 2009: 269). It is in this sense that Vellini's desire here expresses Breillat's definition of the sacred.

Breillat asserts visually that the social isolation of the couple is what kills their child and that the death of the child is what (temporarily) kills the relationship. The novel is more circumspect: perhaps even without this tragedy, time would have done its job (315). And in the novel, the couple's ardent lovemaking resumes following the death, but only after Vellini has gone through a period of violent mourning and depression. In the film, Breillat's elliptical compression of these narrative events makes sex a form of maternal mourning.

PHOENIX MIND FUCK

The next sex scene occurs following the couple's amicable separation. Both have other lovers but remain friends (unlike other men, who, says Ryno, dump their mistresses once they have moved on to the next conquest) and see one another constantly. On one visit, they are in her garden, chatting casually. Without warning, Vellini slashes Ryno's face with her *cuchillo* dagger, smiles, then playfully licks his blood from the blade. Ryno's smiling reaction reveals their ongoing bond. He understands Vellini's gesture as an intimately sexual one, knowingly conjuring the blood-letting that precipitated their love affair and will now set the erotic cycle in motion once more. They continue to chat: Vellini happily recounting her latest conquest, suddenly less relaxed about his. He kisses away her tears.

Cut to a full shot of the two on her divan, naked, she straddles him again: 'Why won't you keep loving me. Not loving is the worst misfortune.' When she tauntingly contrasts their relationship with his new love,

> Marigny angrily overturns his mistress, pinning her under the weight of his body and flipping her into a submissive position with her head hanging backward over the edge of the bed. [...] Breillat relies on these two poses to visually render the struggle for control that characterizes her protagonists' relationship, depicting at times Vellini's psychological dominance over Ryno through her physical placement on top of him and at other times Ryno's efforts to challenge Vellini's authority by destabilizing and inverting her body to the camera. (Brevik-Zender, 2012: 11)

But despite being pinned beneath her lover, Vellini rises to the challenge. As proof that she is without petty sexual jealousy, she dares Ryno to put his hand on her heart and recount his sexual experiences with his new mistress. Reverse shot extreme CU as Ryno describes Madame de Mendoze as a courtly lady, haughty and pious. Cut to a MS two-shot, the two still locked together as Vellini wants to know: 'how does she come?' Her triumphant smile is visible as Ryno admits: 'I don't think she feels pleasure. It's her sense of sacrifice that's sublime.' Vellini counters: 'That's not love. Most women don't know what it means to love a man, to hold a man in their belly.' They continue to battle verbally as they fuck, Breillat's framing switching to the rhythm of their contest. When Vellini suggests that Ryno is a social climber ('Is it her title that turns you on?') he slaps her: 'Be quiet, She's a lady. She's worth ten of you.' But Vellini is unrepentant, sensing the lie. They kiss hungrily and Breillat's camera moves back to capture their orgasm.

The scene is singular in its use of extended dialogue during sex, together with the explicit verbal depiction of sexual rivalry as an aphrodisiac and weapon. The emotionally violent, constantly shifting balance of power is mirrored in framing, dialogues and mise en scène. But the key to sex is always, first and foremost a matter of performance. As Linda Williams (2008) notes, filmed sex necessarily demands a level of actual sexual intimacy 'whether or not one really feels desire for the other person, or whether one really comes'. In her analysis of

Patrice Chereau's aptly titled, *Intimacy* (2001), Williams suggests that to be truly erotic, filmed sex must go beyond performance, in terms of both 'physical motions and the accompanying emotions that might be more real than just acting' (2008: 274–5) This is precisely the level of intimacy that Breillat seeks to achieve from her actors, casting bodies and personalities she feels 'are' her characters (Oumano, 2011: 78). Ait Attou describes his off-screen relationship with Argento as mirroring that of their characters (Bombarda, 2012), a claim which appears borne out by the intense embodiment of their interactions, particularly in evidence in this scene.

The sexual and emotional intensity of the characters' / actors' interaction underlines the gulf that separates the sensual intimacy of the *corps amoureux*, the loving body, from the frigid masochistic piety of women whose sexuality has been socially extinguished: namely, Ryno's latest conquest, the piously frigid Madame de Mendoze, implicitly associated with Hermangarde. Because we never see the former character and because she is described in terms more or less identical to Hermangarde (she is fair, pure, religious, aristocratic, sublimely submissive), the film invites the spectator to associate the two women. In my view therefore, this scene serves as the hermeneutic key to Marigny and Hermangarde's subsequent sexual relationship, which we are never shown.

SISTERS?

If Vellini is no whore, the chaste Hermangarde as envisioned by Breillat, whose casting of Roxanne Mesquida links her character intertextually to the defiled and murdered Helena of *Fat Girl*, is very much a martyred Madonna figure (Keesey, 2010b). In a notable departure from the novel, Breillat erases the strong, sensuous, physical presence of Barbey's blonde heroine, leaving the spectator with a cold, repressed, virgin wife whose (f)rigid subservience to patriarchal codes will ultimately destroy her. True, Breillat's Hermangarde displays a desire for agency and a barely repressed sensuality (Keesey, 2010b). But the film downplays this aspect of her character, accentuating her statuesque beauty, framing her as the immobilized passive object of the gaze. Her adoring subservience to her husband is the materialization of her ultimate obedience to oppressive social codes underpinned by religion and class consciousness. Witness the bride and bridegroom's chosen passage during the wedding ceremony, which emphasizes the eternal nature of the Christian marriage bond and woman's inferiority and necessary subservience to man. Breillat's invention, (absent from the novel), the scene is her reminder that Catholic marriage (and by extension Christian society) is founded on the servitude of women, here openly embraced by Hermangarde.

In a subtle subversion of Barbey's wronged bride, Breillat's editing, costuming and mise en scène serve to constantly pit the hapless, immobile Hermangarde against Vellini's wild, uncontainable agency. We have noted how Vellini's singular unfixableness is underscored by the exotic, unfeminine decor in her living spaces and her bohemian costumes, dominated by sensual lines, warm reds or browns, dramatic blacks. Her off-beat, asymmetrical hairstyles (combinations of metal comb and fresh flowers), jewellery (single earring, serpent bracelet) and ornamentation (Spanish dagger; punk-rock fisherman's cap) are flamboyantly symbolic. By contrast, Hermangarde is always dressed conventionally, in cold virginal white, pastel or dark blues and envious green. Her hair is symmetrically balanced, as smoothly and elaborately contained as her sexuality.

The novel goes to some lengths to emphasize the newlyweds' idyllic months together in the Marquise's Norman manor house before the arrival of Vellini. Another side of Hermangarde is revealed: a robust, wilful, adventurous lover of nature. Breillat replaces this with feeble attempts to please, a form of false subjectivity: wifely submission to her husband's will. In a scene where the couple are out riding, Ryno thoughtlessly gallops off, leaving his tearful wife behind, oblivious to the fact that she is no longer beside him. She is known but in the end, no longer acknowledged. And while the novel insists on the sexual dimension of Ryno and Hermangarde's marriage, Breillat emphasizes Hermangarde's repressed sensuality, accentuating the gulf that separates her from Vellini.

Scenes of Ryno and Vellini are cruelly intercut with scenes of Hermangarde. The lovers' 'first' encounter on the battlements replays the duel of their courtship in reverse: his attempts to resist her sensual pull are doomed, when she almost throws herself into the sea and the scene ends predictably, with his surrendering to her embrace, again renewing the cycle of desire. As with the first sex scene, Breillat cuts to Hermangarde, chastely waiting, in an identical pose and costume. One difference: the absence of sensuality of the marriage is underlined by the Spartan decor of the chateau (homologous to Paul's hospital white apartment in *Romance*) which contrast to the warm opulence of the Marquise's Parisian mansion. Enter Ryno, eager to transfer his sexual energies towards his wife but she rebuffs his amorous advances (ostensibly because her grandmother is asleep in the room), finally sending him off on a domestic errand.

Immediately Hermangarde's pregnancy is announced, we see them naked in bed together. With paternal pride, Ryno caresses her naked belly, kisses her forehead: but what might easily have become a sex scene remains a chaste encounter. And although Hermangarde's Mona Lisa smile is one of pure fulfilment, she remains characterized by immobility and silence. The virgin bride is figured as a Virgin Mother. The immobile, contained object is an object of veneration, no longer an object of desire.

SUCCUBUS OR SAINT?

Perversity is often the result of an unresolvable conflict between desire and duty: one does what one doesn't want (here Ryno is drawn back to Vellini) and doesn't do what one does want (Ryno wants to remain faithful to his wife) (Vignoles, 2011: 60). Thus Ryno rides away from his pregnant wife in her (not entirely) impregnable fortress to Vellini's fisherman's cabin. Still torn between desire and marital duty, Breillat's Ryno suggests to his mistress that his desire arises out of the inadequacy of his sexual relationship with his wife. When making love to his wife, he thinks about her, as we have seen: 'You have been the cause of more kisses, more tenderness for Hermangarde than I would have ever given her if you had never existed ... I kissed her like a drowning man clings to a floating log.' The conversation is delivered in an intimate two-shot, at this point they are lying down, faces almost touching though they are not looking into each others' eyes. We might expect Breillat to have filmed Vellini's reaction to Ryno's confession with a look of unobserved triumph. But no.

As with the first time we see them make love, Breillat cuts elliptically from their two-shot conversation to sex, in medias res. But this time both are naked and fully in shot, their bodies scissored, Fu'ad's body lying passively across the back of the frame, one leg twisted over Asia's torso, his foot in the foreground, close to her mouth as the camera moves in to focus on Vellini's orgasm, her head thrown back, one Amazon breast filling the centre frame. Douglas Keesey perceptively notes how the scene might invite different readings:

> It is possible to view this scene through patriarchal eyes, in the way that Ryno at least in part seems to experience it: he has fallen prey to a

succubus, a female demon (with a snake bracelet) who merely uses his sex for her own pleasure as their conjoined bodies form the shape of a diabolically inverted cross. But we can also see the scene more as Vellini tries to live it, as a mutual giving and taking of love, the consummation of her 'marriage' to Ryno, the height of purity reached through the depths of passion. At the 2007 New York Film Festival, Breillat compared the look on Vellini's face during orgasm to the rapturous expression of Saint Teresa in Bernini's sculpture of the *Ecstasy of Saint Teresa* ... mystical ecstasy, carnal ecstasy. (Keesey, 2010a: 14)

The scene again emphasizes gender inversion; Vellini's active subjectivity and an intimate blurring of the line between self and other, between pleasure and emotional pain. Inspired by a line from the novel (in which 'Vellini had thrown her slender leg over her lover's shoulders' (476)), the lovers' limbs are entwined in such a way their single identities become distorted and confused. Again, Breillat is almost Durassian in her mise en scène of physical passion, the scene evoking simultaneously the opening close-up in *Hiroshima mon amour* and the voice-over monologue later in the film: 'You're killing me, you're so good to me. ... Devour me, deform me to ugliness' (Angelo, 2010: 50, 53; Wilson, 2001: 145). More than ever, the visual focus is on blended identity. Neither is 'on top'. Their contorted bodies display a twisted balance of power. Indeed, the two characters are remarkably similar in their proud wilfulness, their powers of seduction, unconventional social position and perverse gender identity; a point which has escaped reviewers. Rather than the yin and yang attraction of opposites, Breillat's Vellini and Ryno are uncannily alike and they are filmed as such: the violently conjoined 'twin-souls' of Barbey's novel.

The two are contrasted to Hermangarde, the true cold lady. After she discovers her husband's betrayal, her aristocratic pride can have no outlet in action or outward display of anger. More perverse than Vellini, her only defence is false subservience and sexual coldness: a Medea-like expulsion from her womb of her unborn child and passive-aggressive retreat into increasing immobility, all of which effectively drive Ryno back into the arms of his hot-blooded, untameable old mistress.

CONCLUSION: AN UNTIE-ABLE KNOT

The film ends similarly to the novel, 18 months later, in a mirror image of an opening scene, with the Comtesse d'Artelles and the Vicomte de

Prony again discussing Marigny's continued liaison with Vellini. Breillat's final lines (five pages before the novel's end), in discussing Ryno's neglect of his once adored wife, fall like an axe on Roxanne Mesquida's fair Hermangarde, every bit as violently as in the murder of her Elena at the end of *Fat Girl*. Madame d'Artelles is devastated at the news of the once faithful Marigny's return to his old mistress; certain that he truly did love his chaste and beautiful wife. De Prony's cynical retort closes the film: 'It's fitting someone should remember. As for Marigny, it would appear he simply doesn't.' We have noted how the film's disruption of narrative chronology through the embedded flashback structure also disrupts the structure of courtly romance, with its need for the endless deferral of desire to avoid the inevitable fall into disgust that follows (carnal) knowledge. The 'last' sexual encounter before Ryno's marriage is seen first, their first time appears via flashback as both a beginning and a renewal; the last time will not be the last, as the final scene attests. There can be no last time.

We are reminded of Vellini's parting words to the Vicomte, at the end of the expository scene. 'Between Mr. Marigny and myself, there can be no ending.' '*De dénouement à la liaison qui existe entre Mr de Marigny et moi, ... il n'y a pas, Mr de Prony.*' The French term, *dénouement*, literally meaning the undoing of a knot, designates narrative resolution, closure. Though it is a dark victory, Vellini's prophecy is confirmed by the closing line. The film's refusal of narrative closure seals their ongoing attachment. Vellini and Ryno remain tied by a lover's knot which neither man (society), woman (Ryno's wife and female conquests) nor God (social religion) can sunder.

Their enduring passion, Ryno's 'perverse' desire for her, which leads him to sacrifice his pure, beautiful wife for this (un)yielding demon, is constructed as a consequence of Vellini's fiercely brutal reclaiming of sexual subjectivity. Breillat asserts that intimacy is separate from knowledge and that sexual intimacy is inseparable from the spiritual (Flambard-Weisbart, 2013). In *Mistress*, her Vellini's refusal to be completely known, or to submit to anything but passion, however perverse, forces her lover into a violent 'acknowledgement' (Rushton, 2010) that is the closest Breillat has come to image-ining enduring intimacy. Enduring because fleeting. Pheonix-like in its defiance of death and time. Sublime in its intimate blurring of pleasure and pain. Violent in its refusal of conquest. Spiritual in its bodily mortality.

NOTE

1 According to popular French cinema website *Allo Ciné*, *Mistress* scored an average of 3.5 / 5 over a total of 24 press reviews. The two top intellectual specialist film magazines, *Cahiers du cinema* and *Positif* praised the film, scoring it 5 / 5. http://www.allocine.fr/film/fichefilm-55720/critiques/presse/#pressreview18845315 (accessed 17 March 2013).

Chapter 4

HORRIBLE SEX

THE SEXUAL RELATIONSHIP IN NEW EXTREMISM

LISA COULTHARD AND CHELSEA BIRKS

Torture, genital mutilation, rape, murder, cannibalism: with extremes in gore, violence and sexuality, the films associated with European New Extremism mix 'lowbrow' genres of pornography and horror with 'highbrow' art film aesthetics in ways that have provoked and intrigued audiences, critics, and scholars. Featuring films as diverse as *Sombre* (Philippe Grandrieux, 1998), *Baise-moi* (Virginie Despentes and Coralie Trinh Thi, 2000), *Dans ma peau* (Marina de Van, 2002), *Irréversible* (Gaspar Noé, 2002), and *Fat Girl* (Catherine Breillat, 2001), and encompassing works from art cinema auteurs such as Lars von Trier (*Antichrist*, 2009), Claire Denis (*Trouble Every Day*, 2001), and Bruno Dumont (*Twentynine Palms*, 2003), New Extremism is defined primarily by an obsession with bodily excess. Never clearly defined as a movement, school or mode, 'French New Extremity' as a term originated as a condemnatory phrase to describe what James Quandt viewed as an early 2000s trend or aesthetic dominant in a number of films. Primarily linked to contemporary French cinema, New Extremism has moved beyond these borders, recently being applied to films such as *Antichrist* and operating as an aesthetic and theoretical frame for understanding a new mode of provocative cinema based in art cinema traditions but participating in the explicit sex associated with pornography and the gore of horror. Because of their attention to what Tim Palmer calls 'brutal intimacy' (Palmer, 2006: 22), these films are associated first and foremost with explicit portraits of the body in extreme modes of being (sex and violence), a preoccupation that has led critics and scholars to emphasize the tactile nature of this cinema:

as tactile and haptic, the films stress touch, the body, sensation and spectatorial immersion over the merely narrational. More than violence, this tactility has primarily been discussed in terms of the films' explicit and graphic depictions of sex as well as a more generalized emphasis on sensuality and touch. As Palmer summarizes, the 'filmmaking agenda here is an increasingly explicit dissection of the body and its sexual behaviours: unmotivated or predatory sex, sexual conflicts, male and female rape, disaffected and emotionless sex, ambiguously consensual sexual encounters, arbitrary sex stripped of conventional or even nominal gestures of romance' (2006: 22). And yet, for all the accuracy of Palmer's descriptive list, this characterization misses the crucial point that the films most closely aligned with New Extremism (*Dans ma peau*, *Irréversible*, *Twentynine Palms*, *Antichrist*, *Trouble Every Day*, etc.) focus their excessive sex and violence not on transgressive modes of sexuality, but rather almost exclusively on interrogations of heterosexual, sexually active and romantically involved couples.

Although New Extremism is an expansive category, including everything from the explicit sexuality of the films of Catherine Breillat and Patrice Chereau to the art horror of films like *Calvaire* (Fabrice Du Welz, 2004), *Martyrs* (Pascal Laugier, 2008), or *À l'intérieur* (Julien Maury and Alexandre Bustillo, 2007), many of its key texts (including the films that Quandt discussed in his seminal article) focus on the problems of a heterosexual couple and envision their relationship as ultimately founded on an undercurrent of brutality and violence. Not simply explorations of the body, sex and violence, a number of new extremist films locate their explorations of hapticity, violence, sex and the body within the contested territory of the heterosexual relationship itself. This chapter contends that it is this combination of violence, explicit sex, and a concentration on the heterosexual couple that shapes some of the excesses and shocks associated with New Extremism. This is a cinema of provocation – while critically highly acclaimed, all of the films discussed here have met with walk-outs, vituperative attacks and loathing. As Tanya Horeck and Tina Kendall comment, '[i]n their concerted practice of provocation as a mode of address, the films of the New Extremism bring the notion of response to the fore, interrogating, challenging and often destroying the notion of a passive or disinterested spectator' (2011: 2). Although New Extremism's provocations are crucial to any understanding of the movement, this confrontation has primarily been considered in light of transgressive content, a view that ignores that films such as *Trouble Every Day*, *Twentynine Palms* and *Antichrist* concern themselves with the (usually) married heterosexual couple, the most normative of sexual relationships. Explicit sex and graphic violence are not sufficient explanations for the extremes in response associated with these films: it is rather, we argue, the way that these themes expose the fundamental ambivalence and incommensurability at the heart of the romantic sexual relationship that is most shocking.

In what follows, we re-examine the provocations of New Extremism in order to articulate the ways in which the disruption associated with these films is not merely due to shock aesthetics, but to the ways that these aesthetics expose fundamental, unresolved contradictions and ambiguities regarding sexual difference, sexual violence and the heterosexual couple. More precisely, we argue that what is excessive in *Trouble Every Day*, *Twentynine Palms* and *Antichrist* (representative and defining films of New Extremism), is not so much the combination of low and high genres or the explicit sex and extreme violence, but the way in which the sex and violence are left to stand as indicators of the inherent contradiction and irrecuperable aporia of the sexual relationship itself. Discussed in psychoanalytic thought as a fundamental deadlock, the sexual relationship is not about sex itself, but the relation between the sexes and the processes by which sexual difference is established. Lacan's dictum that 'there is no such thing as a sexual relationship' thus articulates the idea that there is no reciprocity or symmetry of the sexes, no 'natural', 'harmonious' sexual relationship against which perverse ones can be defined. Stressing the processes by which sexuation (sexual difference as it is negotiated and determined) defines sexual difference in relation to a third term (the phallus), this statement addresses sexual difference rather than the act. But its resonance for the interrogation of sex is clear – that there is no sexual relationship determines the underlying antagonisms in sexual difference, which in turn relates to the representation in these films of the heterosexual sex act as one primarily defined by violence, whether in fantasy or in reality. As Lacanian theorist Slavoj Žižek notes, because the sex act itself is inherently traumatic, fundamentally both terrifying and obscenely ridiculous, it must by necessity be supplemented by fantasy. That is to say, that there is a minimal idealization required for sex, a fantasy frame that prevents us from disconnecting and experiencing traumatic, depressing desublimation.

As a result, any disintegration or decomposition of this fantasy results in a getting too close that broaches the horror of the Real, an impact that Žižek ties to the depressing effects of films by auteurs such as David Lynch who make emphatic the gap that separates reality from the horror of the Real: in Lynch 'the raw flesh from beneath the surface always threatens to rise to the surface' (Žižek, 1997b: 22), a shift into the Real that causes one to recognize that what was beautiful can quickly and irreversibly become grotesque, its own ugly, obscene underside when there is a gap or a break in the fantasy. In *The Art of the Ridiculous Sublime: On David Lynch's* Lost Highway, Žižek (2000a) argues that Lynch's style, in its movement from sublime to ridiculous scenarios and aesthetics, and attention to the gaps of fantasy, renders his films ideal texts for exposing this obscenity and horror that fantasy attempts to cover and obscure. It is our intention here to apply a similar analysis to the fantasy of the sexual act and the traumatic Real of the antagonism at the core of the sexual relationship in these films of New Extremism, films that are obsessed with sex, violence and the romantic couple. Each filmmaker tackles the paradoxes of the sexual relationship and the necessary supplemental fantasy of sex in divergent ways: Denis's vampiric / cannibalistic story of impossible consummation, Dumont's brutal and microscopic examination of a conflicted couple on a road trip, von Trier's elaborate tale of trauma, psychosis and possession. Although categorized as art films, each has its own signature style as well, ranging from the naturalistic performances and elaborately sublime landscape shots of Dumont to the intense aestheticism of von Trier, to the mixed modalities and wooden performances of Denis's art horror film.

Despite their divergent styles, each of these films interrogates an adult, sexual relationship between a man and a woman, playing with conventional narrative form and stressing ambiguity and a lack of clear causality. In zeroing in on the romantic couple and their sex life, these films can all be seen as love stories. As Žižek notes, however, the conventional film love story can never go all the way, because to do so would disturb rather than engage the viewer. Conventional narrative cinema simply cannot withstand the intrusion of real sex that goes 'all the way'; that is, if at the end of a film like *Out of Africa*, we got a scene showing Robert Redford and Meryl Streep really doing it, 'details of their aroused sexual organs, penetration, orgasm' (Žižek, 1991: 111), the film could simply not regain its footing. The love story requires a proper distance, an idealization, that gets lost if the film directly reveals 'that', in contrast to pornography that trades in precisely showing all, a feature that Žižek ties to its desublimating, depressing effect. The love story must not show all the realistic details of pornography or else it ceases to be a love story. The real act of sex must be obscured, faked, only suggested in the love story or else the fantasy frame is destroyed: 'As soon as we "show it", its charm is dispelled, we have "gone too far." Instead of the sublime Thing, we are stuck with vulgar, groaning fornication' (Žižek, 1991: 110).

This is what we argue is at work in the films we analyse here: although radically different in form, style and tone, each of these three films exposes the radicality of this going 'too far', the 'low art' disruptions of adopting pornographic conventions for art cinema, and the provocations posed by the sexual relationship itself. In these three seminal films of European New Extremism, the provocations of sex are not simply those of violent transgression and the shock of graphic depictions, but rather of a desublimating overproximity to the sex and violence of the romantic couple.

CONSUMING LOVE: *TROUBLE EVERY DAY*

Claire Denis's *Trouble Every Day* exposes the antagonisms of the sexual relationship by explicitly conflating sex and violence, suggesting that sexual desire is inherently associated with a pathological urge to kill. Shane (Vincent Gallo) in *Trouble Every Day* has strange vampiric urges that prevent him from consummating his relationship with his new bride June (Tricia Vessey). Desire is posed not as an essential condition of the romantic relationship, but rather as an impediment, an incurable sickness that precludes any possibility of romantic love. The normal functioning of the heterosexual couple is exposed as utterly incommensurable with desire, since the physical expression of Shane's desire results in the brutal destruction of its object. Žižek argues that desire is constituted by a 'radical oscillation between attraction and repulsion' (Žižek, 1997b: 67): we want to get close to the object of our desire, but not close enough to expose the 'excremental excess constitutive of the kernel of her being' (1997b: 68). Like Lynch's films, *Trouble Every Day* emphasizes this gap and takes it to extremes. Using the shock of explicit gore and brutal sexual violence, it underlines the repulsive implications of wanting to 'get too close', while also revealing that this impulse to uncover the Real of the other person is entirely inconsistent with holding them as an object of fantasy. It is significant that June is implied to be a virgin, exempt (at least at first) from Shane's desirous impulses: unbreached and unpenetrated, she is able to maintain the mystery of the sublime Thing. By separating the two extremes of attraction and repulsion that constitute desire, *Trouble Every Day* discloses their utter incommensurability: as an urge to expose the other's internal being, desire is predicated on a violence that always threatens to intrude onto the Real, tearing open the unblemished screen of fantasy and allowing all its loathsome insides to spill out.

Trouble Every Day, decidedly the most controversial work in Claire Denis's otherwise very highly regarded art cinema oeuvre, counterbalances incredibly graphic scenes of eroticized cannibalism with slow pacing and strangely flat, affectless performances. Shane, a pharmaceutical scientist, uses his honeymoon in Paris as an excuse to track down a former colleague, whose wife Coré (Béatrice Dalle) he believes to be suffering from the same mysterious illness. Plagued by images of his young bride naked and covered in blood, Shane's motivating obstacle in the narrative is that his sanguinary fantasies stand in the way of the consummation of his marriage. And yet, within the diegesis of the film, the problem is framed as a rather banal one – despite the extreme nature of Shane's fantasies, in reality they manifest themselves as ordinary sexual dysfunction. While the horrors of this film should not be understated – Coré's cannibalization of the young boy and Shane's rape and murder of the maid in the basement are particularly significant in this regard, and shall be elaborated in more detail below – it is important to note that Shane does not enact his fantasies until the end of the film. Before that point, his disease finds expression in emphatically more prosaic forms of deviancy than the cannibalism he eventually succumbs to: he fondles a passing woman in a bathroom, ogles a chambermaid at their hotel, follows a blonde woman on a dark road at night, and presses up against a middle-aged woman on a crowded train. When June is out, he masturbates in a prone position (lying face down) – a practice that is considered abnormal by some, and has been seen as both a cause and symptom of sexual dysfunction. After a last, failed attempt at intercourse with June, he rushes to the bathroom, jerks off to a magazine insert and ejaculates in a long stream (which is shown onscreen) – much to June's frustration and disappointment, this provides explicit evidence that his desire *does* lurk in there somewhere, despite his failure to direct it towards her. Aside from the parallel drawn between Coré and Shane (which I will return to below), our access to Shane's fantasy is the only indication that there is anything more sinister going on: if we view his actions objectively, he is merely a rather mundane kind of dysfunctional urban pervert.

Shane's sexual dysfunction is a classic symptom of the Madonna-whore complex, theorized by Freud in 'The Most Prevalent Form of Degradation in Erotic Life' as the primary cause of impotence in men. He argues there that impotence is due to an unresolved neurotic fixation on the mother, and is therefore intimately linked with the trauma of sexual difference: the impotent man cannot desire any woman he loves, and vice-versa, because he associates love with the mother, and the mother with the threat of castration. The complex is exaggerated in *Trouble Every Day*, since loving the object of desire is *literally* impossible for Shane, and not merely psychically so: loving June means not only not wanting to degrade her, but also not wanting to kill her. He therefore must separate his love from his desires and indulge his desires with the 'whores', an impulse that escalates in violence until he finally murders the maid in the basement of the hotel (ostensibly 'eating her out' in a traumatic interpretation of a conventional sex act). The romantic relationship is therefore conditional on this separation, and on the repression of desire for the object of love: repression is the source of Shane's sexual dysfunction, but the problem is that this narrative obstacle is impossible to remove without destroying the integrity of his romantic relationship – doing so means destroying *her*.

Shane attempts to overcome this deadlock by seeking out Léo (Alex Descas), a doctor with whom he had done pharmacological and botanical research in Guyana. Flashbacks and fragmented information suggest that Shane and Léo's wife Coré had been lovers, and that their disease is the result of Shane stealing Léo's work and administering it to himself and Coré. Their cannibalism is therefore implicitly a punishment for adultery and hubris, a narrative detail that seemingly goes against the transgressive spirit of New Extremism by reinforcing the value of the heteronormative, monogamous relationship. The film affirms this institution only to expose the violence that underlies it, however, as the contrasting 'virtuous' relationship between Shane and June is revealed to function only by way of *dys*function; that is, it is revealed not to work at all.

Coré, on the other hand, provides a picture of what occurs when dysfunction is overcome and desire is unleashed. Dressed in high boots and a long skirt, she prowls highways and lures truck drivers with the promise of sex, devouring them during the act. By connecting sexual desire to cannibalism, Denis lays bare the traumatic Real underlying the compulsion to get close to the other: in sexual intercourse, getting close means getting close to the *body* of the other, and the engagement with flesh and bodily fluids that sex requires can evoke a sense of disgust that intrudes on the ordinary, fantasized construction of the body. Žižek writes that

> [i]n our standard phenomenological attitude toward the body of another person, we conceive of the surface (of a face, for example) as directly

expressing the 'soul' – we suspend the knowledge of what actually exists beneath the skin surface (glands, flesh, and so on). The shock of ugliness occurs when the surface is actually cut, opened up, so that the direct insight into the actual depth of the skinless flesh dispels the spiritual, immaterial pseudodepth. (Žižek, 1997a: 22)

By making literal the desire to 'get inside' the other, *Trouble Every Day* makes explicit the ugliness underlying our surface appearance, exposing it as inconsistent with the fantasies that uphold the proper symbolic order. In his essay on the film, French philosopher Jean-Luc Nancy argues *Trouble Every Day* is about the 'real' of the kiss, the 'unbearable tearing apart' that constitutes sexual desire. While it would be a mistake to equate Nancy's concept of the real with the Lacanian real, they are structurally similar in that they constitute a traumatic, impossible remainder that breaks into our reality as an irrecuperable excess. This excess is evoked in corporeal terms in the film, as the 'tearing apart' of desire becomes the tearing apart of flesh; Nancy writes that it opens onto the undifferentiated territory of the real 'by absorption, which opens onto a kind of horrific sublimation: not that of sex in which a body takes pleasure, but that of an entire body in which sex bursts out and is spattered with the body's blood' (2008: 2).

This is most explicitly evoked in the film's most disturbing scene, in which Coré lures a neighbourhood boy to her attic, where she then seduces and cannibalizes him. The scene marks the first instance where cannibalism is explicitly shown, as it was previously merely indicated to have occurred in the ellipses between Coré attracting the truck drivers and Léo finding their bodies in a field. This scene fills in the gap, the cinematography languishing over textural details of skin – moles, hair, veins, nipple, belly button – so as to emphasize its materiality and raw vulnerability. The boy's body is fragmented through these close-ups, echoing similar techniques used in pornography to objectify the body and construct it as a surface open to exploration and penetration. *Trouble Every Day* exposes the violent implications of this construction, as by playing on surfaces the film gestures towards what underlies them: Coré first allows the boy to penetrate her, and then begins to penetrate him. She bites through his lips and throat (Dalle's infamous mouth emphasized by the stark redness of blood and the shadows obscuring the rest of her face), and blood gurgles from his nose and mouth as he screams abjectly; puncturing new holes in him with eager tongue and fingers, she eventually turns him inside out and paints the walls with his blood. This violence is shown to be the logical outcome of the sexual act, as *Trouble Every Day* refuses to differentiate between desire to explore the body of the other and the brutal impulse to tear the other apart.

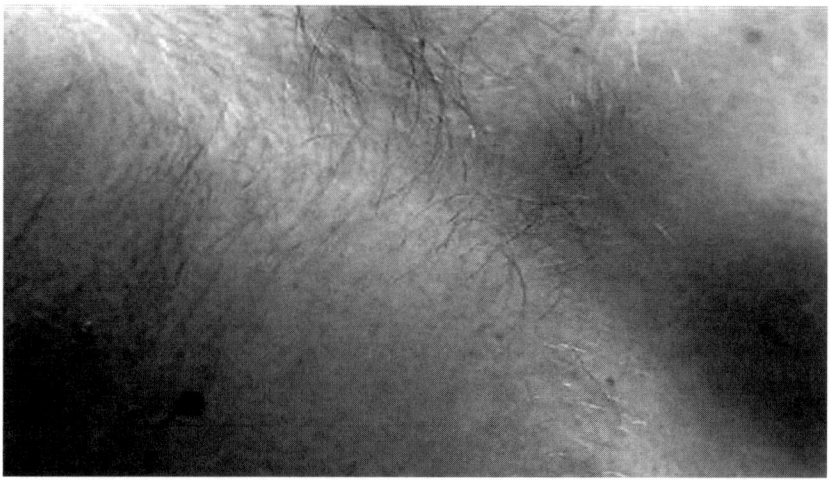

Figure 4.1. The cinematography of Denis' camera languishes over the textual details of skin in *Trouble Every Day*.

This is the desire lurking inside Shane, and while he never fully unleashes it on June, he does indulge his fantasies on the chambermaid. Throughout the narrative the maid seems fascinated by Shane: she lingers at the 'do not disturb' sign hung on Shane and June's door as she passes in the hallway; stays frozen for a few moments in the bathroom when Shane walks into the room as she's cleaning; and, in the scene before she is murdered, pauses after making the newlyweds' bed, sitting down on it to have a cigarette. Her death is further foreshadowed by shots that observe her voyeuristically, following her from behind and focusing on the nape of her neck as she pushes the cart down the hotel hallways, and then watching as she strips in the locker room (where she is later killed), puts on a sweater and washes her feet in the sink (at the end of the scene she glances warily behind her, as if aware of the camera watching her). The camera's perspective is never anchored during these scenes: nobody is watching the maid but us, at least until the end of the film when Shane fills the camera's predatory perspective; until then, it is the spectator that takes the position of the monster.

At first, the sexual politics of the final murder scene are ambiguous. Shane approaches the maid in the locker room and kisses her. She resists (shyly? because she knows he's married? because she has a boyfriend? because she doesn't want to?), kisses him back, and then pushes him away. He pulls her to the floor, takes off her underwear, and pulls himself on top of her. It is at this point that she begins to struggle in earnest, any ambiguity dispelled as she screams and beats against him while he rapes her. He moves down her body and begins to perform what looks like cunnilingus until he raises his head to reveal that his face is covered in blood. Shadows, tight framing, and Shane's body conceal most of what's going on (unlike in the other cannibalism scene, where explicit gory details are made visible despite the darkness of the image), and the shock elicited from the scene comes primarily from sound (her screams, his perverse moans of pleasure) and the visceral reaction evoked by the idea of what he is doing to her. The precise moment of her death is (mercifully) not seen onscreen: Denis cuts to the aftermath, the maid's blood-soaked lifeless body seen for a moment between the lockers before he drags her offscreen (this is similar to the other cannibalism scene, which also elides the boy's death and cuts back to Coré once she has painted him on the walls).

As Nancy points out, this violence is a fury that threatens to be unleashed between Shane and June, a fury hinted at by 'icons' on her flesh: the small bite mark on her shoulder, the cut on her upper lip (2008: 2). It is a fury utterly incommensurable with the daily routine of their love, with June's impeccably prim exterior and Shane's odd tenderness towards her. The flatness of the acting deepens this chasm, as the relationship between Shane and June marks a sharp contrast with the ecstatic abjection of a desire that delights in the traumatic Real of the other, with all its guts and gore. The ending of the film suggests future violence between the couple, however, as June returns home to find Shane in the shower after he has murdered and eaten the maid: her wide-eyed gaze (emphasized in close-up) at the blood dripping from the shower curtain suggests a loss of innocence and her growing cognizance of his brutality. But within the space of the diegesis their relationship is allowed to subsist: Shane's disease is incurable, and his dysfunction the condition of them maintaining the tenuous balance between love and the savage violence of desire.

DANGER AND THE DIRTY WEEKEND: *TWENTYNINE PALMS*

Bruno Dumont's *Twentynine Palms* depicts in slow detail two lovers (Katia and David) having sex, arguing, and making up repeatedly for over 100 minutes, only to end with David's rape by male strangers, his murderous response (he stabs Katia to death) and his resulting suicide (which we do not see onscreen). Stressing boredom and irritation for the majority of the film, the style and narration expertly mimic Katia (Katia Golubeva) and David's (David Wissak) aimless meanderings; the camera painstakingly follows their actions, lingering over petty arguments, animalistic make-up sex, failed sexual encounters. With a cinematic emphasis on landscapes, relative silence (no non-diegetic music), attention to detail, long takes and mobile framing, *Twentynine Palms* invites an almost contemplative spectatorial engagement, despite the conflict, violent arguments and fraught nature of the relationship of the main characters. As spectators we watch every detail, looking for nuance or for clues while we wait for a narrative climax or culminating action. In the last 20 minutes this action arrives in violent spades – rape, murder, suicide follow in quick, fragmented succession. The film's aesthetic shifts drastically as the spectator is launched into the world of the horror film: action and editing speed up, framing is too tight (Katia's murder) or too distant (the final scene) to clearly understand the action, darkness interferes with visual clarity. And yet, with all the surprise of this ending, we contend that from the opening the viewer has been prepared for these moments. Moreover, the violent explosion that erases the characters from the film text demands a retroactive reframing of the previous action. Upon reflection it is clear that from the film's first moments, horror lurks beneath the surface as a palpable unease accompanies these characters on their pointless wanderings. While the last 20 minutes see a superficial calm radically and violently shattered in rape, abuse, murder and suicide, on second look it is clear that this calm was never portrayed as anything but superficial – the violence and aggression of their exchanges is there throughout the film.

More specifically, the film has set the stage for this violent brutality through the depictions of sex that punctuate the film at regular intervals. These sex scenes orient and anchor the action and, although the film's culminating violence seems shocking, these rather banal scenes of daily life and sex between a romantic couple prepare the viewer for the violence that occurs in the last 20 minutes. Throughout the film we witness predatory violence, cruelty, immaturity and childish selfishness between the two main leads and the sex that we witness stresses this combative tone. More than dialogue, character motivation or narrational drive, it is the sex scenes that shape the film's narrative trajectory and tone.

Framing its action within a journey narrative, the film opens with the characters Katia and David leaving the city and venturing into the desert, a landscape that becomes significant in understanding the way that sex and nature interweave in the film's sexual brutality. Critical accounts of *Twentynine Palms* repeatedly reference the primal aspects of the film's landscape and depictions of sexual intercourse: Martine Beugnet stresses the human becoming mineral in the film (2007: 131); Neil Archer notes the tension in the film between the desert as '*tabula rasa*' (2011: 61) and the representatives of civilization (motel, military, vehicles); Nikolaj Lubecker comments on the regression narrative that takes the characters back to a mythical, 'sacred space' (2011: 237). Noting the way the characters become one with the desert landscapes, their regression to pre-linguistic, bodily communication, and the removal of clothing and other accoutrements associated with culture and civilization, scholars have discussed Katia and David as a kind of Adam and Eve in the desert of Eden.

Related to this understanding of David and Katia as Adam and Eve is the attention to the primal, pre-verbal, qualities of their sexual exchanges – grunts, screams, yells, and other bestial noises characterize Katia and David's sex. With significant language barriers (they do not share proficiency in any language and merely stumble through with a very few key French and English phrases), their relationship is presented as a primarily physical one, as body language, sex, physical fights and other non-verbal exchanges stand in for articulate verbal communication. There are five sex scenes in the film before the final rape scene: the first encounter in the motel pool about 15 minutes into the film, which is characterized by awkward fumbling and unsuccessful attempts at underwater penetration; the second scene occurs outdoors hiking in the desert, where they take off their clothes and after a brief period of thrusting from behind (with amplified slapping noises), Katia declares she is too dry and they stop; another motel pool scene where David tries to force underwater sex, and Katia, gasping for air, swims away scared and angry; sex on the motel bed, with Katia straddling David, which ends with a concentration on the faces of the characters as each climaxes; a scene of fellatio in the motel room with David standing and Katia kneeling before him, with the camera focused on the back of her head and on his face as he climaxes. Each of these scenes stresses David's exaggerated performance of a dominant and aggressive masculinity:

grunts, heavy and harsh breathing, yells and screaming, aggressive hand movements and thrusting.

The sex scenes thus are not ancillary to the 'love story' but rather inform the viewer of the characters, their relationship and their trajectory. Controlling and demeaning, David is presented as an arrogant, selfish child-man more concerned about his Hummer (surely a pun intended by Dumont's choice of vehicles) than Katia, while Katia is an equally clichéd portrait of childlike femininity characterized by mercurial mood swings, irrational jealousies, and a dizzying and inscrutable array of emotional highs and lows. The sex scenes confirm these gendered stereotypes by emphasizing David's predatory attempts to assert power over Katia (calling her name, repeatedly asking if she can 'feel it', thrusting her aggressively, pushing her head under water) and stressing Katia's willingness to perform (her loving submission to the aggressive fellatio and the emphasis on her sexual pleasure while having sex in the motel room). In light of this it is notable that the only scene of Katia orgasming occurs when she is on top, in a dominant position.

With the attention to incomplete sexual acts, fumbling, awkwardness and dominance, one can see why Peter Lehman and Susan Hunt come to the seemingly rather trite conclusion that the film is really about David's compromised sexual performance and small penis size (evidenced they argue by the failures of the early sex scenes among other details). Throughout these sexual interchanges, the acts are shadowed by dissatisfaction, predation and violence: several attempts at outdoor sex end prematurely (one in giggles, another in an argument) and the sex scenes that culminate in orgasm erupt on the screen without preparation, are filmed too close for comfort, and are resonant with the discord of this fraught relationship. For instance, after the sequence where they hit a three-legged dog and have an argument, the close-up of the back of Katia's head thrusting back and forth on David erupts suddenly on the screen without preamble, context or framing. This abrupt elliptical editing is the case in every sex scene, except the first one: each begins with a radical break from match on action and erupts on the screen without preparation; each stresses David's predatory, aggressive sexuality; and the last sex scene of fellatio is bookended by arguments, the one afterwards representing significant abuse and brutality. This is not the eroticism of art horror, the perversion of psychological horror, or the sexual explicitness of the slasher genre; instead, we are faced with everyday sex between a (somewhat incompatible, somewhat unlikeable) heterosexual couple on a road trip. These sexual acts thus structure the text in an almost banal, predictable fashion as the couple's days seem to follow a schedule of (in)action: driving in the desert, swimming, having sex, eating, fighting, making up. The most shocking thing about Dumont's film, though, is how dissatisfying these acts seem to be for both the viewers and the actants: the actors seem further apart emotionally with every sex scene and the viewer is left frustrated by the lack of narrative progress and the repetitive nature of the cycle of sex, fighting, sex, fighting, sex. Indeed, the violent ending is perversely welcomed by a viewer annoyed with the lack of action – because the film sets up the feeling that something bad is going to happen throughout the diegesis, when the violence arrives it creates a sense of relief. The submerged but constant tension finally erupts, and the violent ending as a result becomes strangely narrationally satisfying. This creates a sense of spectatorial discomfort as if we are somehow complicit in the violent action of the film's ending – because we have narrationally been given what we were consciously or unconsciously expecting, we are part of the film's final action. It is these final moments and this feeling of complicity that we can relate back to Dumont's comment that *Twentynine Palms* is his engagement with the genre of American horror film – as a critique of American horror, the film opens up spectatorial and voyeuristic pleasure for interrogation as well.

Stressing repetition and stasis, Dumont's film engages in a radically desublimating cinematic experience that stresses the everyday pettiness, irritations, jealousies and aggressions that characterize this couple's relationship. Within this framework, the sex acts stand out not as erotically charged, climactically significant, narrative moments, but as rather uncomfortably intimate portraits of a couple we have witnessed argue, cry and behave childishly over the course of the film. This intimacy is decidedly discomfiting to a viewer desiring either the anonymous sex of pornography (where not knowing anything about the everyday lives, anxieties, worries of the 'characters' is arguably conventionally necessary for detached voyeuristic enjoyment), or the identificatory sentimental comforts of a dramatic narrative (the attractions of which are disturbed by the overly proximate nature of the sex scenes, a getting too close that troubles the distance required for conventional narrative enjoyment). In short, we have seen too much of this couple, their banal, everyday fears and anxieties, and power struggles to wish to see them have sex. Indeed, we have become so familiar with these characters that we have witnessed Katia pee outdoors, something which she forbids David from seeing presumably because it will ruin the mystique and mute his desire. That the camera lingers on her while she urinates in our full view indicates the extent to which Dumont is trying to desublimate, render ordinary and everyday, the actions, characters, and drama we witness onscreen.

This desublimating everydayness is not, however, without a sense of underlying unease and lurking danger, and the intriguing aspect of the film is the way that the sex correlates in a purely structural way with the rape and murder that conclude the film – the violence may erupt suddenly at the end, but the film has prepared us for this sequence of events. The male-on-male rape of David is a crucial reference point for understanding the gendered violence that results, but the representational congruence and similarity of the scenes of sex with the rape indicate a correlation of violence rather than its sudden eruption. Three key factors in the sex scenes suggest this correlation of consensual heterosexual sex with male rape: the male scream; facial close-ups; camera movement. David's scream when his Hummer is pushed off the road by the rapists' large white truck echoes his screams of orgasm heard earlier, which is in turn reflected in the male rapist's scream when he climaxes. This correlation invites the viewer to make a connection to the earlier sex scenes even before the spectre of rape is indicated or the rapists introduced. It is worth noting here that the only orgasm to occur in the desert space in *Twentynine Palms* is the rapist's – the heterosexual lovers are unable to complete copulation outside the confines of the motel room. It is also significant that while Katia is stripped by the male rapists, she is placed in the conventionally masculine position of being forced to watch her lover be raped. Although the rapists strip Katia, setting up an expectation that she will be the victim, Katia is not of sexual interest to them: instead they force her to witness her lover's humiliation, degradation, abuse and violation.

Like the sex scenes, the emphasis throughout the scene is on facial close-ups: Katia's, David's, the rapist's. In the sex scenes the close-ups on David and Katia's faces climaxing ambiguously suggest pain as much as pleasure. Again, this stylistic trope is repeated later in the perverse close-up on the rapist's climax in the rape scene. Moving away from a focus on the victim or the witness, this close-up shot of a rapist's pleasure and subsequent sobbing distorts the ethics, conventions and tropes for portraying rape onscreen – the rapist's pleasure is usually not an object for examination or narrative pronouncement. Indeed to do so would usually be considered dubious and deeply problematic. The rapist is not merely an abstract figure representing violence or a cheap narrative device to push the plot forward, but a character who receives the same focused attention as the main characters via a close-up shot of his sexual pleasure. By stressing the perversity of this shot with an extended close-up, Dumont invites the viewer to make the connection to earlier, similar shots during scenes of consensual sex (one of Katia's orgasms approached sobbing; David's are characterized by Tarzan-like yelling and screaming throughout), a correlation that carries with it thematic import, since to place the rapist within this spectrum is to place him within the context of Katia and David's relationship.

In addition to these sex scenes infected with violence and unease, space in *Twentynine Palms*, both the desert landscape and the town, resonates with menace: the entire region becomes imbued with a sense of danger and uneasiness, confirmed in the small signs that accumulate to suggest that something is awry in the sexual dynamics portrayed: the vehicular scenes of menace, the Hummer's damage and impotence (getting scratched and stuck), running over a three-legged dog (who seems to miraculously recover). In addition to these signs of unease, the film's cinematography stresses hand-held, mobile, long takes that constantly hold out the promise of locating a clue, a hint of what may happen, but that also stalk the characters and lurk in the spaces around them. All of these elements work to stain the fabric of the film's superficial story of a romantic excursion. These elements of menace are further tied to danger, and specifically masculine violence, through the military presence in *Twentynine Palms*, a nod to the base located there that serves as the economic core of the town. When Katia and David see a person in military gear whilst eating ice cream, David pushes back his floppy hair and asks Katia if he should shave his head like the marines. To this she replies that he should not, even though she later comments that they are very handsome. This slight is not merely an indication of Katia's paradoxical and uneven (hysterical) behaviour throughout the film, but a comment on masculinity as such.

It is not surprising, then, that after David is raped by a man with a shaved head, he traumatically repeats the gesture by shaving his own head before brutally murdering Katia (straddling her as he repeatedly stabs her in a perverse reversal of an earlier sex act) and killing himself. Some have read this transformation in symbolic terms as a re-enactment of the earlier failed sexual encounters, with David's knife standing in for his (supposedly unsatisfactory) penis, and his masculinity confirmed through a shaved head, which echoes both the marine and the rapist. For instance, Lehman and Hunt argue that the phallic collapse of his masculinity in the rape causes David 'to transform his entire body into a penis, in this case by referencing the Marine-style haircut' (Lehman and Hunt, 2009: 219). Furthering the act of head shaving, his murder of Katia becomes part of his phallic transformation: 'The target of his wrath is not the men who rape him but the woman who scratches his Hummer, wants "more" from his coital techniques, laughs at his inadequate attempt to clumsily penetrate her in the desert and finally watches him "take it from behind"' (2009: 216).

While this may be an oversimplification of the subtext of his act, it does point to the film's obsession with Katia's role in David's perceived emasculation and humiliation. Reversing the usual trope of rape-revenge or horror films, *Twentynine Palms* has David occupy the role of victim of sexual violence while Katia, his lover, is forced to watch. It is as much for this role as witness as for her place as woman that Katia is murdered. But it is also imperative to note that David kills himself as well – this is not merely an attack on Katia, but a self-destruction as well, and as such, it indicates the extent to which the rape is not merely an act of violent humiliation, but instead a ripping apart and disintegration of David's notion of reality itself. One could posit that the rape rips a hole in the fabric of his tentative reality, exposing him to the recognition of his own predatory sexuality. That is, in experiencing rape, he sees himself reflected in his rapist, an interpretation that is reinforced by the correlation of the sex scenes with the rape scene. Destroying the notion of his masculine identity, detaching him from the minimal idealizing distance necessary for proper functioning in reality, the rape (as well as Katia's witnessing of it and her taking on the role of caregiver) throws David into a catastrophic and irrevocable disintegration. What is crucial for our purposes here is to note that this detachment requires the erasure of Katia as well – the disintegration of his reality means the destruction of Katia as she exists for him (subject to his fantasmatic framing).

THE HORROR OF SEX: *ANTICHRIST*

Antichrist similarly engages with the utter destruction of reality that follows upon recognition of the impossibility of the sexual relationship and concomitant traumatic rupturing of reality. Referencing both occult and rural horror, *Antichrist*'s narrative is ostensibly a generically coherent one of erotic possession. A nameless couple, He (Willem Dafoe) and She (Charlotte Gainsbourg), grieving the loss of their child, head into the woods (their cabin Eden) for a therapeutic session aimed at the female character She's cure (with He, her husband, serving as her lover / therapist). While there, He encounters strange visions of violence and decay in the natural world and witnesses behaviours that indicate She's possession / psychosis, a situation that results in his torture, confinement, escape, and then her death at his hands. With graphic sexual penetration shots, extreme close-ups on sexual organs and a profusion of gore, *Antichrist* is perhaps the most explicitly extreme of the three films we analyse. Not surprisingly, it is perhaps also the most overt in its portrait of 'there is no such thing as a sexual relationship': the sex act roots *Antichrist*'s horror and violence, and is central to understanding its shocking excesses, reversals and subversions.

The film opens with a sublimely portrayed yet domesticated sex act – consensual sex between loving partners with their toddler in the next room, located in the home near the accoutrements of married, banal life (toothbrushes, washing machine, baby monitors) – accompanied by elevating, emotionally charged music ('Lascia ch'io pianga' from George Frideric Handel's *Rinaldo* (1711)) and filmed in gorgeous black and white cinematography. The sequence ends with the child Nic's accidental death: he falls out the window while the parents are occupied in sexual activity. Ranging from an elevation of a quotidian act (consensual sex) to the trauma of a child's death, the sequence maintains an audiovisual emphasis on sublime aesthetics and emotional attachment: beauty and horror co-exist in the sequence as it builds to the shock and extreme sadness at the death of a child. This affectively engaged aesthetic disappears from the film until the final, ambivalent, and aggressively ambiguous conclusion, and what occurs in between these two bookends resonates with uncanny, desublimating disturbance.

After the opening sequence, one of domestic, normative, sexual pleasure (all indicators point to the quotidian experience of a married couple stealing a few moments while their child is asleep and the wash is on), the film destabilizes this portrait, rendering its inconsistencies and ambivalences explicit. In their grief, the couple's inner conflicts move to the foreground and with them the sexual tensions and violence that are retroactively seen to have been present from the beginning, a recognition that reframes the opening as a fantasmatic masking, a sublime aestheticism that covers over both the particular horror of this domestic bliss as well as the more generalized trauma of the Real of sexual difference. This retroactive unravelling finds its most concrete expression in the shot of Nic's shoes in this opening sequence: an easily missed detail, Nic's shoes are shown to be placed below his crib in the wrong configuration (right shoe for left foot and vice versa). This detail is later revealed as proof of She's cruelty and psychosis dating back to the previous year; thus this subtle detail here in the opening operates as a kind of 'quilting point', making sense of the entire film within a single shot at the very beginning: She was cruel and harmful to their child, and He was a distant and preoccupied father who did not notice. Like He, we the viewers are so involved with the ecstatic portrayal of the sexual act with its lush cinematography and sublime music that this detail is overlooked, only to be exposed retroactively as significant.

The shift from sensational immersion into discomfiting recognition is aided by *Antichrist*'s stylistic split that occurs after the initiating sex act that opens the film. Immediately following this prologue, the style of the film changes radically – into colour from black and white, into silence from musical plenitude, into alienation and separation from intimacy. This second sequence is shot from within a hearse, looking outwards to the mourners following the vehicle: the look is as if from the coffin itself, a point of view emphasized by point of audition sound that approximates the silence of this interior space. It also significantly features a washed out palette, and an alienation of human figures: the mourners look forward, walking like the undead, and He and She follow the hearse at a distance from each other. This separation is made emphatic when She collapses and He continues on without stopping for some time – the couple that was so intertwined in the opening moments have become unaware of each other, distant and secluded within themselves. This shift marks the alienating style that dominates the film from this point until the epilogue. Techniques such as obscured speech, hand-held camera movements, disorienting and abrupt zooms in and out, a lack of non-diegetic music, and an amplification of distorted ambient sound all serve to stress an aesthetics of discomfort and desublimation. We are either too close or too far away from the action, the sounds are either too high or too low in pitch, the sex and violence are both too much (too intense, too close-up) and too little (lacking affect, import, or clear meaning). From a sublime beginning, the film descends into aesthetic murkiness, but also into increasingly graphic, overly proximate depictions of sex and violence designed to alienate rather than emotionally engage the viewer.

This aesthetic shift becomes most pronounced after the couple's decision to go into the woods to their cabin, tellingly named Eden. Soon after their arrival extreme violence ensues (She attacks and violently immobilizes him, mutilates herself; He then kills her, burns her remains and leaves), much of it focused on sexual brutality (she pounds his genitals with a block of wood, brings the unconscious victim to bloody ejaculation, drills a hole in his leg and then performs a self-clitoridectomy with a pair of scissors). Referencing witchhunts and historical violence against women, violence in the film is structured by discourses of therapeutic cure and ritual cleansing: stressing feminine weakness and evil, as well as patriarchal power and control, these sacrificial, curative modalities are at the heart of the film's engagement with nature, broadly defined: the natural world; the nature of sexual difference; the nature of evil.

This interpretive complexity of the term nature is foregrounded in the film when He and She play a role-playing game, in which He figures as her fears, which He interprets as 'Nature'. Referring to him as 'Mr. Nature', She asks what he wants from her and He responds, 'to hurt you as much as I can,' 'by killing you'. Highlighting sexual difference as well as violence against women, this discussion regarding nature broaches the infringing Real of the natural world that seems to erupt everywhere around them. As if repeating Žižek's definition of surplus enjoyment as that which has the power to convert pleasure into its opposite, to turn what is beautiful into a disgusting, abject thing (Žižek, 1991: 12-13), She comments on her revelation the previous summer that 'everything that used to be beautiful about Eden was perhaps hideous'. It is this assertion that shapes the representation of sex in the film and its relation to fantasy frames reality and the gap of the Real – without the fantasy that is necessary to keep the Real at bay from reality, we experience a catastrophic disintegration, as evidenced in the increasingly violent 'natural' world in the film (visions of death, decay, physical destruction in the natural world), as well as in an increasing pathologization of female desire and sex itself. His becoming therapist enables him to erect a prohibition on sexual activity, which in turn frames her desire as perverse, excessive, dangerous. This is most readily seen in the sex scenes that follow his self-proclamation as therapist: she bites his nipple too hard, ceasing the foreplay; we have a tasteful fade out on a sex scene, after which he says that's the 'stupidest thing I could have done to you'; she insists that he hit her, which he initially refuses, then happily complies with under the tree outside, a turn that exposes the gap to the Real, as evidenced by the grotesque turn the scene takes. After this sex in nature, which seems to confirm nature's propensity for evil, the film's events quickly move toward the violent climax, that witnesses both male and female sex organs graphically and brutally punished, with her self-clitoridectomy as the most extreme act of physical mutilation.

Central to almost all interpretations of the film, this clitoridectomy sequence is of course crucial to approaching the film's treatment of sexuation and sex: Lorenzo Chiesa analyses her self-mutilation as castration, as an over-identification with phallic logic and the phallus itself that 'unleashes the male protagonist's violence' (Chiesa, 2012: 205); Gitte Buch-Hansen sees it as an attempt to renegotiate gender positions – that is, returning to Eden and removing signs of sexual difference (Buch-Hansen, 2011: 138); Christopher Sharrett contends that 'She, in this film, enacts upon herself what her civilization – right down to the male most proximate to her – has insistently demanded, and continues to demand' (Sharrett, 2012: 26); Terrie Waddell suggests that her self-mutilation is regressive, an attempt at 'ridding herself of the evil of female embodiment and maintaining her girlish affect-ego attachment' (2012: 43). What these interpretations share is a focus on the clitoridectomy as an engagement with sexual difference itself; whether we see her act as one of over-identification with the phallus (a castration of the 'small penis' of the clitoris as Chiesa suggests), an absorption of patriarchal misogyny, an attempt to orchestrate universality, or a rejection of mature female desire and motherhood, the scene clearly stages an engagement with sexual difference and its external, corporeal markers as well as its relation to sexual pleasure. This last point is significant – the cut of clitoridectomy connects us back to the film's beginning and the sexual pleasure depicted onscreen in the opening, a pleasure that is reframed here within the realm of sexual difference. The heterosexuality of the opening act is crucial to the film's logic and the interpretation of this scene – in the opening, sexual difference is foregrounded in the penetration shot, the erotic codes for portraying male and female pleasure (a close-up penetration shot, the voyeuristic camera dwelling on her body, her facial indicators of pleasure) and the concentration of the camera on She during the act. The movement of bodies in that sequence prefigures the violent movements of these same bodies later: for all its sublime beauty, the prologue's sex act is fundamentally destructive (of objects, of a child) and the facial codes of female pleasure can be equally read as those of pain, an imaging of *jouissance* echoed in this later act of self-mutilation.

The climax and conclusion of the film highlights this combative nature of the prologue by mirroring the beginning in perverse ways: after her murder and burning, He escapes into the forest. Repeating the opening's music cue (Handel's aria), the sequence features a multitude of faceless female figures calmly walking past He, an image rife with suggestions of optimistic movement upwards that could be read as an endorsement of the male figure's progress as well as a suggestion of resurrection and rebirth. Where there were two (He and She) there is now just the one (He) and a nameless many shes; She has been erased and replaced by a multitude of women (a clearer articulation of Lacan's 'Woman does not exist' is perhaps not possible). This epilogue returns to the style of the opening, suggestive of redemption, sublimity and affective engagement. The consensual, domesticated sex act that opens the film is paired with She's erasure in the epilogue, an echo that suggests the obscene underside of consensual heterosexual sex is violent antagonism between the sexes and the willed erasure of woman.

CONCLUSION: SEX AS A HORRIBLE THING

Where *Trouble Every Day* examines impossible consummation in the love relationship (the exclusion of sex in marriage), *Antichrist* and *Twentynine Palms* concentrate on sexual desire within the context of the functioning, romantically and sexually involved couple (married in *Antichrist*, lovers in *Twentynine Palms*). Indeed, one could say that *Antichrist* and *Twentynine Palms* pick up where *Trouble Every Day* ends – with the formation of the impossible couple. Referencing horror films (all three directors have commented on the importance of American horror cinema for their films) and shifting the libidinal energies of that genre onto the sexually active couple as the centre point of horror (rather than the group of friends, or isolated individuals), these films subtly posit a brutality at the heart of heterosexual desire and romance, a danger that becomes more pronounced and extreme as each film moves toward violent conclusion. Rendered emphatic through the virginal fantasy of *Trouble Every Day*, the sublime mystification of love as something that only exists with the erasure of sexual desire (his wife is not and must never be his lover) is exposed in all of its dubiousness and absurdity. In *Antichrist* and *Twentynine Palms*, sex and love are shown to be similarly mutually exclusive, but with the signature difference that sex is tied not just to violence but to the violence of sexual difference itself. The representation of the sex act in each of these films is central to achieving these effects – the treatment of sex in each exposes and lays bare the ideological inconsistencies that structure the normative heterosexual sex act. By placing explicit sex within narrative and revealing the ways in which it is sustained and defined through fantasy, *Trouble Every Day*, *Twentynine*

Palms and *Antichrist* lay bare the inherent and standing contradiction of sexual difference: it is left as a traumatic remainder, an indeterminable sexual excess that refuses to be re-repressed. Sexual love is desublimated, rendered ordinary and yet infused with trauma, violence, and the antagonisms wrought by sexuation.

Chapter 5

SHORTBUS

SMART CINEMA AND SEXUAL UTOPIA

LINDA RUTH WILLIAMS

The explicit, theatrically released 2006 quirky sex drama *Shortbus* has been widely billed as the most candid mainstream film ever: in his *Variety* review Todd McCarthy called it 'The most sexually graphic American narrative feature ever made outside the realm of the porn industry' (2009). Six primary characters' sexual and relationship dilemmas form the intertwining backbone of the film; in *Shortbus* all physical dalliances on the road to fulfilment are displayed and enjoyed. Each character is involved in a sexual / identity quest which reaches resolution as the multi-stranded narrative arrives at a more-or-less happy ending: the two primary story threads focus on the uber-rational, over-analytic Sofia (Sook-Yin Lee), a married Chinese-Canadian relationship counsellor / sex therapist who has herself never experienced orgasm and is now in search of one, and a gay male couple – peppy ex-child actor Jamie (P. J. DeBoy) and his depressed lover of five years, James (Paul Dawson). 'The Jamies' (as they are known) visit Sofia for advice on opening up their cosy coupledom to other partners, but begin to betray more fundamental problems. The counselling session goes hilariously wrong: buttoned-up Sofia gets angry, hits Jamie, then confesses that she is 'pre-orgasmic' (to which Jamie dorkishly responds 'Does that mean you're about to have one?'). This sets in motion the main narrative drive of the film: the men encourage Sofia to visit Shortbus, a sex club which also functions as an art-space and consciousness-raising location, which might provide the solution to her problems. Here she meets Severin (Lindsay Beamish), a bondage sex worker, and encounters Ceth (Jay Brannan) and Caleb (Peter Stickles), young men who, independent of each other, secretly obsess over 'the

Jamies'. Other significant characters are Sofia's husband Rob (Raphael Barker), Severin's regular john, the rich 'trust fund muppet' Jesse (Adam Hardman), and Shortbus's flamboyant maitre d' Justin Bond (Justin Bond – credited as 'Himself').

But it is the primary characters whose intertwined individual quests braid together to form the arc of the film: Sofia's search for an orgasm; Severin's desire to be seen as an artist rather than just a sex worker; James's parallel desire to be seen as something other than the hustler he used to be, and his depressed descent towards attempted suicide; Jamie's efforts to keep James committed to their relationship; Ceth and Caleb's individual quests to get closer to 'the Jamies'. The tone is funny and frank, endearing as well as sometimes shockingly overt for a mainstream film (courting theatrical distribution; eschewing pornography or art cinema's niche-outlets). Indeed, *Shortbus* throws down its particularly explicit gauntlet to exhibitors and audiences from the get-go. The opening sequence, which I will discuss further below, features Severin administering B&D to Jesse; James's solo sex including urination, manual masturbation and self-fellatio, secretly watched by Caleb the voyeur; and heterosexual penetrative and oral sex in multiple positions between Sofia and Rob. Later in the film there is group sex, vanilla lesbianism and penetrative and non-penetrative anal gay sex. Activities and body parts are as explicitly filmed as in some pornography, with the proviso that *Shortbus* tends to hold back from close-ups of penetration or (the delightfully termed) 'open / split beaver shots'.

By any standards *Shortbus* is an explicit film, a term which for mainstream cinema has long been yoked to obscenity. For many years, in the UK at least, this was a term intimately bound to judgements and deployment of the Obscene Publications Act, which enabled sexually explicit books to be banned and then unbanned (*Lady Chatterley's Lover*, first published in 1960 when the terms of the act loosened up, is the most famous example), and then became one of the acts under which the British Board of Film Censors (later the British Board of Film Classification) worked. However by the time of *Shortbus*'s release the BBFC had changed its practices and was focusing more acutely on what could be expressed in the category of potential age-groups. *Shortbus* was passed with a mainstream certificate for all viewers of 18 and over. This is crucial in distinguishing the film from pornography: in the UK films meant primarily for sexual pleasure and / or which contain particularly strong images are confined to the R18 category, and can only be accessed via licensed sex shops. However, the word 'obscene' has rather dropped out of British classification language, though it retains a power in the tabloid press whenever a particular scandal film ignites the tinder of the cultural moment.

Obscenity in academic circles has a different currency – arguably it remains a powerful and (for some) necessary word. In academic use, it is etymologically contentious. Liberal-minded cultural critics have favoured a Greek-originating etymology: *ob skene*, meaning off stage or off-scene – that which, in Greek theatre, had to be hidden in the wings of the stage because it was unsuitable for display. Contemporary writing about obscene material is frequently framed as itself an anti-censorship gesture, bringing the previously-hidden into the light. In the UK there is even a funding-council-backed research project called 'The On-Scenity Network' (see http://www.onscenity.org/). However there is some disagreement about the etymology of 'obscene': most published dictionaries cite the word as entering English around 1593 from a Middle French word which itself derived from the Latin *obscēnus*, meaning offensive to modesty, as well as to befoul or bring filth upon something. These meanings chime with contemporary uses – not least the UK's Obscene Publications Act which famously defines material as obscene if it has a 'tendency to deprave and corrupt', resting on a publicly-agreed sense of decency (if such a thing could consistently ever exist). Debate continues (especially in internet-based linguistic discussions) around whether the Greek term influenced the Latin, but though published sources (Chambers, Oxford English Dictionary) have for the moment concluded not, there is a sense that writers *want* the term to still be associated with public concealment in order that liberation and revelation might be championed. Libertarian writers need a censorship-bound concept of obscenity as St George needed the dragon.

However it may be that *Shortbus* short-circuits all of this. In the Greek sense of the term (as well as in terms of its avowed 'healthy' openness), there is nothing obscene about sex here. All is resolutely on-scene, and given its BBFC certification, theatrical release, general-viewer audiences and mainstream newspaper reviews, it seems to obviate obscenity discussions based on a checklist of acts. Whereas at times in the past the BBFC – cited here as a past arbiter of the obscene – had a clear problem with acts such as ejaculation into a woman's face (which caused the French art film *The Pornographer* to be cut in 2002), by 2006 it had no problem with *Shortbus*'s James self-fellating before ejaculating onto his own face (perhaps because the onanistic nature of the act implies no difficult consent questions). This is not to say that *Shortbus* has no spectatorial stumbling blocks or that it now exists in a brave new world of 'anything goes'. I will explore later how its story is partly energized by its negotiation of what it cannot show. However, it has proved something of a touchstone film for changing values in mainstream cinema.

From the moment of its release *Shortbus* proved to be the most likeable of real-sex films, with writers celebrating its human interest focus as enabling engagement with character as well as carnality. Peter Travers wrote in *Rolling Stone*, 'if there is such a thing as hard-core with a soft heart, this is it' (2006), whilst for Jim Ridley in *Village Voice*, 'there's something refreshingly frisky and celebratory about *Shortbus* that offsets its flaws. It's a triple-X midnight movie with a heart of squarest gold' (2006). Of course it is rom-coms or musicals which usually strive for 'heart', not films made with working titles like 'The Sex Film Project' (as director John Cameron Mitchell called it in development). Mitchell's avowed aim was to counter the nihilistic real sex of recent films by the likes of Catherine Breillat and Lars von Trier with something more upbeat, utopian even – sunny American sex to counter dark northern European angst. Tonally, *Shortbus* is certainly a more pleasurable view than, say À *ma sœur* (Breillat, 2001) or *Antichrist* (Von Trier, 2009) – not least because it is funny. Ridley continues in his review, 'given the recent cinema's track record of unfaked hate sex (*Baise-moi*), diseased sex (*Anatomy of Hell*), or just plain lousy sex (take your pick), *Shortbus*'s messianic sex-positive cheer seems more startling than its straight-up intercourse'. However, whilst it is certainly sex-positive (pro-sex, anti-puritanical), it still uses sex as a narrative dilemma which needs solution or resolution, and one question this essay raises is whether sex can be a utopian ideal as well as a problem? *Shortbus* is certainly more rife with contradiction than might initially seem to be the case. Since my concern here is how it tells its stories, and I will be concluding this discussion with an account of *Shortbus*'s particular take on utopia, I will be thinking about sex in this film as catalyst or building block in a cause-and-effect multiple narrative: a utopian romp which also uses sex to stage narrative- and character-problems requiring resolution. Which sounds rather like the disavowing pornography consumer who watches erotic thrillers for the noirish storylines or reads *Playboy* for the articles. How, then, can sex cinema also be narratively interesting and intricate without this seeming like a gateway ploy or intellectualizing justification of unabashed sexual content?

This is complicated by the fact that as a highly explicit film it has also strangely rendered its sex if not invisible then at least normalized for some viewers. Multiple journalists, academics, and internet bloggers note how quickly the overt sexual content here ceases to be the film's primary talking-point 'event', or, as Keith Phipps puts it more eloquently in his *Onion AV Club* review, 'It's remarkable how quickly the explicitness becomes unremarkable' (2006). Humour is key to the enjoyments of *Shortbus*; it may even override sexual titillation, and critics were not slow to engage with this. *Shortbus* is then praised as a sex film where the sex really is second to, or illuminating of, character, and as a feel-good film with a sex-positive attitude despite the fact that its characters experience sex as a problem. Indeed, *Shortbus* makes it easy to valorize complex narrative and quirky characters without dwelling too hard on the sexual action – even though there is copious sex, regularly spread throughout the film. For *Village Voice*'s Ridley again, the film treats explicit sex 'as a facet of shared existence rather than taboo raincoat material'. Whilst certainly this might be a form of disavowal, it is also a symptom of another phenomenon the film revealed: avowed displays of uber-liberal tolerance on the part of viewers replaying, post-AIDS, the earlier porno-chic phase of early 1970s culture (around the release of *Deep Throat*), with self-selecting viewers outdoing each other in bids to be oh-so-very mature about their confrontation with the explicit. A tacit agreement seems to run through these judgements that this is not porn even though it contains many pornographic acts – or perhaps, more slyly, Mitchell uses character engagement and complexity as a Trojan horse, through which the explicit is inserted into a feel-good story of everyday hyper-libidinous New Yorkers.

Shifting the terms towards storytelling, this essay reads *Shortbus* in the frame of 'smart cinema'. In terms of its indie identity, its hyper-narrativized structure, its foregrounding of character and overlapping storytelling modes, it is an exemplary smart film, though, whilst many such films deal with sexual material, most real-sex films of recent times have tended to be read in terms either of pornography or of art cinema. Smart cinema is a genre or cycle first proposed by Jeffrey Sconce in his 2002 article for the journal *Screen*, reworked and expanded in 2006. It is defined as, a mode of cinematic practice that emerged among a new generation of post-baby boomer film-makers during the 1990s. Relying heavily on irony, black humour, fatalism, relativism, and occasional nihilism, this cinema became a particularly active battleground in a larger moral debate over the place of cynicism, irony, post-modernism, secular humanism, and cultural relativism in contemporary popular culture. (Sconce, 2006: 429).

Sconce locates the smart cinematic aesthetic as 'marketed in explicit counter-distinction to mainstream Hollywood fare as "smarter", "artier", and more "independent"' (2006: 429):

> Not quite 'art' films in the sober Bergmanesque art house tradition, nor 'Hollywood' films in the sense of 1200-screen saturation bombing campaigns, nor 'independent' films according to the DIY outsider credo, 'smart' films nevertheless share an aura of 'intelligence' (or at least ironic distance) that distinguished them (and their audiences) from the perceived 'dross' (and 'rabble') of the mainstream multiplex. (Sconce, 2006: 430)

In many ways this is a perfect definition of *Shortbus*'s market and industry/counter-industry location: too funny to be a sober European philosophical tract on sexuality, far too explicit to be squarely mainstream Hollywood, and probably insufficiently sex-obsessed to work as mass-market porn (though porn is of course a broad church), it occupies its own quirky niche. Yet perhaps because of its humour, accessibility and likeability it is certainly the most mainstream-friendly explicit film ever to play on general release in multiplex cinemas – reviews universally applauded its crowd-pleasing good-heartedness and cute characters. Whilst explicit imagery had been increasingly permitted in non-art house, theatrically released films since at least the late 1990s, *Shortbus* crossed a rubicon in terms of sheer quantity of imagery, and the centrality of the sexual quest – even though this was not a key element emphasized in marketing material. John Cameron Mitchell also brought to the project pristine indie credentials: his first feature (*Hedwig and the Angry Inch*) won him the Best Director prize at Sundance, and *Shortbus* was itself a calling-card to move on to Oscar-nominated *Rabbit Hole* starring Nicole Kidman.

Yet the production of *Shortbus* was also influenced by a 'DIY outsider credo', partly because of the particular concerns of its subject matter. Despite some mainstream stars performing sex for real in some recent films (Kerry Fox and Mark Rylance in *Intimacy*; Kieran O'Brien in *9 Songs*), Mitchell knew that he was unlikely to cast something as extreme as he was aiming for from the usual sources, yet at the same time wanted credible actorly performances to be woven around the actual sex. His pre-production task was to train up a bespoke team of uninhibited would-be and more experienced actors using improvization techniques. Cast members discuss in the ancillary material released with the DVD how the process worked for them: over several years the group developed their characters through Mike Leigh-style workshop methods, in the process also developing trust and friendship which would see them through the shoot and publicity of release. All of which feeds into *Shortbus*'s exemplary smart text 'ensemble' focus: one of Sconce's keystone definitions of the form is that its narratives are frequently organized around a principle of synchronicity, borne out by an ensemble cast through an episodic and overlapping structure. Sconce cites Robert Altman as the godfather of the smart film on the grounds that ensemble productions with multiple protagonists like *Nashville* broke open linear narratives to create more complex, overlapping and interpenetrating stories, often imbued with a fatalistic aesthetic. Paul Thomas Anderson's *Magnolia* is also exemplary:

> The favoured narrative structure is no longer the passive observer of an absurd world who eventually experiences some form of epiphany, but rather a range of characters subjected to increasing despair and / or humiliation captured in a rotating series of interlocking scenes in which some endure while others are crushed. [...] The move to an episodic cast rather than a lone protagonist presents a shift in emphasis from 'coincidence' to 'synchronicity', that is, the narrative (and philosophical) investment in the 'accident' yields to a narrative (and philosophical) belief in a logic of the random. (Sconce, 2006: 435-6)

As an ensemble work with an episodic structure *Shortbus* has much in common with this smart formation, but into this episodic brief it injects positivity. Randomness remains; there are despairing characters; there are even characters who run through the film navigating a traditional storyline at the end of which they experience an epiphany (Sofia; perhaps James and Jamie too). And the whole is folded into a dark post-9/11 milieu. But what *Shortbus* gives to the smart film is not just explicit imagery, but an urban sexual utopianism. I will be returning to this in the final part of this essay. First I want to think about the ensemble narrative as a sex format, and – given smart cinema's predilection for either Los Angeles or suburbia – the focus of *Shortbus* as an exemplary New York story.

REAR WINDOWS AND ENSEMBLE STORIES

Our first view is of a graphic drawing of the Statue of Liberty, in extreme close-up. To the breathy swing vocals of Anita O'Day asking 'Is you is or is you aint my baby?' (clearly setting up a story in which much partner-changing will take place), the camera pans lasciviously over, into and around a drawn image of the curves and contours of Miss Liberty's face before taking in her whole body standing proud over New York. An animated camera-eye defines our view, presenting a vision of New York which is rather like an illustrated story-book version of itself. We then zoom across the harbour, weaving in and out of streets and tenements to peer in through promising windows, at which point the animation segues into a live-action vignette of the key characters spied inside the window frame: first the Brooklyn apartment of a depressed James in a bathtub, filming his penis as he urinates into the water. Flying across to downtown Manhattan we then enter an apartment overlooking Ground Zero, where dominatrix Severin whips Jesse. We then return to James, who is now filming himself completing a gymnastic act of self-fellation whilst neighbour Caleb also secretly captures him with his camera from an adjacent apartment window. Then it's on to ritzy Midtown Manhattan, where Sofia engages in energetic hetero-sex across all surfaces of her chic apartment with Rob. Finally, a series of climactic cross-cuts present an orgasmic montage: James ejaculates onto his own face; Jesse's semen splashes in a painterly fashion on what looks like an original Jackson Pollock above the bed; and Sofia's face shows apparent climactic pleasure. The roving, omniscient voyeuristic camera links disparate characters into a common (if differently sexually identified) quest from the outset.

This tour-de-force opening sequence inaugurates the explicit content and narrative multiplicity to come, yet it is not just an overture of body fluids and metrosexual characters. Perhaps more than anything it signals that this is a New York story – or rather a synchronous weaving of overlapping stories featuring swinging New Yorkers of various sexual hues set against Sconce's smart cinematic landscape of post-9/11 secular humanism and cultural relativism. Let us dwell a little more on these through-the-window views, and the narrative multiplicity they set up. Viewers familiar with Alfred Hitchcock's *Rear Window* will recognize such framed views through to private interiors which characterize that 1954 film and to which I think *Shortbus*'s overture pays homage. Mitchell's is a hip, adult New York Hitchcock might have recognized and would probably have relished. Though *Shortbus*'s post-9/11 metropolis in which sexual pleasure and neurosis vie for dominance clearly steps smartly beyond the Hays Code which Hitchcock energetically challenged, this opening sequence is also a 'preview of coming attractions' (as Grace

Kelly naughtily – cinematically – quips when she flashes her nightwear to James Stewart in Hitchcock's film).

In *Rear Window*, incapacitated war photographer Jeff (Stewart) is trapped in his Greenwich Village apartment in a wheelchair with his leg in plaster, distracted only by the vignettes of his neighbours' lives which unfold in miniature through apartment windows arrayed around his courtyard, which functions rather like a Panopticon. Murray Pomerance calls this 'a peculiarly American vista':

> As we look out in accompaniment with Jeff's curious gaze, we see the variegated urban population, each resident going through the day with an indomitable sense of purpose and placement, each with a distinctive, even flamboyant, personality, whether energetic, compulsive, depressive, or distracted. (Pomerance, 2013: 42)

Rear Window's boxed-in vignettes suggest a multiple form of storytelling which is entirely urban, New York-based, and gives *Shortbus* its cue. Through its flying-camera-eye (which re-emerges at key scene-shifts throughout the film), *Shortbus* animates this view of interlocking lives lived on parallel (and sometimes criss-crossing) tracks. Indeed, *Shortbus* has been criticized for characters set up as 'types' rather than fully rounded people, but this is a function of both the film's style and its episodic narrative. *Rear Window*'s Jeff is immobilized, so New York arrays itself before his fixed gaze; *Shortbus*'s multiple cast are seen to be distributed across (the hippest neighbourhoods of) the city's geography, and must gather at the Brooklyn location of the Shortbus club to consolidate their sexual stories. This might suggest that these two films offer entirely separate views of atomized, modern New York life, but what they have in common is a vision of commonly-lived synchronicity.

Let us look a little more closely at *Shortbus* through the frame of Hitchcock. *Rear Window* is an odd format Hollywood film on a number of counts: restricted to the view and limited location of its temporarily disabled protagonist, it uses Jeff's gaze to present the mini-stories of the window-framed protagonists – multiple stories which proceed in parallel with Jeff's tale. Academic analysis of Jeff's obsession with his neighbours is usually framed by theories of psychoanalytic spectacle as a metaphor for cinema itself, with the photographer-protagonist's viewpoint oscillating between film-maker and audience positions. Of course, one particular view (into murderer Thorwald's apartment) comes to dominate his (and the film's) focus. Nevertheless *Rear Window* passes down a legacy of multiple and simultaneous narrative which smart cinema picked up in the 1990s: these arrayed views of atomized urban lives are not just voyeuristic peep shows but mini-dramatizations. The spatial view – of windows / stories opening up to the left, right, above and below each other – is complicated by their development as biographical sketches unfolding over time. Narratively the film is imbued with a strong synchronicity: whilst Jeff is obsessing about whether Thorwald killed his wife, the simultaneous stories of Miss Lonelyhearts, the newlyweds, and Miss Torso unfold.

In the spirit of this essay's refocusing of discussion of mainstream sex cinema from spectacle to narrative, it is then surely *Rear Window*'s example of synchronous storytelling which Hitchcock lends to smart film, which might suggest Hitchcock as ancestor of the cycle alongside Altman. We have already noted that Sconce lays the smart film debt squarely in Altman's court. Even in films as recent as *Gosford Park* as well as *Nashville* and *Short Cuts* it is Altman who most singularly challenges the star / hero-protagonist focused dominance of classical storytelling with an ensemble cast. This term has come to mean a group of actors working in a context in which singular stardom is subordinated to collective effort. Famous faces are still evident, it's just there are more of them, and their presence shoulder-to-shoulder suggests that individual ego comes second to the opportunity to work with an interesting director alongside like-minded performers more focused on role than personal dominance. The phrases 'ensemble cast' or 'ensemble production' have then come to signal particular kinds of film, associated with independent rather than studio forms because of their challenge to star- and protagonist-dominance in production and narrative. Such a film might acquire the artistic prestige of a stage production, with players working together like the members of a theatrical company sharing the limelight. Or it might suggest a rather lower cultural form – the TV soap or series. In this sense the other obvious reference point for Mitchell's film is popular 1990s TV series *Friends*, *Shortbus* plays out like a kind of sexed-up version of the hit series, with its eponymous sex club as an explicit version of Central Perk, both gathering points for groups of metropolitan twentysomethings (which it playfully acknowledges when Severin tearfully reveals to Sofia her real name, kept secret because she is deeply ashamed of it: Jennifer Aniston).

Deriving from earlier French and Latin words, the English word *ensemble* was first used in 1844 to refer to a group of musicians playing or singing together, and by the twentieth century it was also being used in relation to costume (a clothing ensemble, with items put together more or less harmoniously). Both of these common meanings suggest different elements made to work together in a particular moment: spatial distinction (separate players) plus temporal simultaneity (playing together). However this is not how contemporary ensemble films work, because as popular narratives they still must unfold in sequential time. What effectively happens in an ensemble smart film is that the narrative baton is handed back and forth between characters, with each performer taking turns to play out their scenes. Critics persist in using the word 'synchronous' in conjunction with 'ensemble' when discussing this form of multi-narrative smart film, but in fact whilst a cross-cut, montage-heavy sequence of different characters' experiences may be imagined as occurring synchronously, of course it must still be laid out sequentially. Smart films such as *Magnolia* (1999) or *The Royal Tenenbaums* (2001) which deploy ensemble casts are organized around synchronous narrative structures, enabling each actor and story-thread to take its turn to speak. Moving across and between snippets of multiple lives creates juxtapositions and coincidences – sometimes ironic, or opaque, or mystical – and enables a particular style to develop. Hsuan Hsu describes this cross-cutting as 'rhyming visual threads and graphic matches [...] to connect disparate sequences' (2006: 135). Sometimes there is connection between stories – with narrative threads interweaving, or connections and echoes across space within the same moment (the mutual and curiously unexplained singing of Aimee Mann's 'Wise Up', in *Magnolia*, for instance – sung by the whole cast, separated and spread across Los Angeles, though strangely connected by the song). Montage is deployed to connect characters and storylines, but it also sometimes emphasizes their separation. Films like Paul Haggis's *Crash* (Hsu's focus) use such strategies to promote a humanistic contact, but in other films they equally suggest alienation.

The 'smart' editing of the opening of *Shortbus* suggests that the six characters' sexual experiences are all taking place at the same time as well as in the same city, and it is this veneer of simultaneity which joins them in a common sexual quest. At this stage, of course, they are no more together than the alienated LA subjects of *Magnolia* or *Short Cuts*. However whereas Altman's Los Angeles stories (and the ensemble smart films which Clare Perkins identifies as archetypically suburban) all use these techniques to reveal the isolation and loneliness of characters, *Shortbus* moves narratively towards a more connected, utopian (and New York-based) resolution: the gathering of all characters in one place for one purpose with a more-or-less common dream, partly envisioned through utopian group sex, partly fleshed out through a common smart trope – the shared song, a true formation of ensemble action in its etymologically purest form. Quite simply, this is a film which begins with a set of characters experiencing sex whilst separated across the city, and which ends with them in a state of shared togetherness, having sex with each other and singing together. No wonder Justin says that the club is 'like the 60s only with less hope'. I will return to this qualified utopianism at the conclusion of this essay.

VOYEURISM AND THE INVISIBLE

The sequential, scene-shifting handovers of *Shortbus* also often take place across doorway thresholds or through window frames. Caleb, first seen spying on James's self-fellation through at least two window frames, hovers on the windowsill outside Sofia's consultation room as her initial meeting with 'the Jamies' takes place. Once the camera has found him, it then chooses to look past to find and follow Severin walking the streets (the film's *flâneuse*). We then cross-cut between James editing his film and filming himself with Jamie, and Severin alone, taking random Polaroids of New Yorkers to add to her Polaroid artwork. Rita Alfonso reads the turn-taking as a function of the film's scopophilia: '*Shortbus* is structured through this handoff of the plot from one character to another in a chain of voyeurism' (2009: 129). Of course this pervasive interest in peeking and the technology of the look is also very Hitchcockian (though Mitchell does not frame sexualized looking as criminal). Looking through windows in *Shortbus* bridges narrative and spectacle: it offers eroticized framings, and uses the apertures of mise en scène as neat narrative transitions. The opening sequence wittily introduces characters in their class contexts and neighbourhoods (whilst also establishing a strong aesthetic of voyeurism), and suggesting a 'through the looking glass' world of possibilities borne out in *Shortbus*'s wider utopianism. Look through enough New York rear windows, it suggests, and all of life will be there – a message which clearly chimes with how the city has long fantasized about itself (gateway to the land of freedom; celebrating human multiplicity etc.) – though as I will suggest later, these are particularly Caucasian and attractive young New Yorkers. Of course this is a sexually open vision of 'all of human life': Mitchell's version of Hitchcock's 'Miss Torso' (the dancer / model who, in *Rear Window*, never goes barer than her underwear, is courted for sex but chooses love) is exploded through these explicit opening scenarios, with *Shortbus*'s characters being introduced entirely through their unabashed body-work.

The cinematically self-reflexive nods to spectacle through this erotic voyeurism are plain: people filming people filming themselves; voyeurs viewing their neighbours and responding as if they are watching a TV soap; splashed spunk melding into an expensive painting's splashed paint (surely posing a self-mocking question mark over any self-aggrandizing artistic claims Mitchell's sex film project might be tempted to make). But in all this playful visibility there is something not-seen. A pornographic conundrum so eloquently discussed by Linda Williams in the pathbreaking *Hardcore* (1999) is set up here as *Shortbus*'s primary narrative catalyst and jumping-off point. Of course, with the spunky evidence of James's efforts *Shortbus* situates itself squarely in the terrain of the real-sex mainstream film, a phenomenon which had been gaining momentum since the mid-1990s. James's / Dawson's visible semen tells us: 1) he has climaxed, in the story and for real, and 2) this is the kind of film which will show him climaxing. For Peter Stickles (Caleb), the real sex aspect of the project became acutely real when the cast had to have STD tests prior to the improv workshopping; this was the point at which he reports thinking to himself, 'Oh well this is official then. You're going to be having sex with these people, and there's a chance that you will be having the kind of sex where you could be transmitting diseases to each other.' The result is literally on-scene, with fluid evidence of experiential ecstasy, bridging the gap between real event and performance. However, Jesse's orgasmic splash onto the Jackson Pollock isn't quite so clear-cut. Actor Adam Hardman may of course be a seasoned on-cue, accurately sharpshooting ejaculator, and may be more than capable of projecting across the metre or so from bed to wall, on target when the cameras roll. More likely, given the miraculous virtuosity of the act, the splashed sperm is a simulated effect, signalled by a cut to a close-up of the Pollock (though we do see it first spraying across his body), and none the worse for that. In 'real' porn, a male actor capable of long-distance and on-target ejaculation would be showcased for his talent; in *Shortbus* the feat isn't as central as the art-defiling visual gag. Of course, as Davis points out in his reflection on *Shortbus*'s queerness, there's no such thing as an unsimulated sex act anyway (2008: 623). Already, then, we are in the realms of the simulated passing itself off as the real in an ostensibly 'real sex' film.

No such visual evidence presents itself in testament to Sofia's pleasure, except cinema's traditional standby of an ecstatic face accompanied by performed sounds of climaxing. Of course we soon learn that in that opening montage Sofia did not have an orgasm, and – surprisingly – there are several moments in the film where faking orgasm is discussed more positively than one would expect from a sex-positive film. With her therapist's voice fully honed, Sofia reports to her husband (who claims he has had to turn to porn because his wife's failure to climax makes him feel inadequate) that her client Cheryl's faking constitutes 'a completely legitimate strategy to buy time. ... An orgasm isn't something [Cheryl's husband] Brad can give her. She has to claim it for herself.'

So this and the Pollock-esque sperm demonstrate that *Shortbus* has opted for certain kinds of explicitness over others. Certainly it is hardcore on some levels. Unlike much vagina-focused pornography, the primary spectacles of *Shortbus* are largely male and singularly penile. There is heterosexual penetration in the film, but its visual evidence is fleeting. Male excitement is rather more open and visible: due to the sexual peccadilloes of the primary male characters (James and Jamie, who do not initially have penetrative sex), sexual activity is generally oral and masturbatory, and therefore rather more visible than if it were penetrative. Second wave feminist viewers might cheer since here sexual spectacle is not unilaterally female – I have intimated that views of women are generally less explicit than in mainstream pornography: no full on beaver shots, nor do we see undulating vaginal muscles, or squirting (the muchvaunted 'authentic' visual proofs of female orgasm). Female pleasure is then signalled through old school facial contortion. The camera does not delve into female genitalia, even though the story of Sofia's quest for the big O unfolds as the spine of the film. *Shortbus* cannot seem to decide whether this is sexually conservative or radical, so continues to entertain both.

Indeed, for such an omni-liberated film, the narrative of *Shortbus* is supremely goal-orientated. As Williams has pointed out, its primary quest is not that far removed from the principle storylines of 1970s porno-chic: woman seeks orgasm, and goes on a sexual odyssey to reach her goal. Sofia's cause-and-effect journey is also perhaps at odds with the smart film aesthetic which is typically more episodic and synchronous. Each thread of Sofia's journey braids together, leading causally from sexual problem to sexual solution. For Matthew Tinkcom the very notion that sex is the landscape of difficulty and resolution cuts against its libertarian message: the characters' 'common problem – and it is worth underscoring that the film treats sexuality as a problem – is that they each fail to have their sexual desire coincide with the discourses that might reveal and provoke a kind of truth about themselves' (2011: 696). So how can a sex-problem film also have been received as an unalloyed sex-positive film? *Shortbus* is nothing if not contradictory.

GETTING ON THE BUS: GOAL-ORIENTATION AND THE ORGASMIC HAPPY ENDING

If the window views give this film its entries and exits to different stories as well as its voyeuristic inflection, another more classical narrative metaphor drives it along, reminding us that all roads lead to Shortbus as ultimate destination, promising emotional resolution and sexual fulfilment.

One of the mantras of the post-1960s sexual revolution was opposition to hetero-normative goal-orientated sex. This usually meant missionary-position penetration with (male) orgasm as the ultimate outcome. In a discussion of sexual aberrations Freud characterized normality as 'The union of the genitals in the characteristic act of copulation' (Freud); with orgasm functioning as end point and purpose. The eloquent resistance to such restrictive practice by political and lifestyle libertarians from the 1960s onwards on the grounds of oppressive sexual prescription is a well-documented part of Western cultural history, feeding into the queer and women's movements on the one hand and the exponential rise of the pornography industry on the other. By *Shortbus*'s year of release, it might have seemed as if anything goes on mainstream screens – as if a sublime popularizing union of women's liberation, gay rights and pornography had been finally achieved. However, looking at this film narratively rather than primarily for its representational liberties presents a rather more complicated picture.

Let us backtrack a moment to think about the film's title itself. For the benefit of viewers not schooled in the US system, American Justin explains to Canadian Sofia that the sex club in which the multiple narratives and multiple characters intertwine is named after the shorter yellow buses which take 'gifted and challenged' special case children to their special schools. The club is also 'a salon for the gifted and challenged'. Its participants are then defined as sexually non-mainstream: gay and straight, they are hyper-libidinous, exhibitionistic, and questing.

However the image of the shortbus also consolidates a 'driving' metaphor which runs throughout the film. From the opening credits' highly mobile voyeuristic camera-eye zooming across New York from borough to borough onwards, this is a film in motion in a way which

Rear Window can never be. Of course, most narrative films move from location to location and follow more than one character through their distinct stories, and *Shortbus* is no exception (and may not be exceptional in this respect). Road movies place their protagonists in vehicles (cars, usually) and set them rolling over a (usually rural) landscape. Mobile though it is, *Shortbus* only places its protagonists in actual mechanical forms of transport through dreams and imagery: New York is a walker's city. Nevertheless, despite the absence of actual short buses (and, as Davis points out, actual disabled people), *Shortbus* might be a sexual road movie, in the sense that its characters' journeys are articulated as a process of getting on the bus. Orgasm is not just Sofia's own personal objective as primary protagonist; it is the narrative's. The club Shortbus is of course figured as a vehicle which takes Sofia to wherever she needs to go, and once she has got there the film ends. The film's secondary story is almost as conventional: James (who used to be a hooker) finds it impossible to have penetrative sex with long-term lover Jamie because it replicates the power-relationship he had with his johns. After a series of cathartic events (heart-to-heart with Severin; rescue from a suicide attempt; penetrative sex with Caleb the voyeuristic neighbour), James overcomes his difficulties to fully connect with Jamie. However Sofia's quest is rather different. Whereas James's is psycho-sexually rooted in his backstory, Sofia's is rooted in the driver of the narrative itself. She cannot come because she is too focused on coming (clearly she wasn't listening to Frankie Goes to Hollywood in the 1980s – relax is precisely what she can't do). How interesting that *Shortbus*'s narrative goal is to resolve something which repeatedly gets thwarted because its protagonist is too goal-focused.

Two particularly resonant moments develop the film's driving metaphor, and also offer an alternative. Both involve Sofia getting advice from two of the friends she meets on her sexual pilgrim's progress – Severin and Justin. Justin's advice provides Sofia with the most useful key to undoing her sexual lock, and is also a crucial utopian statement for the film, so I will look at this later. Severin's suggestion is more direct. The two women become friends, and decide to visit a sensory deprivation tank on a regular basis for mutual talking cures, with each exchanging their own professional expertise: Sofia will help Severin to connect with people, and Severin will help Sofia to achieve the big O. The two-shot inside the tank is intimate, but the tone is funny rather than aroused. Severin insists that before Sofia tries to come with another partner she must first be able to make it happen for herself, so she talks her through a masturbatory fantasy. 'Feel the thought first,' Severin urges; 'Then get on the bus.' However, true to her key character flaw, Sofia fulfils the brief far too seriously, frantically masturbating with a too-urgent desperation. Severin responds as any responsible driving instructor would: 'Alright, you gotta pull the bus over. You're not riding safely. Park.'

Sofia's character is then partly there to demonstrate that sexual satisfaction retreats the harder it is pursued – and that sometimes in life one can try too hard. The film also more widely suggests that there are narratives which take you somewhere and narratives which don't, which is partly refracted through distinctions of mainstream and art-house storytelling. Justin describes 'a three hour Gertrude Stein documentary' which is playing in the club's performance room as 'a real weenie shrinker'; the pornography which Rob consumes succeeds because it is doing the opposite of this. However Rob feels inadequate because he can't himself lead Sofia down a similar road, and the fantasy film which Severin urges Sofia to play out in her head doesn't succeed either. Perhaps if Sofia were somehow (impossibly) playing out *Shortbus* to herself, the result would be different, since the film offers several images for routes to satisfaction: single roads along which desire travels (perhaps augmented with sexual imagery) but sometimes does not arrive, and multiple stories trying out different thrills. As we will see below, Justin characterizes this as 'trying to find the right connection'. As we leave frustrated Sofia in the sensory deprivation tank it seems that her problem just now is that she sees the journey purely as a linear one, and is trying too hard to follow the map. Of course, cinematic linear narratives often function like roads along which protagonist and audience travel to a goal, but here sexuality will not be channelled down a singular route. Another notion of sexual arrival, and of narrative form, must be explored. For the moment, the best Sofia can do is put the brakes on and stop the bus.

SMART SEXUAL UTOPIAS AND PATRIOTIC PLEASURES

So Sofia must get off the bus in order to get off. But only when another advising friend gives her an alternative sexual vision can she see which direction, or rather directions, she needs to take. Justin and Sofia sit watching the activities of the orgy room, but Justin turns the focus onto Sofia's own quest: 'What's the hold up?' he asks. Ever-cerebral Sofia responds that she has a 'clog' in her neuro-pathways, somewhere between her brain and her clitoris. However, Justin's response suggests that from here on in sexual response (or the lack of it) should no longer be imagined as a teleological journey: sex figured like a linear narrative won't work. Though his customary demeanour is camp world-weariness, this is the point at which Justin delivers the film's key utopian sentiment, providing an alternative to uni-directional linearity:

> Don't think of it as a clog; think of it as some sort of like magical circuit board – a motherboard filled with desire that travels all over the world, that touches you, that touches me, that connects everybody – you just have to find the right connection. The right circuitry. Look at all these people out there – they're just trying to find the right connection. And I personally expect a few blown fuses before the night is over, and maybe one of them will be yours.

Shortbus is of course a utopian film in a number of ways. Manohla Dargis's *New York Times* review sets up the film's free love, consequence-less sexual philosophy, before making wider political claims on its behalf (which I will turn to in a moment):

> As utopian visions go, it doesn't get much better than *Shortbus*, a film in which all you need is love – and sex, lots and lots of mutually, sometimes collectively, pleasurable sex. John Cameron Mitchell wrote and directed, though orchestrated might be the better word for a carnivalesque romp in which men and women engage in sex in a multitude of creative combinations. (2006)

Richard Dyer has written about the musical as a utopian form because it gives audiences an image of 'what utopia would feel like rather than how it would be organized' (1992: 18). He focuses his analysis on *On the Town*, which turns New York itself into a utopia, and for the adventurous swingers of the Shortbus club, it also functions as a kind of erotic Emerald City to which the sexually 'gifted and challenged' flock. The orgy room (known as the 'Sex Not Bombs' room) is then a key utopian space for both the film and the city, and also the crux of its most acute contradictions. Its bodies are multiply interconnected, plugged into each other as they are plugged into this matrix of desire. Goal-orientation hasn't been lost (they all look very much like they want to get to the same orgasmic place as any old school sexual players), but in Justin's formulation this exists side-by-side with a pattern of desire which is also *not* articulated through a simple hydraulic cause-and-effect relationship.

Thus the film manages to keep alive and active two singular metaphors around which its sexual philosophy as well as its narrative principles are organized: the bus (driving teleologically towards a goal) and the network (Justin's motherboard, through which one can multiply connect in many directions, and one also acts as a connector). It drives along a story about goal-orientated sexuality, but it also celebrates other forms of sex and finally a kind of matrix-modelled sexuality comes to dominate. Whilst this might be interpreted as contradiction or hypocrisy, to my mind this is a function of its unwillingness to choose rather than a negative confusion. Though Sofia's driving story dominates, multiple characters in the form of the film's sexual ensemble challenge this singularity. It is both openly exploratory and also tunnel-vision driven. Linearity exists side by side with episodic synchronicity. This 'allowing' contradiction might be why *Shortbus* is finally utopian, not its vision of a more sexually open world (though it offers that too). These might seem like rather grandiose philosophical claims for a small-budget, small-scale sex film, but it delivers (as de Sade would put it) serious 'philosophy in the bedroom'. Bedroom philosophy usually concerns what sex reveals about human behaviour – political power-play, disavowal, the Oedipal. *Shortbus* refuses to choose on both a sexual and on a narrative level – we might say that it wants to have both its narrative and its sexual cake and eat it. It would prefer both / and rather than either / or.

Justin's analogy is also electric, and this resonates. Towards the end of the film we find Sofia trapped in her consulting room with her uptight, faking-it clients. She zones out as Cheryl drones on, mentally escaping through the window into a fantasy Central Park which morphs into somewhere altogether more magical – a beach, with a Narnia-like lamp post next to a bench, on which she lies to masturbate, and may or may not achieve the solo orgasm Severin has prescribed. Whether or not she climaxes, the act synchronizes (perhaps causes) a New York-wide blackout: the 'few blown fuses' are city-wide. Hsu has shown that the threads of recent ensemble smart films are often tied together by a major collective event, which at the same time unites the characters, however disparate their stories have been. The medfly epidemic and earthquake of *Short Cuts*, *Magnolia*'s plague of frogs, the Los Angelean snow and car crashes of *Crash*, all 'provide a vague sense that we are all in this together' (2006: 135). Large-scale, shared environmental experiences which conclude or bookend the ensemble film suggest or reinforce a sense of collectivism perhaps belied by a general tenor of nihilistic isolationism. Hsu seems to suggest that there is something utopian in the ensemble film itself, deploying 'external, geographical connections to demonstrate that dozens of connections exist *in spite of* felt loneliness' (2006: 138, Hsu's italics). It may then be that the ensemble film-making agenda is always incipiently utopian, both in its less hierarchical view of stars and protagonists, and in its drive to connect rather than separate. Of course *Shortbus*'s version of the plague of frogs and flies is this blackout, but music also functions as a collective event. Returning to the animated city of the opening sequence we now focus in on just one singular light – the candles illuminating a now-Edenic Shortbus. Women play in a string quartet; Justin sings a song called 'In the End' addressing the stages of life. The concluding aural spectacle is important to *Shortbus*'s status as both smart film and also a film which flirts with the musical form: Mitchell has said that he wanted 'to use sex the way that I used music in *Hedwig*', but this is not at the expense of music itself. Indeed, there is a musical element to many smart films, usually functioning just like this with a key communally experienced song overlaying a concluding montage or intimating at some kind of resolution. Crucially, the *Shortbus* song is true ensemble work, fully reinforcing the sense (if the group sex hadn't conveyed this already) that all are joined in a unified message. All sorts of reconciliations and resolutions happen in its wake: parted couples come together or reassemble in new pairings (Rob with Severin, James back with Jamie; Ceth and Caleb); Sofia finds herself embraced by the 'beautiful couple' who she had watched fucking in the Sex Not Bombs room earlier. A brass band arrives, and there is a whiff of the 1960s – the 'good' 1960s of Woodstock, of course, not the 'bad' 1960s of Altamont. Soon after, as if the collective had willed it, Sofia gets her wish: her face orgasms, and multi-coloured lights come back on in the animated NYC. One might read this in two mutually exclusive ways: Pandora-woman's sexuality causes metropolitan disaster, or Messiah-woman's sexuality saves New York. These are apocalyptic city-wide events with an individual, intimate origin.

Clearly this is a happy ending for Sofia, but *Shortbus* itself was also lauded by many writers as something of a happy moment in American cinema, especially American critics who seemed to be once again proud to be American if such films could be imagined in their blockbuster nation. This is particularly curious given its post-apocalyptic self-consciousness. The line delivered by Justin as he surveys the orgy room which became emblematic of the film – 'It's just like the 60s only with less hope' – was understood to mean something like, 'in a post-9/11 New York, we might orgy as if the Age of Aquarius is dawning, but in fact we are fucking to the end of the world' (or, as Prince once sang, partying like its 1999:

enjoy yourself, its later than you think – what's around the corner will probably be worse). Less hope implies no better future, yet the film is anything but hopeless. MacDowell sees quirky films as 'A particular type of smart film' (2010: 11); perhaps quirky cinema is smart cinema with more positivity and less irony, and the highly quirky *Shortbus* bears this out. Nevertheless it also seems to be asking whether it is possible to be happy, or at least carefree, after 9/11.

This is a curiously smart phenomenon. According to Sconce, the typical smart film protagonist, director, screenwriter and audience member is a Generation X-er who missed the 1960s and whose stories are characterized more by listlessness and passivity than action or hope. The textual elements of the smart film often include irony, narrative and character-focused incongruity, nihilism and personal alienation, scepticism towards contemporary consumer culture. There is a strong sense of 'dampened affect' – formal strategies designed 'to signify dispassion, disengagement, and disinterest' (2006: 434). Certainly, *Shortbus*'s motley crew are Gen-X-ers in terms of cultural chronology. However the film takes pains to present both ennui and positivity alike as a response to 9/11 as the defining event of their generation. Indeed, the film could be set in a period much earlier (the 1960s or 1970s) if it weren't for its multiple references to 9/11. But the terrorist attack and its televisualization isn't by any means represented as wholly negative: Sofia asks Severin why impoverished young people come to live in an expensive city like New York and is told, '9/11 – it's the only thing real that's ever happened to them'. Indeed, the first time we ever see Severin, flagellating her john in the apartment overlooking the Twin Towers crater, she is asked, 'Are you a top or a bottom ... I mean in real life,' to which she responds: 'This *is* real life.' Jesse pushes her further though, with post-9/11 events forming the primary criteria for dominance in the bedroom: 'Let me put it this way, do you think we should get out of Iraq? ... You're taking a picture of yourself at Ground Zero. Do you smile?' Severin responds to this political philosophy in the bedroom by thrashing him even harder.

These post-9/11 references dominated popular critical discourse around the release and reception of *Shortbus*, but the conclusions weren't that the film danced on the grave of hope, but rather that it emerged as all the stronger in its utopianism for acknowledging and folding dark threat into sexual action. Indeed, it is striking how patriotic the film has made its more liberal critics. Dargis's *New York Times* review further argues that *Shortbus*'s feelgood factor is a symptom of utopian thinking in wider American culture:

> An ode to the joy and sweet release of sex, the film manages to be a sincere, modest political venture that finds humour where you might least expect it ... Part cabaret, part commune, the club functions as an adults-only playground, as well as a testing ground for Utopia; in other words, it's America without the plastic, the fear and the hate. (2006)

Mitchell has said that he wanted *Shortbus* to be 'a small act of resistance against Bush and the America we live in because it's trying to remind people of the good things about America and New York'. Similarly Linda Williams calls this a 'uniquely American film of hard-core art' which leaves viewers 'with a feel-good afterglow' (1999: 284). Perhaps the most striking instance of sexual patriotism inspiring critical patriotism comes with Jim Ridley's celebration of one of the film's funniest as well as most sexually explicit sequences in his *Village Voice* review:

> In what should be the movie's most outrageous scene, Jamie, James and their boy toy Ceth ... spontaneously erupt into 'The Star-Spangled Banner' during a convoluted three-way, using each other as human bullhorns. It sounds like a sneering provocation. But in performance, it comes off unironically jubilant, even patriotic – is this a great country or what? (2006)

Though Mitchell has admitted that 'with the national anthem we're taking the piss a little bit there' he also wants it to be read with positive confidence: 'at the same time we truly are talking about the optimism of the US, the ingenuity [...] there's resonances of the pursuit of happiness' (Kaminsky, 2007). Clearly for most critics Mitchell has succeeded in his quest to inject fresh sex-positivity into explicit mainstream films with a particularly American flavour. *Shortbus* is also acutely anti-nostalgic. I suggested that were it not for the references to 9/11 this could indeed be, to paraphrase Justin, a 1960s sexual spectacle, but in many ways it could only have been made in the first decade of the twenty-first century. Not just because it is allowed to be explicit *and* mainstream. Not just because a woman can go on a sexual quest which is not driven by male sexual solutions (as with hard-core). Not just because its dominant stories and spectacles are queer and straight, and – to some extent – omnivorously accepting of different body shapes and shades, and of age as well as youth. Not just because it reincarnates sexual and social freedom in the wake of the AIDS epidemic and 9/11. But because of all of these things. Justin's sexual motherboard might offer a positive image of a connected, globalized world. Of course, much of this sexual freedom is only available to the privileged strata of arty, articulate New Yorkers who are the focus of *Shortbus*. Nevertheless, the freedoms the film celebrates were hard won, and for the most part only recently achieved, and provoke a curious patriotism in even the most liberal and leftwing of writers. Or, in Ridley's words, 'As long as one man remains free to sing the national anthem into another man's asshole, the terrorists haven't won'.

Chapter 6

BECOMING ANIMAL IN *LUST, CAUTION*

SEAN REDMOND

The first shot of Ang Lee's *Lust, Caution* is a close-up of an Alsatian guard dog staring back into the lens, its eyes looking left, and then right. The camera then tilts upwards to reveal its conspirator-handler, who mirrors the eye movements of the dog. In quick succession, a series of cuts reveal various soldiers or conspirator-guards surveying the streets they are stationed at, using their own trained eyes or a pair of binoculars to see into things, to find people out. A culture of surveillance and suspicion is being established in these opening shots. A caption reveals that we are in 'Japanese-occupied Shanghai, 1942', and the grey, bleak colours, tones and textures of the mise en scène confirm the harsh realities of life under occupation. We then cut inside, to follow a maid delivering bowls of noodle soup to a group of collaboration housewives who are playing mah-jong and gossiping about their husbands and life in general. Light, colour, reflections, pretty fabric, opulent curtains, and decorative jewellery enter the scene through these interior shots, marking a sharp contrast to the outside world previously captured. The cutting and movement has been both comprised of stillness or slowness, in and between shots, and rapid succession, so that even the editing pattern seems compromised. The women exchange a series of glances that suggest suspicion exists amongst them; that they are performing roles to and for each other, further filling the film with paranoia and enigmatic allusions, while introducing character intrigue. The film's attention to historical accuracy, and its attention to aesthetic detail, is immediately recognizable in this opening scene, as uniforms, clothes, hair, cars, interiors, objects and possessions, buildings and streets are finely captured.

All the main sensory and sexual themes, as I would like to explore them in this chapter, are present in this opening scene. The violent correlation between dog and handler suggests a becoming animal (Deleuze and Guattari, 1980) that has both liberating and repressive consequences and implications in the film. For example, the sensorial and sexual relationship that emerges between Mr Yee (Tony Leung) and Wong Chia Chi / Mak Tai Tai (Tang Wei) is animalistic, violent and cruel, and yet it also involves a liberation of the senses, and leads to a love that requires the ultimate sacrifice, beyond the repression of everyday political life.

The pervading sense of surveillance and paranoia that is captured in this sequence is replayed and recast in the rest of the film through oblique narrative devices, suspicious looking regimes, sinister aesthetic design, and paranoid performances. Looking in the film, however, is not simply about controlling the gaze and the subject / object before it, but one that involves hapticity, or the touching of things with one's eyes, and a sensorialization of looking that therefore also desires and invites, in response, a carnal arousal.

Looking, gazing, desiring and devouring is also authorial; one witnesses Ang Lee's own lustful authorship, his desiring eyes and the traces of his fingertips in the film, particularly in the sex scenes. As Lee himself recognizes, the film draws on his 'unconsciousness, to explore guilt, hidden pleasures, childishness, a sense of danger, fear, anger and romance' (2007). Finally, the attention to aesthetic detail, to the sensory value of things, spaces, and people, creates a cinematic space that is pathetic, melancholic, ultimately death-like, and which, nonetheless, simultaneously produces an experiential awakening that is from start to finish deeply erotic and highly charged.

Taking these themes together, the chapter will suggest that this is the lust and the caution of the film, its determining master dichotomy, charged by a magnetic polar opposition that runs through its cold and hot spaces, its frigid and wet bodies, leading to an accumulative experiential realization that we are all capable of animal becomings, if only we dare to (dare we) let go of our encultured selves.

The chapter will be divided into four interrelated sections that navigate the master dichotomy of the film as I see it. First, the chapter will explore surveillance aesthetics and the way looking and seeing is organized in the film, fuelling lust, fostering constraint and repression. Second, the chapter will explore sensory aesthetics and the way *Lust, Caution* creates an experiential world for the viewer that is embodied and invites an embodied response. Third, the chapter will analyse the film's sexual aesthetics and the intimate bio-power that the film directs viewer's attention and affection to. Bio-power is here being defined as involving those bodies that are implicated in controlling behaviour or the attempted subjugation of the other through the exercise of a type of raw sensual power (Foucault, 1977a). Finally, the chapter will assess the way the film enacts a becoming animal that takes over the spaces, places, things, and bodies of the film, opening up its reception to asemiotic feelings and transgressive happenings. In 'becoming animal', all control is lost and one's selfhood is stripped of representational and presentational signs so that one exists beyond language (Deleuze and Guattari, 1980: 272).

SURVEILLANCE AESTHETICS

Lust, Caution is an 'espionage thriller' film that through its visual apparatus, characterization, and narrative structure, creates a culture of surveillance, a pervading, aching sense of paranoia, that forces text and viewer into investigative behaviours, gazing and scanning regimes, and anxious subjectivities. These ultimately fuel and fire the way desire and affection are enacted. In the film, no one can be trusted, spaces are themselves cages or traps, and lovemaking, supposedly the most intimate of encounters, manifests as a form of inside / outside body surveillance, involving the discipline and punishment of the flesh, carried over from a body politic (a country, populace, under occupation) that maintains its power through a network of spies, surveyors, and watchdogs, charged with exposing, torturing, and killing those who resist the regime. Pain and joy, sex and death are closely mirrored in the film, the mirror itself acting as a surface to see through things, to reveal the hidden truth behind the artifice.

The film is marked by its own surveillance gaze either by employing a camera that observes the watchers watching, or which reveals hidden glances and paranoid exchanges, or which looks deeply into things, spaces, objects, faces, and bodies, as if it is scanning them for falsehoods and inner secrets. The camera is itself implicated in this looking regime, is intermittently given a spy-like subjectivity as it swish-pans, tracks, or slowly focuses in on things through what is either a ghostly, unattributed point of view, or through what are revealed to be the literal eyes of the spy, filling the film with a visual embodiment of investigation.

The camera seems to recognize that it promotes, 'the normalizing gaze, a surveillance that makes it possible to qualify, to classify and to punish. It establishes over individuals a visibility through which one differentiates and judges them' (Foucault, 1977a: 25). The surveillance gaze in the film, then, is intricately layered being, public and state sanctioned, domestic and private, acting like a cancerous membrane through society, and personal and intimate, operating through the behaviours, activities, and sexual mores of the main characters.

For example, at the beginning of *Lust, Caution*, Wong Chia Chi / Mak Tai Tai hurriedly beats a retreat from her mah-jong parlour game, wanting to get to a rendezvous that has been immediately signalled as secret. The game itself has been played against a series of suspicious glances, filmed with a camera that seems to be searching for a truth behind the performances that are clearly being acted out before it. As Wong Chia Chi / Mak Tai Tai dresses to leave the house, we see her reflected in two mirrors, the first shows her looking out of the window, in search of someone, or worried that she may be being watched. The second mirror has her looking at herself, perhaps in search of the mask she has on to protect her secret identity, self-surveying to confirm the performative mode she is presently operating under. We watch her scoop up all her possessions, not wanting to leave any trace of the self behind, and when offered a car by Tai Tai (Joan Chen) she at first refuses, only to quickly accept to avoid warranting suspicion.

On the drive over to her rendezvous, we see her give a number of troubling glances, while her chauffeur is caught surveying her through his mirror. He asks her questions that sound like that of an interrogator. Their faces are only partially revealed, as if both are hiding something from the camera, from each other. Paranoia and suspicion floods the sequence, as it will do the rest of the film.

When Wong Chia Chi / Mak Tai Tai arrives at her destination, Kiessling's café, she rapidly scans and surveys the street, the camera taking her point of view, as people she spies at seem to stare back, or deliberately avert her gaze, implicating the viewer in this disorientating surveillance exchange. Inside the café, further furtive and secretive glances are exchanged and the camera itself takes on the mantle of a spy as it pans left and right, seemingly surveying the room as if it too had a paranoid consciousness. Narrative information is slowly revealed, as it dawns on the viewer that a murder or assassination of some kind is being organized. Nonetheless, as Wong Chia Chi / Mak Tai Tai sits down to drink her cup of tea, having just countenanced an execution over a phone call, the camera carefully attends to the detail of her doleful face, trapped in light, to her red lips, and the red lipstick trace she leaves on the corner of her cup (red being a recurrent motif of lust and danger in the film). Gazing and scanning become habitual and intimate, an essential part of the sensual and erotic fabric of the film.

This is the other function of the surveillance regime in the film; it teachers characters to be acutely aware of the complete sense of things, and demands of the viewer that they attend to every detail, gesture, object, light source, colour, or shadowy space in the corner of the room, since everything is, or could be, of sensory significance. These surveillance aesthetics produce a regime of sensing the world that is synaesthetic, cross modular, and fully embodied. In *Lust, Caution*, that is, the viewer is invited to use all their senses simultaneously and in ways that overlap and transfer, so that they are encouraged to touch things with their eyes, to feel things with their fingers, and to taste things with their stomachs.

There is added significance for such sensory immersion and awareness since in the film the continuation of life, the blossoming of desire, and the absence of death, is dependent upon an intimate engagement with the world; one's senses become both deeply suspicious of everything, and supremely heightened; they lead one to exercise caution and yet they put one in touch with the erotic self. Seeing, smelling, hearing, and touching things are rendered acute, and the world is opened up as materialistic, multi-channelled, tactile, a site of olfaction, a place of palpable danger.

For example, when Wong Chia Chi / Mak Tai Tai secretly meets her co-conspirator and love interest, Kuang Yu Min (Leehom Wang), at the local cinema, she draws assumptions about Mr Yee's latest movements by drawing on her memory senses. She says:

> Maybe there's another woman. He took me to the alley 1237 the night before last. There was perfume in the air … jasmine. Not recent, though. There was dust on the pillows. I don't know.

Not only is smell, sight, and touch drawn upon, but insight and intuition, as Wong Chia Chi / Mak Tai Tai retraces her steps that night through all the (super) senses of her body. The scene itself is evocative; she meets Kuang Yu Min in a darkened cinema aisle, with the liquid-like flickers from the film being screened behind them hitting the sides of their faces. The film's melodramatic score and strained dialogue also floods the sequence, drawing or suturing them into that text's spiral of conspiracy. We are positioned deeply within a text that is within a text. Deep red light washes over them, a pathetic foreshadow of their demise, and they are both partially framed in darkness, while their bodies stand in close proximity, their faces, mouths nearly touching one another. The dialogue is delivered with smoky intensity, with husky intimacy, as Wong Chia Chi / Mak Tai Tai's sense recall draws upon the pain she has experienced through her relationship with Mr Yee. However, what is also being suggested is that she is trying to supress the unbearable desire that rises up in her for him; her confession of pain a double bluff, her delivery more a longing for the taboo than a plea for it to end. When Kuang Yu Min passionately says in response, 'I won't let you get hurt. I won't allow it', it is a classic lover's protective plea, but also a faux gesture, a conspiratorial lie, since as he knows, as he has in fact sanctioned, Wong Chia Chi / Mak Tai Tai has been constantly hurt, has been left to withstand alone the sexual assaults of Mr Yee. As Shaoyan Ding concludes:

> The narrative of Wang Jiazhi's experience is a process of cultural politics, exposing the patriarchal inscription of power on the female body. Codes of patriarchal oppression of women are ubiquitous in the film. (Ding, 2011: 97)

Of course, these sexual assaults have led to her loving Mr Yee, or of at least loving the overwhelming or all-consuming lust that it has produced. She enjoys, revels in the sexual pain it has fostered, and has found the violence of the erotic liberating and transformative. In fact, her own surveillance gaze has allowed her to see into the very skin of the man who violates her, revealing a sexual closeness or sameness between them, and that implicates her as willing, complicit partner.

Kuang Yu Min wants to stop Wong Chia Chi / Mak Tai Tai's sexual hurt, but this is not a simple act of protection, or a declaration of romantic love for her, but rather a ways and means to negate her pleasure principle, since it undermines his own patriarchy, his own repressed desires for her. In entering into a carnal pact with Mr Yee she is set free from the patriarchal surveillance regimes that define her relationship to Kuang Yu Min, and this he cannot bare.

Ultimately, the film reveals Kuang Yu Min to be a pathetic character: he cannot protect her; Wong Chia Chi / Mak Tai Tai's fate has already been chosen since she has keenly developed an erotic haptic sight out of the very surveillance apparatus that intended to repress and control her sense of things. She has turned the act of looking and seeing into erotic gestures and encounters, freeing her body absolutely.

One can describe Wong Chia Chi / Mak Tai Tai's lustful vision as a more intimate form of looking, where 'the eyes themselves function like organs of touch' (Marks, 2000: 162), and 'move over the surface of its object rather than plunge into illusionist depth, not to distinguish form so much as to discern texture' (ibid.). For Marks, film and video may be 'thought of as impressionable and conductive, like skin' (2000: xi–xii). In the context of *Lust, Caution*, Wong Chia Chi / Mak Tai Tai's employs her haptic touch on the body of things, in erotic contexts, while the film's own aesthetic framework functions like a skin, that is or can be aroused – a reading I would now like to explore in some depth.

SENSORY AESTHETICS

Terry Eagleton suggests that aesthetics are born as a discourse of the body (1990), and the senses, as Susan Buck-Morss argues (1993), maintain an uncivilized and uncivilizable trace, a core of resistance to cultural domestication. Sensory aesthetics, and sensuous knowledge, have the potential for the radicalization of the body, or a type of liminal becoming that frees one's flesh from its cultural docility and ideological entrapment. Sensory aesthetics can be understood to be a cluster of affects or block of sensations (Deleuze and Guattari, 1980) waiting to be born, free of language, in the (now) unregulated sensorium of the viewer. As Simon O'Sullivan argues:

> Affects are [...] the molecular beneath the molar. The molecular understood here as life's, and arts, intensive quality, as the stuff that goes on beneath, beyond, even parallel to signification. (O'Sullivan, 2001: 126)

One can read or rather experience *Lust, Caution* through its affecting sensory aesthetics, and through the way it activates the viewer's sensuous knowledge of things. The film's shifting visual palette, its sensational attention to detail, to all things material and organic, creates a lustful desire in the viewer, even as the film wrestles with its own constraining forces. The sensory aesthetics in *Lust, Caution*, are a combination and juxtaposition of restraint and expression, of dullness and vitality, of conforming and of letting (oneself) go. One can argue, in fact, that the film's entire narrative and thematic structure is all about the forces and intensities of sex and sexual desire, and nothing else.

One can divide the film's sensory aesthetics into two distinct palettes. First, there is the limited, metallic palette that captures the political essence of state control and state-sanctioned espionage, and counter-espionage. Much of the public world we see in the film is comprised of grey facades, colourless exteriors, supported by the slow and hesitant movement of people, an irregular editing pattern, and a concentration of shadows, frowns, and furtive glimpses. Alexandre Desplat's melancholic soundtrack is composed of wistful strings and pianos that morbidly freezes the temperature of the interactions in the sequence it scores. The music is haunting, casting a death shadow of those who emerge in public, from behind their curtains, or masks.

One can define this limited and lifeless palette as being composed of 'non-representational signs' (Dyer, 1992: 20) that fill the diegetic world with a brooding detachment and a composite structural violence that is deeply unsettling at the level of carnal appreciation. What the viewer sees, hears, feels in their bodies is not easily reducible to discernible impressions; it is not words, narrative action, concrete signifiers that propel meaning but an unsettling sensuous knowledge. This draining away of, or subtraction from, the image can occur in 'private' settings, also. For example, when Wong Chia Chi / Mak Tai Tai enters Mr Yee's private study, to find him manically burning papers, we are thrust into a noir-like mausoleum, a frigidity captured in the room's dark woods and near utter impersonalization. The few military photographs of Yee and his father suggests the brutality of the men, and the father's continuing influence on his son's own brutal self, while the flames from the fire are a destructive force, not light or heat, but the fiery tentacles of death itself reaching out to engulf Wong Chia Chi / Mak Tai Tai, the body of the image, and the body of the viewer.

Second, there is the more extensive palette of the Kiessling café, the domestic mah-jong scenes, and the sexual encounters between Wong Chia Chi / Mak Tai Tai and Mr Yee, where colour, heat, opulent possessions and appetizing impressions bleed into the quality of the image. In one sense, these provide the film with the same sort of 'utopian solution' that Dyer suggests (1992: 26) the classical Hollywood musical supplied for Depression-era America, but here 'abundance', 'energy', 'intensity', 'transparency' and 'community' are directly juxtaposed against the grim reality of occupied Shanghai within the operations of the single text. Such internal aesthetic juxtapositions obviously complicate matters, since they are too incongruous, too self-reflective; to be anything but sensorial ruptures in the way the film is experienced. Further, because the main characters in *Lust, Caution*, are openly performing utopia it is clearly rendered as an intensive sham, not able to mask the deceit and distrust that lies beneath the supposedly open and communal relationships. And yet, the incongruity in aesthetic quality also leads to confessional truths and to the revelation of previously internalized fears, as the sensorial registers become too much to bear.

In one crucial scene that takes place in a Japanese restaurant in Shanghai's Hongkou district, Wong Chia Chi / Mak Tai Tai performs the Chinese popular song, 'The Four Seasons', for Mr Yee. The restaurant is itself situated in the Japanese quarter of the town, which is bustling, full of neon lights, fashionable people out walking, and song and chatter, in stark contrast, then, to the economic scarcity, and blue and grey visuality, found outside of this protected zone. Mr Yee is initially a rigid and isolated figure in the private room he has booked for them. He sits like a stone carving, angular, upright, his hand gestures sharp, his facial expressions limited and stern. The starched suit and buttoned up shirt and tie a repressive and repressing force around his neck. By contrast, Wong Chia Chi / Mak Tai Tai is a fluid figure, her blue dress full of flowers and cherry blossom emblems, and her movements are light and open. When they kiss and embrace she softens him; their bodies composed along gender binaries, she the flame that can melt him. Nonetheless, when she begins to perform the song, a wet aesthetic takes over the scene, foreshadowed by the line Mr Yee delivers before 'The Four Seasons' number is performed: 'They sing like they are crying. Like dogs howling for their dead masters.'

Wong Chia Chi / Mak Tai Tai takes on the persona of a water figure as soon as she begins to sing: her hand gestures are like ripples in a stream, she moves across the restaurant floor like she is floating on water, and her voice and the song's melody and harmony are tearful expositions, while the lyrics refer to tears falling, wetting her blouse. Similarly, Mr Yee's will bends, his posture softens, tears flood his eyes, and his hands begin to tremble as he tries to take a drag on his cigarette. The watery sensory aesthetics here unite them under a cloud of shared repression, she under the yolk of Mr Yee, and patriarchal tradition, he under the tyranny of the Japanese. They both bring stormy weather to the seas that bind them. The wetness of the aesthetics of course extends to the sexual chemistry between them, to states of arousal, to the ignition of desire within them. These wet aesthetics are part of the sexual sensations of the film.

SEXUAL AESTHETICS

Sex scenes are often coded in particular ways and these change depending on the genre, and formal properties of the text and its narrative context. In much of commercial, mainstream cinema, colours are warm and inviting, bedrooms are romantic spaces of enchantment, low key lighting floods the scene, and bodies are slowly undressed, caressed. The camera takes up varying positions, including the close-up of fragmented parts of the body (breasts, thighs, buttocks, arms, necks, lips), and the long shot, sometimes reflected through glass surfaces, or which captures light or flame or fabric as symbols of the smouldering pathetic fallacy inherent in the mise en scène.

Extreme cinema, European art cinema, and cult and underground cinema create a different sexual aesthetic that might include brutal lights, dour or minimalist interiors, a hyper-realist modality, and an invasive camera that capture sexual organs and explicit sexual behaviour between the participants. Porn, of course, is a heady mixture of both mainstream and extreme cinema, creating slim fantasy narratives before penetrative sex, the wet climax and the orgasmic moan confirm the end to coitus (Williams, 1999).

In terms of the sex act, these three different modes of envisioning coitus are problematic in terms of capturing and confirming penetration. Cinema either pretends the act, as in much of mainstream cinema, confirms the cinematic realism of the act (in the European art tradition, for example), or clinically reproduces it through formula, as in the porn film. *Lust, Caution*, certainly slides between the first two forms, but also moves into the third, particularly because Lee has described the sex scenes as painful, laborious, and technical, even while he avows avoiding 'making porn' (Guillen, 2007).

A film's sexual aesthetics can be defined in a more developed way, however, one that takes into account the way non-sex-based acts, objects, encounters, and environments are eroticized, given lustful properties and propensities. Here, the entire mise en scène functions as if it is in a state of heightened arousal, always-on-the-cusp of sexual awakening, heated by the desire that is waiting to happen or be enacted. In *Lust, Caution*, for example, Wong Chia Chi / Mak Tai Tai is repeatedly found delicately removing her earrings. The removal of such jewellery is an intimate affair, involving the finite operation of the fingers, the drawing attention to the earlobe, and the stripping away of artifice, to leave only flesh and bone.

Lust, Caution's sexual aesthetics is composed of all three modes. Its mise en scène is in a constant state of sexual tension and arousal, particularly through the smouldering chemistry between Wong Chia Chi / Mak Tai Tai and Mr Yee, but also through its attention to evocative detail, to sensorial signifiers, such as when Wong Chia Chi / Mak Tai Tai slips off her sheer stocking and slowly smokes a cigarette after first encountering Mr Yee. *Lust, Caution*'s sex scenes are romantic and loving, perverse and animalistic, where one also sees penetrative sex, sexual organs, and one witnesses the twitches and moans of orgasm. The orgasm acts as confirmation of the pleasure of coitus, and the climaxing point of sensation, of the mingling of flesh. Orgasms end scenes since they are the limit point of expression, where viewers are also brought to the limit of their pleasure in the scene.

However, as with the sensory aesthetics in the film, these sexualized palettes are always also built on constraint and repression as much as they are on letting go. And it is here, in these pathetic sexual encounters, that Ang Lee's own anguished authorship comes into troubling view.

There are five main sex scenes in *Lust, Caution*. The first two, between Wong Chia Chi / Mak Tai Tai and Liang (Lawrence Ko) are constructed to be a dry, perfunctory affair; lessons in lovemaking that will allow Wong Chia Chi / Mak Tai Tai to perform the role of seductress in the film. These are scenes of emotional and sexual restraint and awkwardness, which stand in stark contrast to the feverish lovemaking that will consume Wong Chia Chi / Mak Tai Tai and Mr Yee. However, in the second of these lovemaking training scenes, it is Wong Chia Chi / Mak Tai Tai that takes control, taking the expected 'on top' position, in patriarchal and narrative terms, of the man. While it is clear she is getting little from this encounter, the sense that 'she is getting the hang of this', free from being pleasured by a man, opens her up to the possibility of sensorial liberation, to her becoming animal, later in the film.

It should be noted that the actors themselves bring with them something of the binary opposition between innocent newcomer (Tang Wei) and seasoned, older star-performer (Tony Leung), and of the training and transformation that goes into the making of a film. As Wong Chia Chi / Mak Tai Tai learns the subtleties of her performance so does Tang Wei under the guidance of Leung. In a very real sense, then, the relationship between the two characters is one mirrored in the representation of the two actors. And yet, both idealized figures, they mirror one another from the start of the film, as objects of desire, not only for each other, but for other characters, and for the viewers.

As I will now go on to analyse, the three impassioned sex scenes between Wong Chia Chi / Mak Tai Tai and Mr Yee take different thematic and sensorial turns and are meant to be read as progressive, each one leading to a new erotic understanding between them. All three sex scenes involve a degree of sadomasochism; the first involves a violent assault and a rape, and the last auto-asphyxiation. An invasive camera that sees into everything captures all three scenes. All three scenes are a wild mixture of unleashed desire and of continuing restraint or repression, of shadowy performance and verisimilitude, most notably played out through the quietness of the sexual tumults as they are in train, since language, it is implied, might give them away. All the scenes are a combination of pain and pleasure, of violation and intimacy. As Ang Lee commented:

> I think it's true. That pleasure you feel when someone is smiling and being tender to you: you don't know if they are pretending or not. Through their lovemaking you can see he wants the truth, though he doesn't know what that is any more. Sex becomes a kind of interrogation, escalated by violence, through which they both have an actual taste of love, although of course they have to deny it [...] We're just common people. It felt pretty harsh. But we used the pain. We enjoyed the pain. (Bunbury, 2011)

The first sex scene between Wong Chia Chi / Mak Tai Tai and Mr Yee emerges as a sensorial shock, because while the film has burned brightly as an erotic tableaux, the violence of the encounter is directly taken from the surveillance palette, from the repressive forces of the text. The scene is set up through sensorial, non-representational signs (rain, reflections, dust, the slow removal of stockings) but these quickly lurch into the blocks of uncontrollable force and aggression.

Wong Chia Chi / Mak Tai Tai is driven to an abandoned hotel / residence and is given a room number by the chauffeur. She enters the room, surveys it, but doesn't at first see Mr Yee, who is quietly sitting in the shadows. It is only on closing the window to the room that she sees him in the reflection cast. She is startled, a carnal foreshadow of the shock that will engulf her, the body of the screen, and the body of the viewer once the violence ensues. She chastises Mr Yee for scaring her, takes off her coat and walks slowly towards him, first taking a cigarette off him and then stamping on it. Mr Yee forcefully stands, then violently pulls her towards him, pulls her hair, saying 'are you playing hard to get'. Each of the actions that precede this line of dialogue are brought back sharply into view because of it. Wong Chia Chi / Mak Tai Tai is playing the role of mistress and seductress; even her startled shock can be now read as performative, lulling the viewer into what they might now think will become a cerebral game of chess.

Wong Chia Chi / Mak Tai Tai is attempting to get the upper hand, to exert her sexual power, as she did in her lovemaking training scene with Liang. She imagines herself as a gifted spy, a skilled femme fatale, lifted or copied from the American films she is so enamoured with. Wong Chia Chi / Mak Tai Tai presses Mr Yee back down in his chair and walks to the other side of the room where she begins to slowly undo the clips to her stockings, an act that itself refers back to her training days. The scene is echoing with the intensities of its own confused and duplicitous erotic callings. Mr Yee is momentarily captured in the rocking chair he was first found in, an incongruous, domestic object rendered strange by his brooding presence. He is upright, erect, his eyes flittering and his fidgety hands the main indicators of the sexual fury that we will soon realize lurk beneath the surface. The forces in the scene, then, are a mixture of pulling towards and away, repulsion and attraction, desire and loathing, and these calibrate the vibrations and intensities that will now consume the scene.

Mr Yee rises to his feet and quickly walks towards Wong Chia Chi / Mak Tai Tai, where he pulls her hair and slams her into the wall. He then rips the inner lining of the dress, the clips to her stockings, her pink silk underwear. This is done with proximate force, captured by a hand-held camera that places the viewer within the scene, an embodied camera that follows hands, rips, falls, and penetrations, with close proximity. Mr Yee then throws Wong Chia Chi / Mak Tai Tai on the bed, removes his belt and begins to whip her with it, before he binds her hand, lifts up her dress, pulls down his trousers and enters her from behind. This frenzy of his unleashed desire is nonetheless marked by two moments of softer intimacy. Against the wall, she lifts her head to meet his and their eyes meet, and on the bed their eyes meet again and they momentarily kiss. Eyes are culturally understood to be that which reveals all, while the kiss is a recurring motif in much of art, confirming an intimacy beyond say, functional sexual matters. The implication here is that Mr Yee cares for her and that she may care for him; that this transgressive and brutal lovemaking may be born of mutual attraction and shared desire.

The scene, nonetheless, also has the hallmark of the type of discipline and punishment that Mr Yee would utilize in his interrogations of spies and collaborators. He is skilled in his ability to overpower her, bind her, and subjugate her to his bio-political will. Similarly, Wong Chia Chi /

Mak Tai Tai's face is unreadable, or unrecognizable in this scene, like a doll's mask. She is either paralysed by the shock of the animal-man before her, or is lost in the performance, in her (their) disgust at what is taking place.

Conventionally speaking, the scene is morally disgusting; it involves violence, coercion, rape, and the (imagined) complete control of a living thing; it rubs against the grain of accepted ethical behaviour, of conventional identity positions and sexual relations. It is coded to be obscene and pornographic. Mr Yee seems disgusted with himself, nauseous at the actions as he undertakes them, and yet it ignites and electrifies him. Wong Chia Chi / Mak Tai Tai is disgusted by his actions, and perhaps at her own pleasure in the pain he metes out. Disgust, then, is a 'gatekeeper emotion', one that tries to stabilize the self in time and space, and yet it is also 'anti-democratic', unleashing forces that cannot be contained or constrained by normative ideology, by the repressive apparatus of conventional life (Miller, 2004). The whole sex scene is enacted without words, as if the acts and actions go beyond language, to animal sounds and becomings.

In the second sex scene, the sense that their lovemaking is subhuman, animalistic is cemented through the way intercourse is cross-cut to a nameless exterior street, where an armed guard and an Alsatian dog is being walked. The correlation can be read as:

> Conveying the message that sex is the most sensual enjoyment in a circumstance imbued with white terror, yet the parallel editing also helps the audience to read the intercourse as the most inhuman, bestial behavior at the time of national humiliation, both metaphorically and metonymically – and under the surveillance of an invisible force, just like the dog is being drawn by its master whose face is not shown. (Wang, 2010: 579)

I think the cross-cutting also draws attention to the fact that the wolf is already in the room, not just through the figure of Mr Yee, who is connected to the implicit violence of the dog handler and dog, as their uber-spymaster, but through the danger and desire and anatomical exploration that both the bodies undergo. It is like the Alsatian dog senses the animals that are engaged in bestial acts behind the closed curtains. Of course, the curtains are not quite closed, a tiny gap between them allows a 'slash of sunlight' to cross their bodies 'like a knife [...] representing them, the danger and also the violence' (Rodrigo Prieto, in interview with Lindsay Coleman).

The sexual aesthetics employed to capture their lovemaking reveals the body in all its fine detail. It is forensic in its revelations, taking the rawness of the two figures into its ocular and haptic operations. Just as in this scene their hands, fingers, mouths, and sexual organs paw / pour over each other, and penetrate one another, so does the camera. This is sense-based lovemaking, and cross-modular aesthetics combined, where sight, smell, touch, and taste eroticize the skin of the sexual beings, and the skin of the film.

The scene calls forth a primordial synaesthesia rather than a linguistic or representational interpretation; it draws one's senses to, the coarse hair of the protagonists, the thickness of pubic hair, wrinkles, melancholic expressions, smoothness, extended veins, taut muscle, supple arches, probing tongues, salty tears, and wetness. Both Wong Chia Chi / Mak Tai Tai and Mr Yee are driven by animal instincts, held out in a shadowy lair. The bodies are photographed as completely entwined, reduced ultimately to one organic truth, and the camera itself seems to be enmeshed in this carnal togetherness. Bodies also seem to extend beyond their normal physical parameters, to merge with fabric, sheet, light, colour and shadow, so that the sexual aesthetics, the primordial disintegration, permeates every flickering flame of the scene, exactly like an infectious membrane. In Deleuzian terms, this assemblage involves a certain kind of becoming-imperceptible.

Becoming-imperceptible is a process of elimination whereby one divests oneself of all coded identity and engages in the abstract lines of a non-organic life, the immanent, virtual lines of continuous variation that play through discursive regimes of signs and non-discursive machinic assemblages alike (Deleuze and Guattari, 1980: 73).

Hate as well as love fuels this sex scene; the hating of their political circumstances; the hating of the pain they endure; the hating of the intense sexual satisfaction they get from one another, and from their anti-democratic disgust. In the very next scene, during a drive to their next sexual encounter, Mr Yee aggressively places his hand up Wong Chia Chi / Mak Tai Tai's dress, presumably penetrating her with his fingers, while he tells her of the bloodshed and torture he has dealt out to traitors and spies earlier that day. His description of these open wounds, of bodies turned inside out, is monstrous, and yet it is seductively delivered, has the terrifying sound of an intense romantic calling. Mr Yee ends the refrain with a description of one of the dead men on top of Wong Chia Chi / Mak Tai Tai, where 'the bastard's blood spilt all over' his shoes, and he had to wipe it off. This mental image of a dead man's carcass penetrating the body of Wong Chia Chi / Mak Tai Tai, in a setting drenched in blood, as Mr Yee watches on, is the most violent of the film, although it is later matched by Wong Chia Chi / Mak Tai Tai's own confession that she feels steeped in his blood. Wong Chia Chi / Mak Tai Tai is heard moaning but the sounds are themselves caught between abject fear and arousal. Lust, carnography, and necrophilia merge and converge in a phantasmagorical horror show, where 'meat' is murder.

However, what is particularly potent in regards to the investment in sex and death here is the match cut that follows from this mental image of a dead man copulating. The car scene is immediately replaced by Mr Yee and Wong Chia Chi / Mak Tai Tai's naked bodies, writhing in ecstasy on a bed, his front to her back, his hands between her legs, her aroused sounds the acoustic mirror of those that fell out of her mouth previously. It is as if they are animated corpses, are aroused by the scent of death and biological negation, by their own willingness to take sex to its limits, or rather to beyond the threshold of the limit.

This is the third and final sex scene of the film, it heralds the dominance of the death instinct, and yet it also confirms their mutual lustful love for one another. They are gentler, delicate with one another in the final sex scene, and yet they push each other closer to death. Wong Chia Chi / Mak Tai Tai begins to again take up a dominant position in the encounter, at one point she takes the 'on top' position, and she smothers Mr Yee until he is forced to pull the pillow away. They have both fully succumbed to the animal within, a primordial force or intensity that knows no language, and that cannot be understood except as a moment of pure becoming.

BECOMING ANIMAL

Lust, Caution involves a series of border crossings in its complex play of performances, so that the opportunity to occupy a stable identity position is rendered null and void from the very beginning of the film. Wong Chia Chi / Mak Tai Tai moves through various roles; naive student, militant, reluctant spy, middle-class housewife, mistress, concubine, femme fatale, victim, lover, animal, and traitor. The roles she undertakes deepen and thicken, they transgress traditional gender roles, as each performative turn takes her away from a constrained and constraining core identity. Once she embraces the dark desires that lie within her, once she moves through the limit of semiotic experience to become a sexual animal:

Her unconscious becomes indifferent to her identity and language system, and the 'limit' or division between the Self and the Other disappears, so that she becomes a nomadic subject. (Ding, 2011: 99)

Mr Yee also moves through various roles; collaborator, spy, husband, torturer, rapist, sadomasochist, lover, executioner. Once he embraces the type of liberating sex that Wong Chia Chi / Mak Tai Tai offers him, he experiences a type of death that he finds intoxicating, liberating. Wong Chia Chi / Mak Tai Tai feminizes him, renders him abject, while he turns her into wolf.

This becoming animal sits at the very core of the aesthetic apparatus of the film; its sensory and sexual aesthetics foster a primordial violence and sexuality that vibrates in and across every scene. The sentient presence of Ang Lee is pivotal in this respect since the experiential traces of his authorship are found right across the film. He becomes animal too; he is also the wolf of the piece.

One can view the character of Kuang Yu min as Ang Lee's stand-in. He directs the student play at the beginning of the film, orchestrates the violence of the first murder scene, and directs and in part shapes Wong Chia Chi / Mak Tai Tai's performances. Kuang Yu min is all passion, strives for perfection, but is inadequate, not quite up to the task; the events he tries to control can only end in tragedy. Kuang Yu min, however, is also about constraint; he holds his desire for Wong Chia Chi / Mak Tai Tai at bay, and under orders agrees to sit tight. This oscillation or mixture of lust and caution is Ang Lee's too, bound by convention, under the politics of his own sexual mores, but wanting to explore the pain that desire fosters, he sees his authorship disintegrate in the very process of perverse film-making. Kuang Yu min's death at the end of the film is recognition that a text is always lacking, no more than a ragbag tissue of quotations (Barthes, 1977); his death is the death of the author. As Kuang Yu min, Ang Lee dies from a bullet to the back of the head, to fall away into a deep mountain pit. Given the perversity of the film, of Ang Lee's authorship, one sees this as his own sanctioned moral retribution of order, the killing of the wolf at the cinematic door.

The surveillance camera that operates across the film can be seen to be Lee's own conspiratorial eyes, the haptic eyes of the tactile director, the violent eyes of the taskmaster, ringing more from cast and crew. The sex scenes involved many hours of footage, and Ang Lee would explore these scenes in great detail, wrestling with shapes, angles, sightlines, fine lines, gradients, and texture. His own body is found in the interwoven structures of these scenes; it is his skin that is being turned into animal, which turns people into animals. Lee's desire for authenticity is pivotal here: the sex had to be seen as penetrative, as actually taking place, even if prosthetics and camera trickery and optical illusions were in play (but we can't be sure of this). Lee was after the full sensorial affects of desire, beyond the limit. His own commitment to capturing the essence, the taste, touch, and smell of violent sex, is itself perverse, turning the director into a becoming animal, free from the repression of his stand-in, of the film's master dichotomy.

What of the viewer, their senses activated, their haptic visuality honed in on the tactile detail of things? Faced with anti-democratic disgust, with constant border crossings, with bodies being undone and extended, and without the crampons of language to root their experiences of perverse acts and exchanges to, they come face to face with the wolf. Their bodies are drawn into the entwined bio-politics of the film, taking them to or through experiential limits, to leave them at death's door, if only they dare to (dare they) let go, let go, let go of their constrained and repressed lives.

Chapter 7

SEX, DRUGS AND ROCK AND ROLL

ANALYSING AESTHETICS, PERFORMANCE AND PLEASURE IN *9 SONGS*

BETH JOHNSON

Showcased at the Cannes Film Festival and released in 2004, Michael Winterbottom's British film *9 Songs* broke new ground with its fearless portrayal of explicit 'real' sex. Chronicling an intense love affair between Matt (Kieran O'Brien) and Lisa (Margo Stilley), the visuals intercut nine live rock gigs at Brixton Academy with nine extended scenes of real sex, including vaginal penetration, cunnilingus, fellatio, ejaculation and masturbation. Despite this placing of sex front and centre (taking up approximately one third of the screen time), *9 Songs* is very much a film about absence as well as presence. Indeed, according to Winterbottom the raison d'être for making the film was one concerned with omission. As he noted in an interview with Adrian Hennigan for the BBC:

> One of the starting points of *9 Songs* was: why do films NOT show sex? So many films are love stories, so why not show a love story through two people making love? Why is it that you avoid two people making love when you do a love story? It seems perverse. (Hennigan, 2005)

While the sex acts screened are ones most commonly associated with and depicted in hard-core pornography, the context of *9 Songs* was not judged to be pornographic in the sense that its primary intent was not, according to the British Board of Film Classification (BBFC), to arouse the viewer. As Derek Malcolm of the *Guardian* noted: '*9 Songs* looks like a porn movie, but it feels like a love story. The sex is used as a metaphor for the rest of the couple's relationship. And it is shot with Winterbottom's customary sensitivity' (Higgins, 2004). In addition, film critic Roger Ebert noted that: 'The nine sex scenes [...] lack the choreography of pornography, and act as a silent rebuke to the hard-core image of sex. Winterbottom seems deliberately reluctant to turn up the visual heat; he accepts shadows and obscurities' (2005). As well as the shadows of the film, Todd Konrad of *Independent Film Quarterly* noted the non-pornographic context of the film in the naturalism of the sexual performances and their sensual rather than solely sexual quality:

> The sex scenes in this film are among the closest ever made to real life in that, it is not merely about the actual act itself. It is about the intimacy of touch, the smells of skin and hair up close, the airiness of light, panted breath, in short, the scenes attempt as much as possible to engage all the senses in portraying the sex as a living, breathing, and deeply sensual activity. (Konrad)

Indeed, as a case-in-point, the BBFC awarded the film an '18' certificate, releasing it uncut and allowing it the accolade / kudos of being 'the most sexually explicit film in the history of British cinema'. The awarding of an '18' certificate to *9 Songs* was so unusual and significant that it remains on the BBFC website as an exemplar case-study and the DVD version of the film now includes an extra feature – an introduction to the film by Tom Dewe Mathews, the author of the 1994 book *Censored: The Story of Film Censorship in Britain*. The assessment of the context rather than content alone of Winterbottom's work led the BBFC to the conclusion that the film was 'not a sex work' (works, normally on video or DVD, whose primary purpose is sexual arousal or stimulation) but rather was a piece that used sex as a means of 'exploring a narrative about a relationship' (BBFC).

Framed primarily as Matt's recollection of a year-long love affair, his dominant perspective is signalled from the outset via his voiceover: 'When I remember Lisa, I don't think about her clothes, or her work, where she was from, or even what she said. I think about her smell, her taste, her skin touching mine.' Matt's statement can also be understood aesthetically as a declaration of intent – intent to convey *through* the sex scenes the real of what Melanie Williams (2006: 61) nominates as 'what we really remember about a past love affair [...] sex and music'. Matt's memories of Lisa are, for him, affective however, for the audience they are cartographized through sex and rock music (the latter being synonymous with the former) – the acts that the couple engaged in and the gigs that they attended. The fact that both sex and music are capable of stimulating emotional responses that lie beyond language is key to their status as dominant modes of expression. The stylized manner in which both are presented in the film is also of note here in that both are captured via hand-held digital video and in a sense, this creates a strange aesthetic – a sense of acuteness, a high, an emotional experience and an immediacy that is haunted – that is both of the present and the past and that we, the audience, are distanced from. The result is grainy and the contrast acute but captivating. This focus on fucking and gigging is then carefully aestheticized through a keen consideration not only of theme but also of form, intended to convey not the affective arousal of the sex and sonic experiences but rather, to make visible – to amplify – the importance of these experiences in the rhythm of a real relationship. Indeed, form has clearly been carefully considered by Winterbottom and the sex and musical set pieces are framed in interesting and frequently playful ways.

The first sex seen in *9 Songs* occurs approximately 20 seconds into the film. Framed from above and in the half light, Lisa is seen in a medium close-up shot, make-up free, her head on a pillow, her mouth open, chin tilted back, moaning in time with the sexual thrusts of a male, on top, who enters only the peripheries of the frame. Heavy breathing can be heard (the actors are closely miked) and shadows permeate the frame before a longer and lower moan by Lisa suggests a possible climax. The screen fades to black, silence follows and the white bold title '9 SONGS' appears on screen in a cut-out, ransom style typography. This conscious invocation of newspaper cutting stylization perhaps hints at and signals Winterbottom's knowingness regarding the press outrage that was to be directed at the text, and in particular, at its female lead Stilley on its release.[1] Moreover, the typography also perhaps speaks to a dialogue of musical and cultural resistance, most obviously evoked by the Sex Pistols on their 1977 punk album cover *Never Mind the Bollocks: Here's the Sex Pistols*. Over the '9 SONGS' typography, a rock soundtrack starts up, steadily increasing in volume before the band – the Black Rebel Motorcycle Club – are introduced – firstly by an external shot of the Brixton Academy in London with the band's name in lights above the entrance and then by a shot of singer and guitarist, Robert Levon Been launching into a performance proper of 'Whatever Happened to My Rock and Roll'.

While it is impossible to know the exact ways in which being filmed may have changed the band's performance, the fact that they played live for both a musical audience and a cinematic audience goes some way to suggesting a doubling up or amplification of their rock performance. The performance of rock as erotic is itself important. As Roland Barthes points out in *The Grain of the Voice* (1977: 188) 'The "grain" of the body is in the voice as it sings, the hand as it writes, the limb as it performs [...] I am determined to listen to my relation with the body of the man or woman singing or playing and that relation is erotic.' In essence, Barthes' idea is that, in untrained voices (like a rock star's in comparison to an opera singer's), the body leaks through; the more trained the voice, the less you get a sense of the cavities, membranes, mucus and so on, because the voice is purified (amplification, of course, amplifies all the imperfections of an untrained voice, and obviously this is something people find pleasurable, as when a voice 'breaks' on a high note in a track).[2] In this way, the untrained voice of Been leaks an eroticism through its grungy grain. The dirty sound as a result of amplification and variations in volume, pitch and pace key out the fact that the Black Rebel Motorcycle Club are playing 'live'. Due to this 'liveness', they in no way threaten the previously established authenticity of the (sex) scene but rather, add to it by way of a vérité or documentary feel.

Shot from the point of view of a member of the crowd stood about 30 feet back, the backdrop of the stage is a digital screen dominated by blue and black moving image graphics that, to borrow a phrase from Sheila Whitely, appear to 'sequence and respond to the underlying rhythm which appears to lead both the ear and the eye' (1997: 260). Smoke obscures the stage, the excessive lighting creates blind spots, and figures in front are seen in silhouette and occasionally obscure the view. A close-up shot then shows Been beginning to sing (the sound quality is grainy) before the camera slowly pans down his body to focus on his guitar and his hands aggressively and repetitively strumming (a synonym for masturbation). As the song begins proper, the point of view returns to the audience, this time from in front, revealing a sea of moving bodies and outreached hands tinted red by the stage lights before a whip pan returns us back to the frontman on stage. The clear ecstasy of the crowd is reflected in the kinetic energy of the scene.

The euphoric fervour experienced by the crowd links back to Lisa's previous experience of intense pleasure. While the prior and present sequences are linked, they also reveal a point of difference (one which arguably permeates much of the film) in that the lineage and scene / seen of rock is associated with what Sara Cohen notes to be 'a male history, [...] canon and legacy full of male bravado, male comradeship and collectivity. The masculinity of the scene is influenced by a more general rock ideology. Within that ideology [...] rock is commonly associated with "the street" and opposed to the bedroom' (1997: 30). In opposition, in the bedroom, female Lisa is the focus of the scene / seen but the problematics of this apparent binary will be addressed later.

The lyrics of the Black Rebel Motorcycle Club track are particularly revealing in their ethos and focus on both an apparent anticipation of and desire for pleasure by another, and the desire for pleasure by and for the self. The first verse focuses on desire that is undoubtedly sexual:

> You want a part of me
> You want the whole thing
> You want to feel something more than I could ever bring
> You want it badly
> You want it tangled
> I want to feel something more than I was strangled.

Singing about sexual desire and indeed the pleasure of anticipation hints, as Matt is seen on screen smoking a cigarette and moving to the rhythm of the track, that perhaps hitherto, he can identify with the theme of wanting. Indeed, this possible identification seems to link to what the band themselves have said about the meaning and punk origins of the track in regard to the real experience of what guitarist Peter Hayes refers to as the 'soul or sex of the music' (Bateman, 2007). Interestingly, the following chorus of the track seems to shift in time from a lyric of the present written about the future, to a lyric of the present written about the past. The past tense 'I fell in love' rather than 'I'm falling in love' implies or perhaps forebodes a narrative of a relationship gone wrong – a relationship in which the rock 'n' roll (the sex) eventually fails to fulfil:

> I fell in love with the sweet sensation
> I gave my heart to a simple chord
> I gave my soul to a new religion
> Whatever happened to you?
> Whatever happened to our rock'n'roll?
> Whatever happened to my rock'n'roll?

The repetitive structure of the song and indeed the questioning of 'whatever happened to my rock 'n' roll' encapsulates what is so captivating about the song. Here then the song exposes or tells of a strange eroticism, a highly charged sexual encounter that repeats again and again, reaching a regular crescendo before, coming to an (anticipated) end. As such, it seems that rock music is not interested only in lyrics but, more specifically is interested in and associated with the reading of active movement[3] and an aesthetics of sensuousness. As Peter Wicke notes speaking of rock:

> The ceaseless repetition of the basic musical elements had a hypnotic effect [...] Instead of transposing emotions into musical structures [...] these emotions were *presented* in movement, a movement which demanded the active participation of the listener so that the emotions could be created in reality. [...] Here musical performance takes place according to an aesthetics of sensuousness. (1990: 53)

The repetition in the song is, I suggest, a deliberate device that Winterbottom employs in *9 Songs* (thus the title) to express and portray the sensuous pleasures of engaging in new experiences albeit in the Brixton Academy / The Forum / Hackney Empire / Hammersmith Apollo or the bedroom.

PERFORMANCE, GENDER AND THE PORNOGRAPHIC

As hinted at above, the repetitive structure of live songs and real sex scenes function as markers of authenticity. Interestingly however, in this film the real constantly bumps up against issues of performance in that the bands / artists and actors clearly both engage in the real of music and sex and yet are also, undoubtedly performing for an audience – either at the Brixton Academy or for the film audience. In this sense, it could be suggested that the nine sex acts and nine songs function as set pieces of performance – musically or pornographically yet, the use of these scenes is, I contend, much more complex and linked to the politics of representation and in particular, the politics of gender.

In the first sex scene proper (immediately following the first gig by the Black Rebel Motorcycle Club) Lisa and Matt are seen in a close-up shot in the lounge of his flat. Akin to the characters of Claire (Kerry Fox) and Jay (Mark Rylance) in Patrice Chéreau's British real-sex film *Intimacy* (2000), Lisa and Matt have sex prior to talking. Indeed, as in *Intimacy* we infer that Lisa and Matt are interested in the sexual connection over and above a spoken or emotional one (at this point in the narrative), which is, in contrast, awkward. Their faces fill the screen, the lighting is muted (tinged barely yellow by a small lamp) and their features are partially obscured. The lighting employed here is absolutely distinct from pornographic lighting which is generally highly amplified to ensure maximum visibility. Instead, the interplay of light and shadow used by Winterbottom works to draw attention to specific features such as the wet lips of Matt and, when the camera pans down and pulls out, the small peach coloured nipples of Lisa. The natural erotic appeal of the performers is emphasized in details such as these and works in clear opposition to the dominant and conscious artificiality of high-end pornography. Indeed, their 'ordinary' bodies (ordinary despite Lisa's model figure and Matt's generously sized penis) and the fact that they are so frequently both seen without clothes, stresses the intimate knowledge that they each have of the other's body in its natural state – the body un-groomed, lacking in the professional pretence of work attire, bushed hair or make-up.

The next shot continues this aesthetic and is a medium shot angled above Matt and Lisa, who, now naked, breathe loudly (with anticipation) while Lisa sits on top of him and, we infer, penetration begins. Unlike the usual projection of moans over mainstream porn films, the sound of breath alone here again serves to reinforce the naturalism of the scene. The following shot is a close-up however, unlike the aesthetics of pornography, it is the faces of Matt and Lisa that are made the focus of the shot, rather than their genitals. The next shot is again a medium one and shows the couple in a different position (an ellipsis is inferred). In a long shot lasting approximately 15 seconds Lisa is seen to plunge her fingers into Matt's open mouth. When she withdraws them, his saliva can be seen and this clear reference to the real wetness of the body has continued resonance as the camera, amidst deep shadows, moves downward, showing (in shadow) the sight of Matt's erect penis entering Lisa. As this sequence is shot from above rather than below and because any clear view is obscured, the composition obviously works to deny pleasure unto the filmic audience, instead, giving the pleasure over to Matt and Lisa. Indeed, the moment is so intimate and so estranged from the over-exposed genital spectacles often found in porn, that the audience are potentially alienated or purposefully set apart from the connection and closeness that they see on screen. Such a moment of course further distinguishes the sex seen here from typical pornographic representations that are intended not to convey an intimate closeness but to arouse. This clear attempt to show the truth of the body while refusing a solely pornographic positioning demonstrates or perhaps provokes what Linda Williams refers to in *Porn Studies* as: 'a curious mixture of boredom and titillation; or perhaps more precisely, a mixture of boredom and titillation inflected in a different manner than that usual to the experience of watching pornography' (2004: 52).

The issue of sex, boredom and the banal is bound up with the representation of sexual politics in *9 Songs* in various ways. Arguably, the role of boredom has a double function in *9 Songs* – in terms of how the film was received by critics (and the affiliation between the BBFCs nomination of the film as a 'non-sex work' and what some have referred to as the films 'yawn factor' (implying interestingly, that where arousal is exciting, non-arousal is not) and secondly, in terms of the representation and repetitive strategies touched upon earlier in this essay. In terms of the latter, various cultural commentators including Linda Ruth Williams have noted what she nominates as the film's banal and troubling approach to its heroine and, more specifically, the 'stereotypical [...] way Lisa's pleasure is conveyed' (2005). In particular, Linda Ruth Williams (2005) notes the issues associated with Matt's and indeed the director's own nominated (in voiceover) and pictorial comparison of Lisa to the white, vast and recently colonized continent of the Antarctic (Matt is a climate scientist). This link is made on six occasions throughout the film; in the opening shot, where a biplane flies over the icy landscape and Matt notes that he remembers Lisa in terms of her smell, her taste and her skin touching his; directly following Matt and Lisa waking after their first night together when he sees her naked in the bleachy morning light; following Primal Scream's performance of 'Movin' on Up' when Matt notes that 'the Antarctic is the planet's memory'; immediately after Franz Ferdinand's performance of 'Jacqueline'; again moments later as Matt explains how Lisa bought him a book on the Antarctic for his birthday (Michael Nyman plays in the background as cross cuts show Lisa and Matt and the rippling, shadowy sea punctuated by melting bergs); and finally, the Antarctic is seen after Lisa's departure to the States when Matt, from the plane proclaims 'it's beautiful'. Notably, Lisa explicitly mentions the topography of the Antarctic (a topography that she is linked to by repeated intercutting) referring to it as 'an exercise in reductionism' and 'both substance and symbol'. These two phrases seem to capture some of the criticism directed at the film (Melanie Williams, for example (2006: 61) notes that the former description is apposite while Natasha Walters of the *Guardian* writes that *9 Songs* is 'Kinsey-esque in its unsmiling celebration of "sex reduced to its physiological functions"' (2005)). The notion of sex occupying a position of substance as well as symbolic importance is offered up by other critics in response to such judgement. Linda Williams argues, for example, that: 'the sensual substance of a love affair can just as well be captured through sexual and musical lyricism as through dramatic event or extended dialogue' (2008: 261), and she certainly has a point. Yet, as Melanie Williams notes, the most problematic aspects of the film concern not the sexual sustenance but the pictorial comparison of Lisa to the craggy plains of the Antarctic – a trope borrowed from 'the opening scenes of *The English Patient* (Anthony Minghella, 1996), which compares the undulating desert dunes to the contours of the female body' in the same way that scenes depicting 'Matt's plane flying over the polar landscape and his hand roving over her naked body' (2006: 61) are continuously intercut. This visual tactic objectifies Lisa and yet, it is arguable that in various ways, Lisa both desires and invites her own objectification.

While Lisa's body is undoubtedly seen more than that of Matt, in terms of how she is shown and indeed how she wants to be seen by Matt, Lisa actively invites if not demands an objectifying gaze saying to him, for example: 'Hey baby, pay attention to me', while dressed in a T-shirt and knickers, and later: 'I've brought you a present (she turns to one side, lifts up her skirt and shows him her silk bowed lingerie). Me!'[4] It is also worth pointing out here that, as noted at the very beginning of this essay, the film is one based on Matt's memories rather than Lisa's own. Thus, while the seeming comparison of Lisa to the Antarctic (continents to be conquered or colonized by man) is undoubtedly problematic, the very appearance and performance of traditional gender politics are also challenged in various other sequences. Immediately after the Antarctic is discussed by Matt for a second time, Lisa and Matt are seen, again in bed, naked, laid down. Rather than Lisa being dominated or conquered she is positioned on top, her mouth exploring his skin before biting his nipple and pinching his shoulder. This active and semi-aggressive acting out of female desire is shot in close-up not, I argue, to draw attention to her role as either a party to whom sex is 'done' or a nymphomaniac who cannot be satisfied, but rather to highlight her dominance and agency. Indeed, it is Lisa's choice to go to Matt's house and it is Lisa not Matt who not only asks him to fuck her, but tells him what she wants and how she likes it. In addition, as far as the narrative allows us such knowledge, Lisa and Matt are understood to be faithful to one another during their year long relationship.

Interestingly, though Lisa and Matt are understood to be monogamous, Lisa's personality also connotes elements of the 'ladette' – a term that, as Angela Smith notes is: 'widely used in British culture [particularly in the twenty-first century] to describe young women who adopt "laddish" behaviour in terms of boisterous assertiveness, heavy drinking and sexual promiscuity' (2011: 165). Though Lisa is, as noted above, faithful to Matt, she has, she tells him, enjoyed previous sexual relations with men from a variety of nations. Unlike the virgin Antarctic then, Lisa is not virginal but a real woman with a real past. Lisa is also heterosexually appealing and perhaps, could be considered via both her own previous erotic encounters and her American heritage and stereotypical US confidence, to exemplify an exotic and assertive otherness. In many ways, Lisa can be understood to play on her assertiveness, enacting for Matt, a fantasy performance. She is American (not British), young, beautiful, carefree, likes drinking, sex, drugs, rock music and playing with her vibrator. Indeed, her oft repeated phrase 'fuck me, Matt' could be inferred to be an example of her being a ladette / male fantasy. This blurring of traditional gender roles is implicitly addressed after the second sex scene of the film when Lisa stands naked in front of the bathroom mirror and asks Matt: 'Do you think I look like a boy?' While clearly referring to biological sex rather than gender here, a playful link is made between the two. Lisa and Matt are situated in his bathroom where Matt is shaving his face (enacting a performance of masculinity) while Lisa stands at the mirror sideways on, stooping over and then arching her back repetitively with the accompanying words 'boy', 'girl', 'boy', 'girl'. Such a playful construction of Lisa's sex and her gender as both feminine and masculine is important as a political display of otherness. Lisa's 'otherness' is however also signalled in another way. The construction of Lisa as a 'ladette' arguably fails to tell the full story of Lisa's sexuality. While the heterosexuality of the ladette is an integral aspect of such an identity, various sequences in Winterbottom's film hint that Lisa's sexuality is not so 'straight' forward.

On various occasions Lisa's characterization – her gestures and behaviour – hint that she is attracted not only to men but to women also. While Matt reads a regular magazine on his bed in one scene, Lisa interrupts him, reading out a passage of Michel Houellebecq's novel *Platform* to him. The scene that she chooses (one which clearly turns her on) is a scene in which a woman, Valérie, admires the 'delicate slits' and 'pussies' of other women and says how she'd like to 'slip her finger inside'. Fantasizing and role-playing with Matt moments later, she whispers her own fantasy: 'There's a couple behind me to my right. I can feel them looking at me. I put my hand between my legs. I'm so wet. As she slides down her boyfriend's body, she has the most amazing breasts and she's rubbing them. Ummm ohhh. And she's covered in oil. Ohhh and she leans over to her boyfriend, grabs his balls and puts his cock in her mouth. Fuck me, Matt. Come up here and fuck me. Fuck me. Matt.' On another occasion, Lisa and Matt are seen to attend a local lap-dancing club, aptly named, Venus. While Matt leads Lisa by the hand, clearly initiating the visit, once inside it appears to be Lisa rather than Matt who is particularly excited by the experience. As a young blonde woman gyrates in front of her, Lisa mouths the words 'Oh my God' and stares at the woman's genitals transfixed. Matt, sat next to her, looks only at Lisa. While Lisa refuses to return his gaze, Matt, appearing increasingly bored by the spectacle and, as indicated by his pent-up facial expression and taut unsmiling mouth, appears jealous / angry that Lisa's desire for the woman does not extend to him. As Lisa is seen in medium shots placing her hands either side of the woman's naked and gently gyrating bottom, flashbacks show Lisa caressing her nipples and beginning to masturbate. The exclusion of Matt from the scene results in him leaving the club. Lisa stays, her eyes drawn to and flirting with the female dancer.

The transformation of Matt's heterosexual porno fantasy into Lisa's own which seemingly excludes Matt is a powerful moment of rupture in the relationship. In excluding Matt and flirting with the dancer, Lisa sabotages their sexual harmony and calls her commitment to Matt and their relation into question. As Adam Phillips argues:

> Flirtation has always been the saboteur of a cherished vocabulary of commitment [...] The generosity of flirtation is in its implicit wish to sustain the life of desire; and often by blurring, or putting into question, the boundary between sex and sexualization. Flirting creates the uncertainty it is also trying to control. (1994: xvii–xviii)

Lisa's gender and sexual identity can also be seen as uncertain or complicated in relation to the other performances that she attends. Interestingly, when at the rock gigs with Matt, Lisa is far less engaged while watching the rock frontmen than she is watching the female nude dancer (or the female guitarists, in particular Carrie Smith of The Von Bondies). At the various gigs, Lisa is seen laughing and enjoying herself but is also, where the bands are male dominated, not always fully engaged, pictured looking a little bored and resting her head on Matt rather than singing or dancing along. One reason for this might be the prevalence of gender divisions within the realm of rock. As Norma Coates argues:

> Rock is indeed a technology of gender in that 'masculinity' is reinforced and multiplied in its many discursive spaces. However, what is reiterated in and by rock is a particular type of masculinity, one which was 'fixed' in the early days of rock and roll. Rock masculinity, at least the stereotype which, I assert, is still very much in play discursively and psychically, is one in which any trace of the 'feminine' is expunged, incorporated or appropriated. (1997: 52)

Where pop has for a long time been understood as a feminine domain (one associated with the music of the bedroom), rock has frequently been seen as a masculine domain, connected to the real and the outside. While many of the rock frontmen in *9 Songs* can be seen to perform a clichéd type of masculinity, the focus on Lisa in the bedroom juxtaposes the gender division where she is the sexual focus. Such a division could also be applied to the genres of rock and pop, with rock understood as a domain connected to the real while pop is seen as feminine and inauthentic. As Coates also notes:

> Consider, for example, the discursive and stylistic segregation of 'rock' and 'pop'. In this schema, rock is metonymic with 'authenticity' while 'pop' is metonymic with 'artifice'. Sliding even further down the metonymic slope, 'authentic' becomes 'masculine' while 'artificial' becomes 'feminine'. Rock, therefore, is 'masculine', pop is 'feminine', and the two are set in a binary relation to each other, with the masculine, of course, on top. [...] Furthermore, according to this schema, authenticity in rock is something which, like pornography, one is supposed to know when one sees it. 'Rock' is not so much a sound or a particular style of playing music, but represents a degree of emotional honesty, liveness, musical straightforwardness, and other less tangible, largely subjective aspects. (1997: 52–3)

While this division and binary can be seen as problematic in that in *9 Songs* the male is the site of rock and the female the site of sex, I'd like to suggest that it is in the sexual arena where Lisa's power really emerges. Indeed, at the end of the film it is Lisa not Matt who is literally and figuratively 'on top'. The relationship ends because Lisa chooses to go back to her home country leaving, in her wake, Matt and a plethora of memories written into the body.

The term 'wake' can also be understood as doubly relevant in that, following the departure of Matt from the Venus club, the relationship is on a downward spiral and while it occasionally shows signs of life, it never fully recovers. The next morning, Lisa is seen in bed with Matt, silently weeping. While no explanation is given in dialogue, we can infer that the couple had a fight following Matt's vacation of the club. The fact that Lisa was seen masturbating alone with her vibrator implies that even though she and Matt shared a bed that night, Matt could not fulfil her sexual desires. As Matt tries to soothe her in the morning light, she clings to him. While the act can be read as implicitly feminine – a need or desire for protection by an active male – as Linda Williams notes in *Screening Sex*: 'it is the clinging of a partner who best knows that the end is near and is mourning the relationship's loss' (2008: 264). In this sense, rather than Lisa's desire for another and her masturbation being accompanied by a sense of guilt or regret, the alternate reading here, as Linda Williams suggests, is that Lisa is far more attuned to the new disaccord that has crept into her and Matt's relationship than he is. Indeed, in this sense it is Lisa who, though branded egotistical and childish by Matt, is in fact far more aware of the emotional complexity – fluctuations, of the closeness and distance between the pair – than he is. Here, Lisa, despite her tender age – Matt points out that she is only 21 – is awarded an emotional intelligence lacking in Matt (who looks approximately 10 years older though his age is never specified) whose responses are most frequently sexual rather than emotional.

CRITICAL RESPONSES, FRAMES OF REFERENCE AND REPRESENTING THE REAL

The issue of gender politics isn't only addressed in relation to the gendered and sexual representations within the film and readings of it, but also in relation to the critical responses to it. While a number of commentators (including Patrick Marmion of the *Daily Mail*) noted that they found *9 Songs*, and in particular, the sex scenes in the film 'boring', or banal, as Melanie Williams (2006: 60) pointed out, Peter Bradshaw of the *Guardian* asked if such commentators were, in fact, being truthful: 'Boring? Gosh, really? Is that why all those male journalists in the audience were gulping and surreptitiously re-crossing their legs?' (2005).

This questioning of the distinction between the real and the performed 'professional' is a significant and relevant one in relation to the principal actors in the film, Stilley and O'Brien. Due to the inclusion of real sex, *9 Songs* is in part, a text that demonstrates the blurring of boundaries between performance and the real. In performing the real of sex, Stilley becomes intimate with O'Brien in spite of the fact that her character's demand for sex is not her own. Though Stilley in particular stressed in countless press interviews her and O'Brien's professionalism and denied any genuine or real connection (noting, for example, in an interview with Andrew Anthony of the *Guardian*, 20 February 2005 that 'real stimulation was never an option. We were working [...] and we were super professional'), Stilley and O'Brien do engage in intimate acts; however, as Linda Williams suggests, the term 'act' may be best replaced by the term 'performance' due to the actuality of penetration, that is, a penetration of 'safely contained boundaries of acting'. To explicate further Williams notes:

> [P]erhaps acting is not the right word here. Acting implies artifice, being precisely what one is not, through drawing on what one has been in order to create an appearance that is credible. To 'act' a scene in which the action is sex is [...] to really engage in sex. [...] Actual sexual intimacy with another person does take place in the sex scene whether one 'really' feels desire or whether one 'really' comes. This may be one of those occasions where the word performance – connoting an avant-garde edge challenging the more safely contained boundaries of acting – is more appropriate. (Williams, 2001, 'Cinema and the Sex Act')

The notion of an avant-garde edge in relation to *9 Songs* is certainly an interesting one. Making explicit diegetic reference to artistic or avant-garde works such as Michel Houellebecq's aforementioned novel *Platform*, the real sex performed in the film can also be contextualized within a broader artistic or avant-garde frame of reference.

Though in many ways *9 Songs* is purposefully unpretentious in its sexual depictions, the avant-garde European 'cinema of the body' that came before it prefaced the acceptability of real sex on film in a non-pornographic context. Though inspired, according to Winterbottom, by the Japanese film *Ai no corrida* or *In the Realm of the Senses* (Nagisa Oshima, 1976) which told the story of an intense sexual love affair between Sada Abe (Eiko Matsuda) and Kichizo Ishida (Tatsuya Fuji), the more recently '18' certified European films starting with Catherine

Breillat's *Romance* (1999) paved the way for explicit depictions of real sex to be passed uncut and viewed by mainstream audiences. While Breillat's film is a particularly interesting example in that it starred a combination of mainstream actors such as Caroline Ducey (playing Marie) alongside famous porn actor Rocco Siffredi (who plays one of her lovers, Paolo), it also, like *9 Songs*, had something important to say about both the censorship of sex and the politics of representation and gender on screen. While Breillat's discussion of the censorship of *Romance* had a feminist focus (she declared that censorship was a male urge, and the X certificate was linked to the X chromosome), (Palmer, 2013: 93), the film purposefully placed female sexuality at the centre of the narrative. As Peter Bradshaw of the *Guardian* noted in his review of the film:

> It must have been a while since mainstream cinema audiences were invited to view a young woman submitting to be tied up by an older man […], the cord tied between her legs, through her vagina and pulled up good and tight: the unlovely impress of rope on genitalia represented in unforgiving close-up. Then the young woman interrupts the process in tears, not through rage at phallocentric oppression in life and art – nothing so dated – but rather anger at her own timid refusal of this adventure and naturally a vertiginous sense of the profound 'enigma' in female sexuality. This is the burden and the song of *Romance*, Catherine Breillat's opaque essay in eroticism, a film controversial for its explicit portrayal of male arousal: a pink orchard of erect penises. (1999)

That Bradshaw notes the significance of gender politics in and to the film, points to the significance of film form and refers to *Romance* as an 'essay', demonstrates the serious and avant-garde positioning of it. Following Breillat's film, other directors such as Virginie Despentes and Coralie Trinh Thi, Gaspar Noé, Michael Haneke, Claire Denis and Patrice Chéreau also released features that included real sex but took it seriously such as (respectively) *Baise-moi* (2000), *Irréversible* (2002), *The Piano Teacher* (2001), *Trouble Every Day* (2001) and *Intimacy* (2001). As Lisa Downing notes, such directors have: 'spawned a genre that seeks to dismantle the prohibition regarding the exposure of the body and of "real" sexual activity in narrative film, within a cinematic climate that has seen a concerted return to the tenants of realism in other contexts' (2004: 266). While *9 Songs* can undoubtedly be positioned akin to these texts in the sense that it is what Tim Palmer labels a 'narrative of the flesh' (2006: 22), a striking difference between the texts nominated above and Winterbottom's own concerns the distinction between mood – both that represented and potentially experienced by the audience. Whereas 9 *Songs* is in many ways a text that treats sex seriously, sex is also, importantly, keyed out as an activity both of the 'everyday' and as something celebratory, an act of fun, of play; a source of pleasurable intimacy. In opposition, *Baise-moi*, *Irréversible*, *The Piano Teacher* and so on tend to depict sex as part of a serious strategy concerned with displeasure. While intimate, Palmer uses the title 'brutal intimacy' to refer to these displeasurable texts, pointing to and keying out their 'close relationship to contemporary French-language literature [where] leading practitioners are Michel Houellebecq and Frédéric Beigbeder' (2011: 63).

This return to Houellebecq in relation to the deliberately displeasurable cinema of the body raises important questions regarding the intention of 9 *Songs*. Though, according to the BBFC the purpose of the film is disconnected from 'the primary intent to arouse', it is worth questioning if the BBFC can indeed predict what effect the film is likely to have on viewers. While the primary purpose of the film is, according to Winterbottom to explore a relationship through the dialogue of sex rather than to arouse, arousal for a heterosexual audience may indeed be a pleasurable by-product. For me, the emotional and bodily honesty written into the sexual and musical performances coupled with the minute gestures of intimacy shown, such as the momentary rests indicated by the hanging of the head and the gentle brushing of the finger against the other's cheek, effect, at times, a mindful and joyful arousal. That this does not take away from the film is significant. Such a response, for me at least, adds to it in that it embraces and affirms the tactile and intense qualities of cinema and the powerful ways in which it can make us 'feel'.

The realist approach to sexual performances on display in 9 *Songs* does, at times, move away from the natural and consciously closer to the artificial conventions of hard-core pornography. Two scenes in particular, both occurring toward the end of the film showcase Winterbottom's purposeful blurring of the art / porn binary. In the first, we see Lisa masturbating Matt to the point of ejaculation. In the second, we see Lisa and Matt have sex for the last time. The first sequence opens with a slightly high-angled medium shot of Lisa and Matt in bed. Matt is closest to the camera and turned toward Lisa (his back to the camera) who touches her nipples before speaking: 'Do my nipples feel sore to you? They are.' That the form of the shot emphasizes their interaction before the dialogue highlights the mutuality of their bodies and sensations is telling. Indeed, as Michael Ryan and Melissa Lenos point out: 'In a medium shot, one can see the bodies of the characters [...] The emphasis is usually on the interaction between the[m]' (2012: 52). Matt and Lisa then kiss, slowly and sensually before Lisa progresses the physicality by licking Matt's neck. As he responds, rubbing her shoulder gently, Lisa shifts the weight of her body onto him, kissing his chest. The two lie still for a moment, their arms wrapped around each other before a cut shows Lisa in a close-up shot kissing Matt's naked thigh. The composition of the shot is tight with both Lisa's head, Matt's thigh and his semi-erect penis in the centre of the frame. In shadow, due to a strong natural back light, Lisa briefly flicks her tongue over Matt's testicles before, with her lips parted, she moves her face silently and effortlessly upwards – above Matt's now erect penis. Lisa's grace and ease in her movement and the fact that at times she obscures the view of Matt's penis suggests a certain naturalness. This continues as Lisa runs her nose gently back down the length of Matt's shaft. Unlike the frequent or what Linda Williams refers to as 'reverential penis worship that so commonly occurs in hard-core pornography' (2008: 272), Lisa's interaction with Matt's penis conveys in Lisa an ease with her sexuality and her desire. In the next shot, Lisa is seen in close-up, eyes closed, calmly sucking Matt's testes before the camera pans to the left to show him watching her. The sound of Matt's breathing – a single, audible anticipatory outbreath – discloses his desire as Lisa continues kissing and licking his penis. Interestingly, at this point in the sequence, the framing of the shot changes, eschewing the 'naturalness' of the previous actions and ushering in a more pornographic set of aesthetics. Firstly, the camera is now placed at the bottom of the bed, showing and indeed emphasizing the curve of Lisa's buttocks and waist as she hovers over Matt's body. The next shot which moves back to capturing the couple from the side, is a medium shot rather than a close-up showing Lisa taking Matt's penis in her mouth. The next shot, a close-up show's Lisa propped up on her elbows, playfully running her tongue around the tip of Matt's foreskin. Rather than looking down at his body, Lisa here looks directly forward – toward Matt – smiling. Matt half-laughs before Lisa takes the shaft of his penis back into her mouth causing him to breathe deeply. The shot then again changes to an end of bed perspective showing Lisa's curved spine and her head moving up and down. A close-up shot next shows Lisa continuing to fellate Matt as the dull and wet sound of her lips moving quickly over his skin can be heard. Matt's face is again seen in close-up, before Lisa fills the screen repetitively moving her mouth back and forth over his penis. The next cut takes us back to a medium shot which immediately shows Lisa holding Matt's penis in her left hand while he ejaculates onto his own belly (the first '18' certified film to show such a sight). Lisa smiles in response.

This scene of ejaculation is interesting in that on the one hand it is a staple of pornography – its purpose being to articulate the authenticity of the desire on show – and yet in 9 *Songs* the so-called 'money shot' is markedly distinct. Whereas in heterosexual porn it is customary for the man to come, most often, the site of the ejaculate is the belly or face of the woman, not the man. Arguably, the reason for this is to attempt to show *on* the female performer what cannot be seen *in* the female performer – her own wet climax. Lisa's pleasure is not implied by the sight / site of Matt's ejaculate but is rather seen in her brief smile as he 'comes'. Indeed, her feelings are conveyed through such small gestures. As Linda Williams notes, these types of gestures 'make us believe in the reciprocity of one touched body part to another' (2008: 273). While this sequence can be seen as a stylized nod to hard-core, its representation is not straightforwardly pornographic but rather, a mixture of what Tanya Krzywinska might refer to as pornography and art or 'explicit art cinema' (2006: 225).

The final sex scene in the film – a scene that follows Lisa's admission that she is going back to America – is closer to the aesthetics of hard-core than the former in that the framing of Lisa and Matt ensures that in as many of the shots their genitals are centre screen – what Williams refers to as 'penetration staged for maximum visibility' (2008: 5). As such, the audience are shown in the 'light of day', Matt guiding his condom-covered penis towards Lisa and penetrating her as she straddles him. While the positioning is pornographic, Matt's thrusting is not in the sense that it is neither particularly fast nor mechanical. Rather, Matt's slow thrusts denote a sensual longing, a revelling in the moment. From this, the audience can connote that while the penetration is framed like hard-core, this sequence in fact denotes something closer to 'making love' than fucking. Indeed, the sex portrayed here does not appear to be about climax, but rather about love, emotion and connection. The shots in this sequence are all from a fixed perspective (below the couple – bottom of the bed – or, a long shot of the penetration from side on) and are reasonably long, the majority lasting about ten seconds. This focus on the lovemaking is so intimate, so personal to the couple, that it arguably works against identification with the characters. Instead, I'd like to suggest that this sequence functions to question strategies of screening sex and regimes of perception as well as the classification of sex and moral judgements that are often made about it. What this final sexual swansong points to then is a tension – both an intimacy in and a struggle over representation and its meanings.

CONCLUSION

The struggle over the representation of sex on screen is not new but is one that Winterbottom explicitly noted he wanted to address via a mainstream twenty-first-century film in the hope that it would resonate with a mainstream twenty-first-century audience. His serious and determined approach to the subject of sex belies his serious attitude regarding its representation, censorship and regulation. Talking about and responding to the designation of *9 Songs* by some critics as porn, he noted in an interview with Margaret Pomeranz:

> It isn't pornography, the truth is, you know, this was an attempt to show two people in a relationship, to show two people making love. It was not an attempt to excite the audience, or arouse the audience. You know, if you watch a porn movie, you watch a bunch of porn movies, and then watch *9 Songs* – however you define pornography, *9 Songs* just doesn't look like the porn movies, doesn't sound like them. It just doesn't have the same effect as them. It's just a completely different thing. That's not to say it's better than pornography, or worse, it's just different. (2006)

The last point that Winterbotton makes – that *9 Songs* is no better or no worse than pornography – is, I believe, an important one and one that I support. As noted above, Winterbottom's film is clearly an example of narrative cinema that does not look or feel like high-end glossy porn. Winterbottom's denial of its classification as pornography occurs because *9 Songs*, while making a series of nods to porn, is not porn. For Winterbottom, and indeed myself, no moral judgement is attached; sometimes sex on screen is intended to arouse, sometimes it is not. Both are valid forms of expression and representation. For Winterbottom then, an honesty regarding the tenants of the real is more important than a reductive moral judgement. In many ways, it seems straightforward, sensible even, to show a love story through showing a couple making love. Another tongue-in-cheek response to such accusations of *9 Songs'* pornographic status may be eluded to in the theme of resistance nominated in the 2006 album title of British rock band, The Arctic Monkeys, *Whatever People Say I Am, That's What I'm Not*. In the same way that many have noted this to be a concept album, Winterbottom's film can be understood as a concept film. Both attempt to represent the real of modern-day experiences, sounds and sex. Speaking of the inspiration for the album title (besides the original Alan Sillitoe novel, *Saturday Night and Sunday Morning*), the parallels between the ways in which the musical work of the Arctic Monkeys and the sexual and cinematic work of Winterbottom has been wrongly labelled becomes clear: 'there's a lot of people saying a lot of things about us and you don't have control over it." (*NME*, 2005).

Serving formally as points of punctuation in the film, the nine songs, like the sex scenes, are rhythmically and lyrically in sync with the state of the relationship providing a mirroring function. Franz Ferdinand's 'Jacqueline', Super Furry Animals' 'Slow Life', Elbow's 'Fallen Angel', Michael Nyman's sombre 'Debbie', Primal Scream's 'Movin' on Up', Dandy Worhols' 'You Were the Last High', The Von Bondies' 'C'mon C'mon', and Black Rebel Motorcycle Club's 'Love Burns' and 'Whatever Happened to My Rock and Roll' thus serve to both clarify and add another textual layer of meaning to the narrative. Indeed, the lyrics of the tracks can be understood to provide what Rick Altman calls a 'unique opportunity to editorialize' (2001: 26) – in essence, the song titles and lyrics are used relatively straightforwardly as subtle titles of subtext. In addition though, as Simon Frith points out, music and sex are interlinked: 'Music is "sexy" not because it makes us move, but because (through that movement) it makes us feel; makes us feel (like sex itself) intensely present' (1996: 144). While then, as I mentioned at the very beginning of this essay, the inspiration for Winterbottom's film concerned omission, the eventual presence of the film in the canon of screening sex is important in that, to borrow a phrase from Linda Williams 'screening sex, has, at each new stage, proffered an opportunity to see and to know what has not previously been seen so closely' (2008: 326). As Matt points out at the end of *9 Songs*, the past harbours a beauty – and that beauty infects and inflects our understanding of the present and our desires for the future. For Winterbottom, his desire was a simple one; that the film would capture a sight of beauty that was usually ignored and that the primal scene would be seen differently. What he also achieved in his process of socio-political provocation was the creation of a set of diverse critical responses to his work which map the very real struggle at the heart of sexual representation.

NOTES

1. For example, Charlotte Higgins of the *Guardian*, Thursday 20 May 2004 (accessed 1 October 2013) wrote:

   You could, perhaps, have seen it all coming. Or maybe not, if you were a 21-year-old with no significant acting roles to your name. What is clear is that Margo Stilley, the female lead in Michael Winterbottom's film *Nine Songs* – already famous as the most sexually explicit film in the history of mainstream British cinema – is at the centre of an almighty media ruckus. On Tuesday, tabloid headlines gleefully announced the arrival of the "Muckiest Film Ever" and the "Rudest Film Ever to Hit Our Cinemas". By yesterday Fleet Street's finest had caught up with friends and family in Stilley's native North Carolina. "Mother of Beauty in 'Real Sex' Film Shocker Prays For Her ... Oh God! Oh God!" trumpeted the *Daily Express*, on startlingly baroque form. "My Prayers For 'Porn' Daughter" and "Bible Belt Mum's Fear For Her Sex Movie Daughter", were the contributions from the *Daily Mirror*.'

2. I am immensely grateful to Dr Nicholas Reyland, Senior Lecturer in Musicology at Keele University for drawing my attention to this.
3. An early example here is Elvis Presley and his gyrating and supposedly corrupting hip swivels (Elvis the Pelvis).
4. Interestingly, Stilley's background prior to acting in *9 Songs* was modelling – implying perhaps that she has a degree of comfort with being objectified. In interview however, Stilley notes that she in no way equated her performance in the film to exhibitionism, but rather stressed her professionalism and the serious nature of the role and theme. See for example: http://www.guardian.co.uk/film/2005/feb/20/features.magazine, http://www.guardian.co.uk/film/2004/may/20/cannes2004.cannesfilmfestival and http://www.guardian.co.uk/film/2005/jan/24/1 (accessed 17 October 2013).

Chapter 8

TRAGEDY OF HANDS

RAPE IN GASPAR NOÉ'S *IRRÉVERSIBLE*

DAVID ANDREWS

Gaspar Noé's *Irréversible* (2002) made an unmistakable impact on its audience, an impact first registered through the scores of viewers who walked out of the film's Cannes premier. Much of this brouhaha arose in response to Noé's use of graphic violence and the movie's unapologetic homophobia (Wood, 2003: 5-6). Add to this the film's arty structure, which runs backward through just over a dozen narrative episodes, and the director's effort seemed almost tailor-made to *épater le bourgeois*.

Plainly, though, if there was one specific thing in *Irréversible* that left an indelible impression it was the rape scene. In this sequence, the film's heroine, Alex - played by Monica Bellucci, whose exceptional beauty has been recognized by magazines and websites as well as by films like Giuseppe Tornatore's *Malèna* (2000) over the past 15 years - is assaulted and anally raped in a Parisian underpass, then beaten until comatose and disfigured. The sexual assault plays out in real time, running more than 11 minutes, much of which is recorded by a static camera that faces the victim on the ground, while her rapist - a psychopathic homosexual pimp known as Le Tenia (Jo Prestia) - lies atop her, holding her from behind. The largely unedited rape scene (which contains just one 'invisible cut' that reportedly occurs before the sodomy even starts) generates such immediacy that, according to Noé, some viewers were tempted to see it as unsimulated, as if it were part of the 'real sex' trend popular in global art cinema at the beginning of the new millennium. This temptation was exacerbated by the presence of a bloody, semi-erect penis at the end of the rape. But it was all an illusion - including the penis, which was added in post-production (Sterritt, 2007: 311-12). Instead, the rape sequence's tremendous immediacy derives from something much more old-fashioned: terrific acting in the service of cinema-vérité minimalism.

One particularly powerful aspect of this minimalism is its use of the characters' hands, especially those of the victim. This subtle choreography hasn't elicited the critical comment it deserves, despite the fact that it is one of the scene's most active components and arguably one of its most haunting, too. On a first viewing, the audience can decipher this choreography through its repetitive motions in an otherwise barren visual tableau - and if that audience has been schooled in the erotic grammar of postwar art films and exploitation films, it will be in position to read this choreography as signalling the rape victim's consistent non-consent as well as her increasing pain and trauma. On a second and third viewing - after becoming familiar, that is, with the events leading to the rape, which in the film's reverse structure are revealed only after the rape is shown - viewers can glean further meaning from this tense choreography. These hand gestures are integral to a larger system of hand gestures that help tie the movie together through doublings that communicate a decidedly fatalistic vision. In other words, Noé's hand choreography is one of the film's most fundamental interpretive keys, something that makes it possible to understand the tragic philosophy of the film as a whole.

The chapter below begins with a brief overview of *Irréversible*'s reverse narrative followed by a close description of the rape scene itself. Once these summaries are in place, I proceed to a close reading of the hand imagery within the scene. I contextualize that imagery by touching on the erotic grammar of hand gestures that developed through postwar art films and exploitation films, from Louis Malle's *Les amants* (1958) and Russ Meyer's *Lorna* (1964) to Sam Peckinpah's *Straw Dogs* (1971) and David Lynch's *Wild at Heart* (1990). *Straw Dogs* offers a particularly useful comparison, for like *Irréversible*, this rape-revenge film is governed by a tragic, fatalistic sense of sex and violence. But at the textual level, Noé's hand imagery is quite distinct from Peckinpah's, in part because *Irréversible*'s narrative structure requires multiple viewings but also because its rape scene, unlike that of *Straw Dogs*, is consistently non-consensual - a difference inscribed in the hand imagery. To make all of this clear, I examine Noé's imagery in the context of *Irréversible*'s elaborate narrative doublings. I close by contemplating what it means that one of the most disturbing, inhuman scenes in film history may be understood in terms of such an understated and *human* form of bodily imagery.

* * * * *

When related in forward order, *Irréversible*'s plot is simple. Taking place over the course of a single day, the action begins with heroine Alex reading in a park. Later, she frolics in and out of bed with her boyfriend Marcus (Vincent Cassel, Bellucci's husband), a man who is goofy and affectionate when sober. Through most of this sequence, the characters are naked; they have just awakened after a post-coital nap, a moment that is conveyed with uncompromising realism. The couple must get ready to go to a party accompanied by Pierre (Albert Dupontel), Alex's ex-boyfriend. At one point in the scene, Alex indicates that she might be pregnant and waits to gauge Marcus's response – which is affirmative and quite buoyant, much like Marcus in general. When he goes out to buy liquor for the party, Alex takes a home pregnancy test and happily confirms that she is pregnant. The plot darkens just slightly when Pierre comes into the picture. On the train to the party – the pair were supposed to take Pierre's car, but it had broken down that day – Pierre grills the couple about their sex life, demanding to know how Marcus, that 'primate', could supply Alex with orgasms when he never could. Marcus accepts Pierre's ribbing in good humor. At the party, Marcus over-imbibes – partly, perhaps, because he is happy about Alex's condition, but mostly because that is Marcus's nature. He kisses girls, takes coke, and dances sloppily, even urinating in a kitchen sink. Pierre is unhappy with Marcus's unhinged behaviour and scolds him out of deference to Alex, whom he still loves. Alex accepts Marcus's behaviour until he interrupts her attempt to reconnect with a pregnant friend whom she hasn't seen in some time. Shortly thereafter, she angrily leaves the party on her own, despite Pierre's and Marcus's efforts to restrain her.

As Alex makes her way through an underpass to cross a street and reach a taxi, she comes upon the pimp Le Tenia (literally, 'the tapeworm') as he beats Concha (Jara-Millo), a prostitute who we later learn is a transvestite. When he notices Alex, Le Tenia lets Concha go and assaults, then rapes, Alex over a long sequence. A misogynist and an apparent psychopath, he verbally abuses Alex as well, reacting with fury and desire to her revealingly 'high class' party dress and beautiful face. After he finishes sodomizing her, Le Tenia continues this verbal assault, which he punctuates by kicking her ferociously and slamming her face to the concrete, presumably to destroy her beauty and upscale allure. Marcus and Pierre discover all this as they leave the party and find the comatose Alex being taken away on a stretcher. At first numbed by the news (and still under the influence of drugs), Marcus is roused to anger and revenge by a pair of locals who promise to help him find the rapist

Figure 8.1. In this frame capture, Marcus misbehaves at the party. He restrains Alex in an evocation of the rape sequence that viewers have already witnessed.

in return for money. This, the two strangers suggest, is the 'natural', 'manly' course of action. Marcus and Pierre go with them and are led on a frenzied journey toward Le Tenia, during which Marcus's dark side – characterized by rage, violence, homophobia, and racism – becomes apparent. Though Pierre tries to stop Marcus, he never actually leaves his side. Eventually, they get Le Tenia's name and possible whereabouts – a gay sex club called 'The Rectum' – from Concha, whom Marcus assaults. After stealing a taxi from an acutely distressed Asian cabbie, they locate The Rectum and proceed to explore it. Pierre continues to implore Marcus to reconsider, to stop, since Alex wouldn't approve of his plan or tactics.

The Rectum is a nightmarish place of public sex, masturbation, and threatening sadomasochistic behaviour. Marcus leads the way through the darkness, making many false moves. Eventually, he and Pierre come upon two men who refuse to say whether either one is Le Tenia – which leads Marcus to assault the wrong man. That man gets the better of Marcus, breaking his arm in retaliation and attempting to sodomize him. Pierre 'rescues' Marcus by clubbing the man's head with a fire extinguisher – an action that he persists in long after the stranger is incapacitated, thus reducing the man's head to mush. Throughout the melee, the second man, later identified as Le Tenia, looks on with grisly fascination as the crowd cheers the spectacle. Marcus is then taken away on a stretcher and Pierre is led off by the police. The men who incited the vendetta meet the pair outside the club and hurl epithets at them, desperate to get paid. The action ends in a seedy hotel. There, the naked

Figure 8.2. In this frame capture, Marcus reveals his dark side while in the taxi en route to the sex club The Rectum.

anti-hero (Philippe Nahon) of Noé's previous film, *Seul contre tous / I Stand Alone* (1998), waxes nihilistic while telling a companion about his sordid past, which also included revenge-gone-wrong. He jokes crudely about the noise coming from The Rectum, which is located below them. '*LE TEMPS DETRUIT TOUT*' – 'Time destroys all things' – flashes on screen to close the plot.

* * * * *

These are the major plot points of the film – but because these details are *not* related in forward order, their violence is frontloaded and confounding, making it difficult for first-time viewers to understand the causes of the violence or the personalities involved. The shaky, hand-held camera-work, which is most emphatic over the first half of the film, only adds to the confusion. However, in the rape sequence, this kaleidoscopic intensity is mostly absent. The contrast with the previous scenes, which have been characterized by a swirling camera and a frenetic visual confusion, is plain. It is as if the auteur is instructing the viewer to see and hear every detail of the rape – which makes a scene of intense sexual violence more authentic and immediate. Indeed, this intensity even makes it more difficult to remember that the actors are by necessity *simulating* the sexual action – and that it is that necessity that dictates the position of the camera, which is focused on the victim's agonized hands and face rather than on her violated lower half.

The rape sequence, which has but one 'invisible cut' in it (Sterritt, 2007: 311), may be broken into six separate segments. The sequence begins with a hand-held camera following Alex voyeuristically from behind into the red-tinted underpass. In this interval, Alex's face is not directly shown and is only briefly seen from the sides. That changes in the next segment, when Alex tries to pass Le Tenia and Concha in the tunnel. Suddenly, Le Tenia begins to hit the transvestite, violence so shocking it stops Alex in her tracks. Here she is shot from the side, a visual shift that accents the departure in the mood. Alex begins to run in the direction she came from but is pursued by Le Tenia, who lets Concha escape. It is at this point in the sequence that the camera focuses frontally on Alex for the first time, emphasizing her panic and loss of control. Le Tenia blocks Alex's retreat by putting his hands to either side of her body. Noé's camera moves with the action, tracking the developing assault as it shifts from one side to the next.

In the third segment of the sequence, the action is quieter and more static – as if in response to the knife that Le Tenia puts to Alex's cheek. It is at this point that the sexual part of the assault begins. Le Tenia forces Alex to the ground and climbs atop her back, pinning her. The camera follows this downward movement and settles on the ground, where it remains motionless, close to the heads of the rapist and his victim. During this segment, Le Tenia is occupied with keeping Alex quiet and pinning her down even as he caresses her body and prepares to violate her. Just before the penetration commences, a stranger walks into the underpass, unseen by rapist and his victim; he assesses the scene for a moment before retreating in the direction from which he came. This detail, which might get missed by the inattentive viewer, is one of the bleakest moments in the assault, for someone who could have responded to Alex's cries for help chooses not to, walking away instead. At this point, the sodomy itself gets underway as signalled by Le Tenia's hip-pumping and the rhythmic, muffled noise from Alex's mouth, which is covered by Le Tenia's hand. This fourth portion of the rape is punctuated by Le Tenia's insults and his use of poppers to heighten his sexual pleasure during the act. The camera is static on the ground throughout.

The last two segments are marked by extreme violence. The fifth segment starts with Le Tenia rolling off Alex, a hint of his semi-erect penis visible for several seconds. Alex is shaking and whimpering; she begins to crawl backward, struggling to her knees, her head down. Le Tenia gets up to block her escape, insulting her again with comments aimed at her beauty and class status. Traumatized, she is unable to look him in the eye as he commands, so Le Tenia kicks her in the head and in the back and in the head again. At this point, he says, 'I'm not through

Figure 8.3. After blocking her exit with his hands, Le Tenia puts his knife to Alex's face in this frame capture. The change in camera angle reinforces the change in mood.

with you, but I will be,' and 'I'm gonna fix your face.' He climbs atop her again and punches her. Her face is hidden – the camera still has not moved significantly – but the force of Le Tenia's blows is registered in the spasms of her legs. Then he asks, 'You want some more?' He turns the defenceless Alex over to slam her face into the concrete. This begins the sixth and final segment, as the camera abruptly begins moving again, whirling in on the violence. Le Tenia finishes his assault, wipes his hands together and fixes his suit to signal the end of the deed. Then he spits on Alex, calling her 'Dead meat.' The camera then swirls away, back to the party scene. The entire sequence, from the moment that Alex leaves the party to the end of Le Tenia's vicious onslaught, takes 13.5 minutes of screen time. The assault itself takes 11.5 minutes with four of those minutes occupied by the graphic but sexually inexplicit documentation of Alex's anal rape.

* * * * *

The most conspicuous part of the movie's hand choreography takes place in the third and fourth segments of the rape sequence, when Alex is forced to the ground and sodomized. Here she makes three repeated hand motions, each with its own function and meaning within the mise en scène. Alex's hand gestures also draw power from other sequences in the film as well as from sources beyond the film. One of the inevitable difficulties of this scene involves the fact that it poses the classic problem of the rape-revenge genre and of so many other exploitation forms: the violence is horrible, excruciating, and realistic, and yet the victim is desirable, even beautiful, in all her pain. It is not too much to say that an effective rape scene in a high-end rape-revenge movie such as *Irréversible* will horrify and disgust viewers even as it seduces them and turns them on. No matter what one ultimately thinks of this movie, it is impossible to overlook the fact that Noé has mastered this contradictory effect in *Irréversible*. And it is my belief that his subtle use of hand imagery is a very significant aspect of that sort of mastery.

In the third and fourth segments – which together form the tragic, traumatic heart of the film as a whole – Alex's hands do three things. First, they repeatedly try to remove Le Tenia's hands from her mouth, which prevent her from yelling for help or even from breathing freely. These efforts cause Le Tenia to use his own free hand to struggle with hers, which typically ends with him slamming her arm to the ground. But when Le Tenia tries to use his free hand for other purposes, Alex's hand springs back in a ritual struggle to free her mouth. By my count, this stubborn, hopeless dance of hands is repeated at least a dozen times before Le Tenia achieves penetration, becoming a major motif at a climactic moment in the film. During the fourth segment of the sequence, this movement is repeated three more times – but at that point, Alex is clearly more interested in using her free hand to dislodge Le Tenia's penis. In the previous segment, Alex had also used her free hand to interfere with Le Tenia's genital manipulations, but she seemed most interested in freeing her mouth. In the fourth segment, when Le Tenia carries out the violation, this order is reversed, with Alex now much more interested – again, judging by her hand motions – in interfering with the sodomy. The fourth segment also depicts a third set of non-functional motions, which are stressed by the position of the camera on the ground in front of the victim's head. The most heart-rending of these motions features Alex's outstretched hand unfolding in the air, as if to scratch it. Again, because the mise en scène features close-ups with the camera on the ground, a hand reaching toward the camera, fingers rigid and apart, is a dramatic sight, indeed.

These motions are functional in the scene as elements of the hand-to-hand combat of rape. But they are also meaningful in that they provide glimpses of the victim's interior world. For instance, the hand-to-mouth choreography signals Alex's relentless struggle, which communicates in turn her consistent non-consent. *What Noé is doing is ripping away any possibility of reading ambiguity into this rape.* There is no ambivalence here, no emotional complexity at all, just victim and victimizer. This is a horrifying scene filmed by an auteur who wants no question about his feelings or those of his heroine. Besides non-consent, the heroine's feelings include

Figure 8.4. Throughout the lead-up to sodomy, Alex struggles to free her mouth from her rapist's grip. Notice the figure in the background of this frame capture; the figure soon retreats, signalling the pessimistic outlook of the film.

Figure 8.5. In this frame capture, Alex tries to use her hand to dislodge her rapist after he penetrates her.

Figure 8.6. The third function of Alex's hands in the mise en scène of *Irréversible*: to signal trauma.

Figure 8.7. Hands as symbols and indices of trauma in *Irréversible*.

Figure 8.8. This frame capture presents what is perhaps the most poignant, shocking shot in the film: Alex's outstretched hand, which measures the extent of her pain.

pain, anguish, and trauma. Alex's outstretched hand, in particular, functions in the scene as a sign of the physical and psychological traumas of rape. Noé has reported in interviews that he 'could not think of doing a rape scene that would not be painful' (Sterritt, 2007, p. 312) – and Alex's hand captures that pain, which inevitably reverberates beyond the crime. One important way in which this pain reverberates is its effect on the viewer. Noé's insistent lack of ambiguity, the realism of the scene, the incredible agony endured by Alex: this only makes the dilemma of rape-revenge that much more difficult for the viewer to endure. For, in the end, even as she is being beaten and raped, Alex is still beautiful, still desirable. The highly effective way in which Noé constructs the complicity of the audience is what makes the duration of the scene seem longer than it is.

These meanings are apparent enough in context, but they draw further force from their film-historical context. If viewers are familiar with a wide array of art films and exploitation films, they will see in Alex's hand gestures clear references to the many postwar sex scenes and rape scenes in which the explicitness and intensity of the shot was communicated through the hands of the actors, most often through those of a woman. Two iconic examples of this tradition include Malle's *Les amants* – with its famous visuals of Jean Moreau's ecstatic hand suddenly interlocking with that of her lover – and Alain Resnais's *Hiroshima mon amour* (1959) – which features erotic body imagery, including hand imagery, in extreme close-up. In these and other movies, sexual pleasure, and especially orgasm, was often registered through fingers going rigid or a fist balling up around a sheet. Of course, the utility of such scenes was industrial and cultural as well as aesthetic, narrative, and psychological, for one purpose of this imagery was to indicate what was happening to the individuals on screen without violating any market regulations or other censorship concerns. A similar functionality has been achieved by focusing on faces – a tactic that European films have employed at least since Gustav Machatý closed on Hedy Lamarr's face in *Ekstase / Ecstasy* (1933) – but the motif of fingers going rigid or of hands balling into fists gave directors another visual option, one that mimicked the muscular contractions of orgasm in a distinctive, seemingly authentic way. Though such imagery quickly became cliché and is today taken for granted in contemporary cinema, it was introduced to American markets well before the lapse of the Hollywood Production Code in 1968, meaning it was edgy and controversial in its time. This ooh la la factor was heightened when such imagery was combined with rape.

Here it is worth pointing out that in rape scenes this imagery had another narrative function: to demonstrate the victim's non-consent, as in *Irréversible*, or to indicate the victim's coerced pleasure, as in the 'semi-consensual' rape scenes of films like *Lorna*, *Straw Dogs*, and *Wild at Heart*. As I have explained in other writings (Andrews, 2006: 56, 63–5; Andrews, unpub.: 18, n. 21), a semi-consensual rape scene is one that begins non-consensually but that moves toward coerced consent, implying that the victim's sexuality is not fully subject to conscious control. Even after the lapse of the code, this coercive imagery was sure to spark controversy, particularly among feminist commentators who rejected as dangerous and just plain wrong the implication that rape victims could ever take pleasure from a sexual act that had begun non-consensually. In the hands of an exploitation auteur like Meyer, who was happy to court publicity

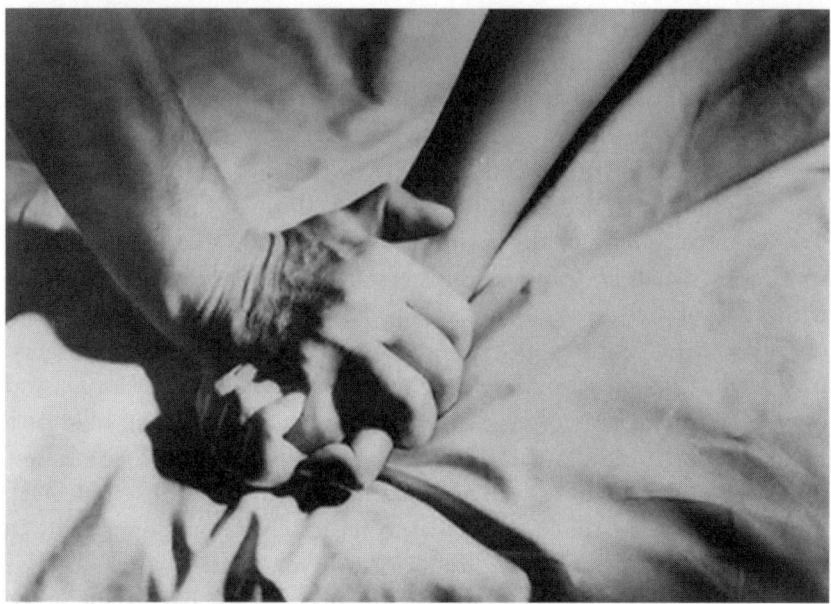

Figure 8.9. Hands signalling orgasmic connection in an iconic art film: a still from *Les amants*.

Figure 8.10. Close-ups of the heroine's hands in erotic imagery from Alain Resnais's *Hiroshima mon amour*.

Figure 8.11. Historically, faces have been used to show female sexual pleasure in art films, with hands being secondary. Here is a shot of Hedy Lamarr in *Ekstase / Ecstasy*.

through controversy, such a scene could factor into an awakening-sexuality narrative in which rape is just one stage in the heroine's journey toward sexual discovery. But directors outside the exploitation circuit tended to use such imagery in more complicated ways. For example, in *Wild at Heart*, Lynch points directly to the hyper-mediated nature of this orgasmic motif through the movie's parodic and patently post-modern repetition of hand images in a trio of sex scenes, including one sequence of coerced pleasure. In that semi-consensual scene, Laura Dern's hand – which has already been established as the main sign of her character's sexual pleasure – is used to show in a peculiarly undeniable way the effect that Willem Dafoe's unwanted clutch has had on her.

Straw Dogs is more analogous to *Irréversible* than either *Lorna* or *Wild at Heart* because it is a serious film that uses naturalistic imagery, including highly realistic hand gestures, in its rape sequence. However, the distinctions between the films are important, too. Ultimately, the films use hand gestures in distinct ways due to broader differences in their narrative and style. Unlike *Irréversible*, *Straw Dogs* has a straight, linear narrative with a great deal of subjective editing to take viewers inside its characters, particularly Amy (Susan George), the rape victim.

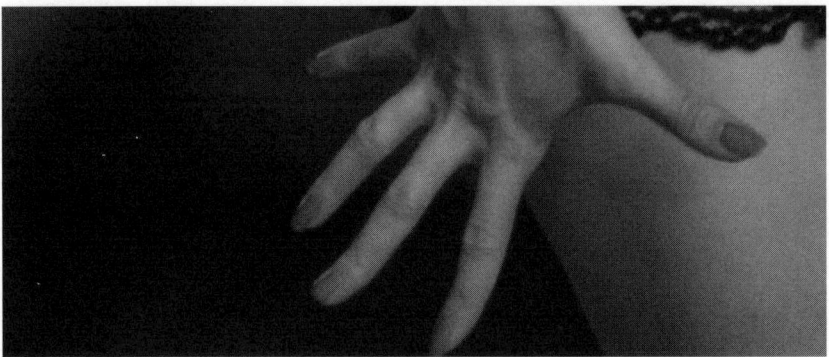

Figure 8.12. Because a wide variety of postwar art films had used hands as sexual symbols, hands could also be used to indicate pleasure or pain in rape scenes. In this frame capture from Lynch's *Wild at Heart*, a film in which the hand is an important sign of sexual pleasure, the heroine's orgasmic hand is used to indicate the 'semi-consensual' trajectory of a psychosexual conflict with a coercive male.

This subjective strategy – which is fundamentally different from Noé's documentary minimalism – entails a focus on faces during the rape sequence that renders the hand imagery secondary. Peckinpah's seven-minute rape scene depicts a double rape scene, including a semi-consensual rape that is by turns brutal and tender as well as a fully non-consensual anal rape in which the rapist (Del Henney) of the first segment is forced to hold Amy down for the second rapist (Ken Hutchison). In the semi-consensual portion, Peckinpah uses George's hands to show his heroine's ambivalence and emotional conflict. At first, the heroine uses her hands to slap and to push her rapist away; then she uses her hands to caress him, to draw him closer. In a pivotal shot, Amy's outstretched fingers are used to show ecstasy – proof, it seems, of her changed feelings. However, the main focus of even this shot is George's face, which twists and turns and mimes pleasure in the standard way of such scenes from Lamarr's time to ours – and this composition reflects Peckinpah's subjective pattern, which places his heroine's hands at the margins of the mise en scène in order to foreground her face. This emphasis on faces makes it easier to understand the director's use of flashcuts, which indicate what is going on inside his heroine's head at times of intense stress. Through this interior compositional method, Peckinpah demonstrates how the trauma of rape causes the rape victim to come psychologically unmoored – to the extent that she eventually sees her husband (Dustin Hoffman) and her assailants as virtual doubles of one another.

Irréversible contains no comparable editing. The film employs a highly objective style that minimizes subjective effects. However, Noé is able to generate a similarly rich and meaningful cinematic texture replete with doublings through careful manipulation of his backward structure – and like Peckinpah, Noé seems to use this texture to argue that violence shrinks the distance between the rapist and those who would avenge the victim.

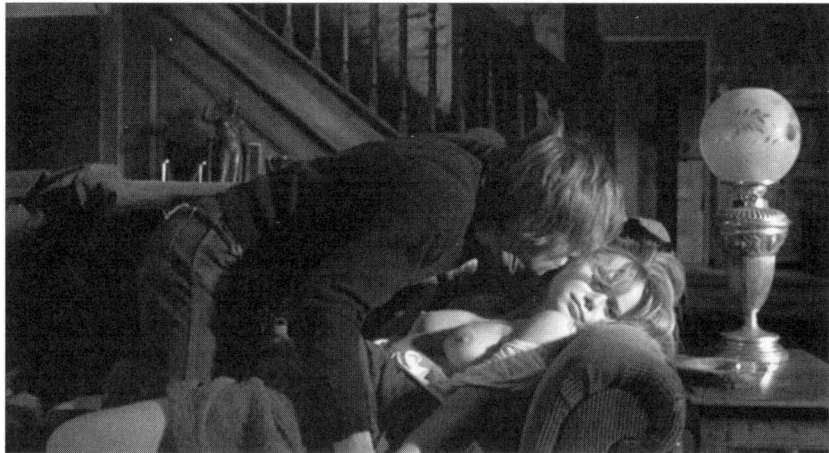

Figure 8.13. This frame capture depicts the hand-to-hand struggles of rape during the non-consensual portion of the semi-consensual scene in Peckinpah's *Straw Dogs*.

Figure 8.14. Frame capture of struggle becoming the hand-to-hand embraces of coerced consent in *Straw Dogs*.

Figure 8.15. From there, the heroine's face is used to indicate her sexual pleasure in the semi-consensual rape scene of *Straw Dogs*, with her hands becoming marginal to the mise en scène.

Because his style is not interior, Noé assigns no less significance to the hands of his main characters than to their faces. Thus, through an elaborate but very subtle pattern of motifs that tie the two domestic scenes (that is, the one at the party and the one at home) to the rape-revenge violence that follows those scenes within the plot, hands emerge as crucial motifs – and predictably it is the hand gestures of Marcus, the boyfriend, and of Pierre, the ex-boyfriend, that mimic the hand gestures of the rapist. For example, Marcus uses his hands to restrain Alex during their dispute at the party – which is characterized by Alex repeatedly pushing Marcus away and finally yelling 'Don't touch me!' at him. During their affectionate post-coital romp before the party, Alex and Marcus seem to double the rape in a different way when Alex moves Marcus's hand away from her mouth as they are waking up and throughout their playful tussling, during which Marcus repeatedly holds Alex down by restraining her hands. If there were any doubt that these motifs are meant to anticipate the rape (in terms of the plot) or to recall it visually (in terms of the backward structure), such doubt is dispelled when the cheerful combatants spit on each other during their romp, which calls to mind Le Tenia's final degradation of Alex. Though the domestic scene is bright and gentle, because of the backward structure, its every frame is fraught with knowledge of the coming violence – and this knowledge is, ironically, darkened further by the perfection of the acting, the realism of the scene and all its touching details, as when Marcus rolls Alex over and reveals her smile using his hand to delicately remove her hair, strand by strand, from her lovely face. Conversely, when Pierre beats the wrong man in The Rectum, rendering him unrecognizable, it calls to mind the moment at the end of the rape when Le Tenia uses his fists to disfigure Alex. In this film, senseless rape violence begets senseless revenge violence in a tragic, ineluctable pattern that interlinks victims, victimizers, and avengers.

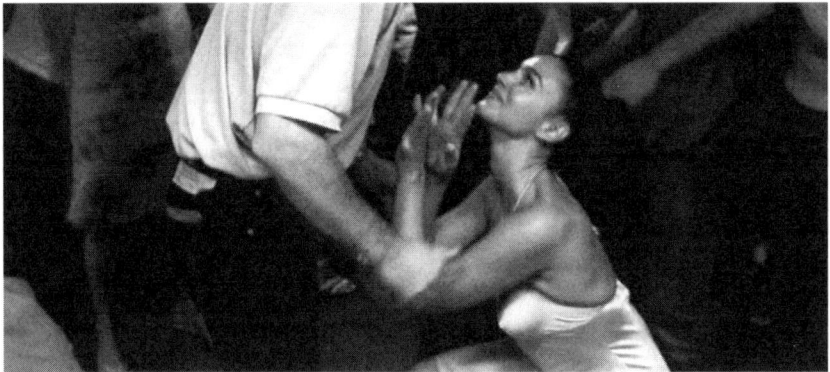

Figure 8.16. After viewers have seen the rape, Alex's hands become ironic symbols of an event that hasn't happened yet in the plot, due to the reverse structure. In this frame capture, she attempts to dance with Pierre at the party.

* * * * *

Noé distinguishes drama from tragedy on the basis of the relative sense of inevitability that is conveyed by a narrative. Thus, as he puts it in an interview, 'in a drama, dramatic things *happen*,' whereas 'in a tragedy, they *unfold*' (Sterritt, 2007: 309; Sterritt's italics). Noé uses his backward structure to short-circuit the drama of *Irréversible*, the sense that *anything* could happen in its plot, while at the same time using that structure to heighten the tragic inevitability of the pain and violence in the film – despite the light and tender scenes that arrive, with their acid irony in tow, at the end of the film. Because the plot unfolds backward, the horror is frontloaded, which means that there is never any sense that the characters can escape their fates or do anything but what the viewer has already seen them do. Marcus will always anger Alex, causing her to leave the party early; and Alex, who mistakenly thinks herself queen of her own fate, will always go home alone, unaware of what awaits her on the way.

Noé believes that there is truth in tragedy, for he does not think that people have anything but 'present freedom', by which he means the ability at any given moment to choose between coffee or tea, i.e., between relatively trivial and momentary specificities. But in a general and ultimately more significant sense, '[y]ou're not free from fighting for your survival, and the survival of the species,' for 'you're not free from your genes' or your 'genetic code' or your 'guts,' which lead you on 'above anything your brain can tell you' (Sterritt, 2007: 309). According to this logic, Marcus angers Alex not because he makes some bad choices but because he is *Marcus*, while Alex leaves the party so impetuously not because she is unaware of the dangers of the Parisian streets but because she is *Alex*. The same personality dynamics that made this couple so charismatic in the post-coital scene make it likely to blow up in unpredictable ways. The only character who on first glance seems to go against his 'guts', i.e., against his manifest personality, is Pierre, whose misdirected violence seems excessive and just plain odd, given how self-possessed and self-conscious he has seemed until then. On the other hand, in bludgeoning the wrong man to death, it may be that Pierre has simply chosen that moment to apply the advice that Alex had given him on the train. There, she counselled him that the key to giving someone else sexual pleasure was to think only of oneself. (The irony of this advice, of course, is that it describes fairly exactly the way in which Alex's rapist behaves.) According to Alex, Pierre needed to do less thinking and more *feeling*, more *acting*. When he kills the stranger in The Rectum, Pierre, who still loves Alex, may be struggling to do just that: he is trying to *feel* and to *act*, hoping to avenge the crimes against her. But the strain of self-consciousness that hovers over this disastrous violence reminds the viewer that no one can act out of character. From this perspective, Pierre kills the stranger not because his blood is boiling but because he is bloodless *Pierre* – a man who has always been too self-conscious for his own good.

The choreography of hands that unfolds in the rape scene fits into this narrative texture. It is a mini-tragedy that captures in microcosm the tragic dimensions of the film as a whole. Throughout this sequence, Alex continues to resist her attacker. But there is no sense that she will ever be successful. Her free hand goes to her mouth, it is wrenched down; her free hand goes to her mouth, it is wrenched down. The unbearable sadness of this real-time ritual goes a long way toward explaining what exactly it was that so upset viewers during the film's festival exposure at Cannes. After all, they were not seeing anything particularly explicit during the rape scene; indeed, the only truly graphic shots were those of Alex being beaten after the rape itself was over. Indeed, one of the main reasons that the camera was placed in *front* of Alex was that Noé needed a compelling way of showing the rape without showing the penetration. (For, of course, there was no 'real' penetration; in that sense, the audience infers a physical violation that does not actually happen on the acting plane.) Noé was able to do this by focusing the viewer's attention on the smallest, most human of gestures: a woman under sexual siege trying to free her mouth, her voice, and having no luck, never having any luck.

Noé has claimed that he has never made a film in the hope that its violence would cause viewers to flee the theatre. But he has not minded that viewers sometimes have. As he tells interviewer David Sterritt, he walked out of *Straw Dogs* during its rape sequence when he first saw the film. Nevertheless, he now considers *Straw Dogs* a 'great' film (Sterritt, 2007: 312) – which explains, perhaps, why he asked Sterritt early in the same interview whether the viewers upset by *Irréversible* in Cannes ended up liking his movie later, much as he had ended up admiring Peckinpah's movie (Sterritt, 2007: 308). Like Peckinpah before him, Noé set out to film 'the greatest rape scene ever' (Weddle, 1994: 420), but the crassness of that shared intention never disrupted the sophistication of their success. One reason for this was that visual explicitness wasn't crucial to the outcome of their work. What was crucial were all the little things done well and acted perfectly, like the choreography of hands in *Irréversible*.

It is worth noting that Peckinpah's tragic vision is similar to Noé's in several key respects. As a film-maker who came of age in the wake of second-wave feminism, Noé is much more sensitive to the plight of women than Peckinpah ever was. But neither auteur compromises his tragic vision in order to satisfy what he considers progressive wishful thinking. What I mean by this is that neither auteur is willing to say that people, and men in particular, can through education and reform civilize themselves away from their chemical propensity for violence. Peckinpah signalled this attitude through his fascination with the writings of Robert Ardrey, a popular anthropologist of the 1960s who claimed that violence was integral to humanity's ancestral inheritance. No matter how liberal Peckinpah was himself – and he was surprisingly liberal, given his badboy reputation – he never let his ideals interfere with his conviction that violence was a fundamental part of human nature (Andrews, unpub.: 3–5, 15–16; also Weddle, 1994 and Prince, 1998). Similarly, Noé does not seem capable of making a movie in which his characters do not suffer violent ends. Though his characters often have light and hopeful dispositions – except, of course, in *Seul contre tous* – it rarely makes any difference. Thus, even Alex, a strong-willed optimist who tells Marcus that 'women always choose' their sexual partner, is forced during the rape sequence to recognize that women do not *always* choose. As a consequence, Noé has been no less controversial in his offerings than Peckinpah, whose incredibly subtle treatment of sex and violence almost inevitably elicited charges of misogyny and brutishness.

* * * * *

What does it mean that much of *Irréversible*'s power – which emanates most forcefully from its rape sequence, with its violence, degradation, and dehumanization – may be felt through quiet imagery like the aforementioned interplay of hands? Brinkema (2005: 50) places Noé's use of hands in a Deleuzian framework, arguing that the force of this imagery is meant to invoke a 'traumatized body [...] as a constitutively decentered filmic and metaphysical space' that erases gender. But these obtusely *academic* statements seem more than a little uncalled for. A better way to look at this imagery is to see in it Noe's tragic vision in miniature. This asserts something basic and human, even animal: persistence in the face of hopelessness. The haunting ordinariness says it all.

It is a *constructed* ordinariness, of course – for it was made from allusions to the hand play of a thousand other sex scenes and rape scenes in a thousand other art films and exploitation films. And it was made from the skill of its actors. Those hands, whose movement is so fragile and human, are part and parcel with the craft displayed by Belluci throughout the rape sequence. There, Bellucci's acting is neither overdone nor falsely erotic or 'semi-consensual'. Indeed, if one really looks, one can see that the scene, which is allegedly so over-the-top (MacKenzie, 2010: 162), is so minimal as to seem real. For example, the penis of the rapist – an effect added in post-production – is both there and not there, neither grandly phallic nor entirely tucked away. The dress, the scenery, the duration, everything is so understated as to remain credible. As noted, this minimalism led some viewers to think that the sex, though not exactly rape, was at least real for the actors (Sterritt, 2007: 311–12), qualifying the film as a 'real sex' rape-revenge flick like Coralie Trinh Thi and Virginie Despentes' *Baise-moi* (2000). But it was not – and the viewers did not have any real reason for thinking it was. They were instead led to this false conclusion by terrific film-making – and by a tragedy of hands.

Chapter 9

ANTICHRIST, EXPLICIT SEX, ANXIETY, AND CARE

TORBEN GRODAL

Lars von Trier's *Antichrist* is an art film and it is also a film that has a 'pornographic' explicitness in its portrayal of the naked human body and sexual intercourse. On the one hand the film brutally exposes the human body, its lusts and painful frailty, with the intention of creating strong bodily arousal in the viewer, seeking to 'turn them on'. On the other hand the film has very many lyrical images of landscapes which evoke a sense of serene detachment, or perhaps a sense of romanticism. The film also wilfully presents images which evoke a visceral sense of bodily disgust or fear, as in central scenes where the character 'She' masturbates the character 'He' to the point of his ejaculating blood – a pinnacle of 'orgasm as a bodily mutilation', or when the camera lets us witness in detail how she cuts off her clitoris.

In the following chapter I will argue that the film is centrally about the experiences of being imprisoned in the body and about the multiple strategies which characters take in the film for gaining control by a series of different fantasies. Intriguingly this control is achieved through the painful but sometimes also gratifying feelings of being in the grips of bodily arousal.

MODESTY AND OTHER CONTROL MECHANISMS OF SEX AND EMBODIEDNESS

Because sexuality is such a strong, basic drive, sexual behaviour and the communication of sex-related phenomena are strongly regulated and negotiated in real life as well as in media. Without regulation our lust would likely cause a level of chaos in our society. There are several interpretations / rationales behind this phenomenon. One dominant explanation of this is prevalent within the monotheistic religions: sexuality has its roots in the animal aspect of human beings and should be strongly suppressed; sexuality should be used only for procreation within the framework of marriage and therefore the presentation of the body should be ruled by modesty. The good aspects of humanity therefore rest in its immaterial body-less soul. Another explanation is the emancipatory one that has been important in the twentieth century. According to this sexuality is a good, natural thing that has been suppressed by an authoritarian society, and any modesty is a sign of suppression. Any restrictions on the display of and unfolding of sexuality are evil and should be abolished. Neither of these dominant explanations or normative positions are very helpful.

Let us first look at some of the regulatory mechanisms that may have a direct biological foundation due to evolutionary processes. Let us start with Darwin and his idea of sexual selection. He argued in *On the Origin of Species* (1859: ch. 4) that a central driver of evolution was sexual selection because of an evolutionarily driven fight for good genes by mating with somebody that triggered feelings of selective advantage. Thus, on the one hand, sex is strongly gratifying and thereby strongly compelling; it needs to be in order to guarantee an urge to procreate, and all of the attendant difficulties and competition which comes with finding a mate. On the other hand, evolutionary processes strongly support choice, especially female choice, as argued by Darwin, because females bear the larger part of the cost of having offspring, and therefore have the largest advantage of choosing optimal partners. The motives for selection are in some respects more important for humans than for other mammals, because the burden of rearing children stretches for long periods of time.

The concern for procreation and the concern for choice motivates two strong, but opposed mechanisms to regulate sex: the sexual urge on the one hand, the wish for having control over one's own body, including who penetrates / is being penetrated by whom on the other hand. The urge for control is reflected in mechanisms such as modesty, a control of whom to give access to one's tender parts and restrictions of who may have visual or acoustic access to your sexual processes. The reason for this is that visual access to organs related to sexuality and sounds related to sexual intercourse may inspire unwanted sexual attention in onlookers and those hearing the sounds. The sexual flirting and foreplay that is partly built upon care and playful behaviour are behaviours that are centrally aimed at overcoming control functions and wishes for body autonomy. Negotiation of sexual relation is a universal fact of most of the animal kingdom that may rely on dominance-submission patterns, but also on playful negotiation and caring intimacy.

This conflict between autonomy and heteronomy is not only something that is linked to sexuality. At a certain age all children will have an ambivalent attitude to being cared for: I can do this and that by myself, I want to put on my shoes myself, I do not want to be embraced right now. Violation of body autonomy is in *Antichrist* not only linked to sexuality by the way in which the woman brutally mutilates the man and his tender parts by force. One of the strangest elements in the film is that the mother may have caused issues in her son's (Nic) physical development by giving him the right shoe for the left foot and vice versa: a perversion of care. The bottom line is that modesty as a control mechanism for sexual engagement is not only something that is based on cultural effects in socialization, but also has components that rely on the fitness-enhancing aspects of a certain level of self-control that has biological underpinnings, for the reason mentioned above that those that choose a fit partner for having children - good DNA and / or resources - will have children with better survival chances.

The rape is the ultimate confrontation of urges of autonomy in conflict with the desires of others, and the rape or the sex act under some external pressure is one of the central themes in von Trier's oeuvre. The rape exemplifies how one person regulates his or her sexuality by violating the other person's strong urge for autonomy, as in the continuous forced scenes of sex in *Dogville* or the way in which the heroine in *Breaking the Waves* is forced by her love of her husband to submit herself to sex acts with those whom she has no emotional connection nor physical attraction. Sexual intercourse in von Trier's films very often involves violations of body integrity. Intercourse cannot be negotiated through situations of care and mutual consent, only forced upon the other by rape.

I mentioned above that considerations of freedom of choice of partner are a motive for modesty as a regulator of sexuality that explains why modesty may be rooted in biology. There are additionally also other strong reasons for a certain regulation of the audiovisual access to tender parts and sounds, one of them being the wish for conflict avoidance. Sex creates strong conflicts in most of the animal kingdom by male competition for mating rights and female competition for male resources, and humans are no exception. Many crimes in society are based around sexual jealousy.

Furthermore, sex is also linked to the distribution of resources and the build-up of social networks for instance through marriage, prostitution or sex-based favouritism. Modesty-related considerations are the reason why, universally, there are restrictions on the display of sexual behaviour in public and rules about how to display the naked body. The purpose of course being that the visual access to sex-related phenomena may ignite onlookers in inappropriate ways and create conflict.

The precise expression of such modesty-behaviours is, however, strongly moulded by different cultural practices. Tropical hunter-gatherers may only cover the genitals whereas certain Muslim women are fully covered. The signalling of erotic attractiveness and erotic desire are therefore often an act of balancing two opposed wishes and may cause the emission of contradictory signals: to signal erotic attractiveness and to signal modesty and control. Nudity not only becomes a mere fact, but a sign of sexual accessibility. However, the very acts of partly shielding the visual access to the naked body may also fuel types of signalling that activate seeking, the dopamine-based craving for pleasures which demand some active striving to achieve.

The same balancing acts between speeding and braking sexual signals, which are an inherent characteristic of modesty, are also found in the audiovisual representations of sex-related phenomena. In the prologue to *Antichrist* the full view of penetration is counterbalanced with slow motion and black-and-white photography to provide indications of reduced reality. It is a far cry from the high-definition colour cinematography found in contemporary cinematography.

Furthermore, some of the sexual images later on in the film are imbued with associations to cultural phenomena from earlier ages such as when an act of intercourse is linked to images similar to those of fifteenth-century painter Hieronymus Bosch, or the lore surrounding Blocksberg, a German mountain believed to be the home of witches and fertility rites. Similarly some medieval pictures of the torturing of women, that are supposedly working material for 'She' in her dissertation, provide the explicit sexual scenes with a cultural and associative frame. That the scenes on some level are exhibitionist, directed at creating arousal in viewers is obvious, especially within the framework of Trier's oeuvre, and it uses the art film framing to make it acceptable. The art film framing consists in the claim that what is on the screen should not be regarded as pure entertainment but as film elements pointing to some higher and more abstract ideas and meanings similar to religious rituals that are not to be taken in a literal sense (Grodal, 2009). To use cultural frames to

Figure 9.1. In this picture from *Antichrist*, the intercourse between 'He' and 'She' is foiled by a mythological frame. Thereby their intercourse becomes abstract and anonymous, a symbolic manifestation of the human condition.

expose and control at the same time is an old business, as when biblical or mythological themes have been used as excuses for portraying nudity, portrayals of paradise being an obvious excuse for nakedness.

The twentieth century has witnessed a long process of balancing ideas of public modesty versus ideas that viewing audiovisual representations of hard-core sex in cinemas or in private should be considered as taking place in private, unregulated spaces. Opponents of free access to audiovisual sex representations think that such explicit portrayals would provide a moral contagion, whereas adherents have used different arguments. In the 1960s, art films and art novels had a central role in this negotiation because those in favour of explicit representation argued that such portrayals were not only made to create sexual arousal, but served higher ideals of portraying reality etc. When hard-core porn was legalized it had some years as a cinema event, but with the advent of channel TV and the VHS–DVD-revolution hard-core porn functioned as a private experience, so that people in the public space might live by the same modesty rules as before the porn revolution but witness sexual acts in their private spheres. Whether this will also be the case in the future is not easy to predict.

Viewing porn film as opposed to viewing sexual organs and intercourse in real life relies on the way in which the relation to other people's bodies has become audiovisually concrete, yet abstract in relation to other senses: the actors are out of reach and therefore cannot provide a concrete experience of touch, smell and taste. The audiovisual nature of porn films further emphasizes those aspects of sexuality that may become visible; the positions and activities are aimed at providing a maximum of visibility, such that oral sex has prominence because it is observable. Furthermore, it is an anonymous relation that has no direct social consequences; the interaction emphasizes that this is an 'abstract' pleasurable relation between the two sexes; any healthy individual of the other sex is OK, the problems of choice and negotiation have become negated. The sex act is not passionate, not an expression of a high arousal. This is in stark contrast with most hard-core sex scenes in von Trier, that either describe the sex act as an expression of force, of the rape type, or of the 'romantic' passions that override the rational parts of brain control, or out of social obligation, including the 'love' that motivates Bess in *Breaking the Waves* to prostitute herself. Von Trier creates a series of situations where Bess gives up her body autonomy without gaining any personal pleasure in order to provide the 'dirty details' to the man she loves.

BODY DISGUST AND IDEAS OF SPIRITUAL PURITY

Central in *Antichrist*'s use of cultural associations to frame its strong images of sexuality are its references to the biblical story of the fall from innocence in Paradise. The vacation cabin that is the location of the majority of the film's action is Eden. In the Christian tradition the exodus from Paradise – that represented a kind of natural innocence without sexuality and therefore no need for modesty – is linked primarily to a misogynistic idea that an awakening of female sexuality is the primary reason for this sinfulness.

Ideas of purity as the negation of sex and body is based on the idea that the essence of humans is their soul, their spirit that may sometimes be controlled by something physical and impure, the human physical body. To negate the cravings of the body is to set the immaterial soul free, hence it achieves autonomy vis-à-vis the cravings of the body. The idea of the soul is therefore often heavily based on recruiting basic emotions related to disgust directed at all aspects of our bodily existence. Disgust proper has evolved as a tool to avoid contamination from bad food, rotting corpses, faeces and other bodily fluids and the extreme form of corporeality, death. In those discourses that use disgust as a tool for extreme sexual abstinence, sexual intercourse is mentally linked with such experiences of contamination by ingestion, and touch, and the sexual organs are indeed both sites of pleasure and desire, and sites of possible contamination of various kinds. The scene in *Antichrist* that shows a deer with its bloody offspring nearly fully born might strengthen such ideas of the uncleanliness of embodied processes, as opposed to the fresh and clean images of the plants in the final images of the film and the relative purity of the intercourse in the prologue in its black-and-white and slow motion dream-purity (although this intercourse represents the 'aboriginal sin' in which the parents' lust blocks care). Those sex scenes that take place after the prologue are perhaps meant to provide arousal, but not pleasure in the minds of the viewers, because the sex scenes are strongly linked to the feelings of a painful, horror-like experience of being possessed. The emotional urges from deep down in 'She's brainstem and limbic system cannot be controlled by the rational arguments from 'He's forebrain. 'He's arguments in relation to 'She' are based on cognitive therapy, and via the links to Christian and heathen mythology (the idea of witches, for instance), the urges from the old parts of the embodied brain are provided with demonic overtones.

The body is thus the site of an ongoing ambivalence: the body is a site of heteronomy, as when it is hurt and its frail physicality is exposed, it is a site of uncleanliness and contamination. The urges of the body are seated in the lower parts of the brain, outside rational cognitive control. A long tradition therefore blames the body of the feelings of heteronomy when the (rational) mind is overwhelmed by cravings of the body and the lower parts of the brain. But the body is also a site of pleasure as in the intercourse of the prologue.

The purity ideas in the film are linked to disinterested perception, of a consciousness that is not forced by any emotional urges to do anything special, but just perceive and contemplate. This is in accordance with many traditions of so-called spirituality, Western as well as Eastern: because any situation that may cause arousal may also cause negative emotions linked to a strong sense of a lack of control of the strength of arousal. To link the body and its physicality with disgust and pain may therefore be regarded as a control procedure to avoid arousal, just as the transformation of action-oriented emotions to contemplative feelings are control procedures (on feelings see Damasio, 2012, and Grodal, 2009 that lay forward a model of brain processes – the PECMA flow model – that explains the difference between narrative emotionality and lyrical portrayals of atemporal feelings).

LUST, ANGER, FEAR, PANIC, SADNESS, CARE, AND AROUSAL

Arousal control seems to be the central problem in *Antichrist* and other von Trier films. So let us look at the physiology and psychology of arousal and how it sets the stage for the different scenarios in *Antichrist*, caused especially by lust, rage, and fear. (My references for the description of these emotional systems are especially Panksepp, 2005 and Panksepp and Biven, 2012.) At the top of our brain we have the voluntary nervous system that controls our (striated) muscles so that we may control our actions. The voluntary 'top' of our embodiedness is supported by a series of processes that are controlled by the autonomic nervous system, called autonomic because it is outside our voluntary control. The autonomic system consists of two subsystems, the sympathetic nervous system that is in charge of arousal. The sympathetic nervous system is the system for energizing the body for action and provides maximum energy to the muscles. It may cause heavy breathing, fast heartbeat, muscular tension, sweat, dry mouth and so on, regulated by different neurotransmitters such as adrenaline (Gazzaniga et al., 2009: 88). As directly mentioned in *Antichrist* by 'He' in a 'lecture' in Eden to 'She', such mechanisms will for instance prepare for fight and flight (anger and fear) but are also partly responsible for the unfolding of the physiological responses which accompany sexual lust.

The parasympathetic nervous system has the opposite effect. It relaxes the body, provides saliva for food intake, prepares the stomach for food, switches on the cooling of the body from sweat by causing the dilation of blood vessels in the skin (Gazzaniga et al., 2009: 88f). In addition, deep grief and depression are also parasympathetic reactions, but of course not motivated by pleasure, but by giving up all action tendencies. Sexuality is ambiguous, because the giving up of autonomy and acceptance of physical union relies on parasympathetic elements, erection presupposes a relaxation to let the blood flow to the penis, and often a relaxation to accept bodily proximity; however the act itself has strong sympathetic elements (Zillmann, 1998). A few times in *Antichrist* there are moments of playful, parasympathetic-evoking foreplay, but mostly the eroticism is sympathetic, based on violent craving.

That sympathetic bodily arousal underpins several rather different emotional reaction patterns may however create confusion, a confusion that is central to the many emotional ambiguities in *Antichrist*, and the basis for many of those behaviours that previously were called perverse. An emotion is a motivational urge to achieve some goals. An enemy may cause anger and rage that create bodily arousal as a support for confronting the enemy with actions that will create relief so that the arousal disappears. Sexual lust creates arousal that should lead to actions leading to orgiastic pleasure and relief. Fear creates arousal that should motivate for actions such as flight to create relaxation. Panic by separation from significant others such as the separation of mother and child creates arousal that should motivate for striving for a reunion with the significant others to create relaxation.

In principle arousal is linked to some action patterns, some 'narrative scripts' that outline what actions to perform in order to achieve the goals inscribed in the emotions. Normally therefore the arousal is linked to an awareness of what goal-situation would bring an end to the arousal. The script might in the case of sexual arousal be: search for sex partner, have sex, have orgasm, after which sympathetic arousal stops and is transformed to parasympathetic relaxation. The generic patterns are often such macro-formulae for the relation between emotions, actions and release conditions (Grodal, 1997: 2009).

Except by contextual analysis it is however often difficult for a spectator to figure out what a given sign of arousal links to and whether it creates pleasure or pain. Some of the signs of sexual arousal and of anxiety are similar because they are two different aspects of bodily arousal. The heavy breathing, and the moaning expressions may not provide a clue as to whether breathing and moaning is an expression of sexual arousal and orgasm-induced pleasure or whether it is caused by an anxiety attack, or whether, as with the female tennis player (Sharapova) the moans are signs of her extreme effort to hit the ball (modesty considerations have led to restrictions on her moans).[1] If no context is given, the facial expressions of a tortured person may be interpreted as pleasure. Sadists are ignited by the sheer signs of bodily arousal in their victims, whether these signs have a pleasant or an unpleasant cause and feel that they may get outlet by pain-inflicting actions. Sex is a social bond between people and a central part of the pleasure is that one's partner also enjoys the act, but for sadists the sheer arousal of the other is pleasing, whether the arousal of the other is due to pain or pleasure.

If a person confuses or misinterprets the causes of arousal he or she may then switch action goals and relaxation means. He or she may non-consciously be sexually aroused and try to get relief by anger (instead of by intercourse), eventually enhanced by disgust at the target of desire or getting relief by the agony-arousal of the victim. He or she might be in a stage of panic arousal and try to get relief by sex or by self-inflicted pain or even suicide. Or he or she wants to get aroused to circumvent strong modesty functions and try to create a panic situation as in bondage situations. Or create such fear that it creates submissive freeze reactions typical of total surrender (Grodal, 2009). What if facial expressions of pain are confused with facial expressions of sexual pleasure or sounds of orgasm confused with sounds of suffering? I will show that such experimentations with a steady emotional re-contextualization of arousal are central to *Antichrist*.

PANIC AROUSAL

A key scene early in the film is when 'She' experiences a violent panic attack shortly after she has complained about 'He' that he has always been distant. It starts with the rumbling, scary sound from 'nature', a variant of which will reappear in *Melancholia* as a sign of the end of the world. We then have a series of stylistically very elaborate ultra-close-ups, of an eye that anxiously looks around, of the skin of her neck that is vibrating, a close-up of a trembling hand, the skin above the breasts engaged in breathing, a mouth deformed in pain and so on. Then sounds of heavy, panicked breathing. We exit the ultra-close-ups and see her body jerk with muscular activity that points to panicky pain. This is the central scene of arousal in the film, and all the other arousal scenes are, as we will see, efforts to transform the panic arousal to other forms that may have releasing mechanisms like orgasm or death or the aggressive mutilation of others or even being a masochistic object as when 'She' wants 'He' to beat her to heighten her arousal.

It is no accident that the pictures of arousal are made in ultra-close-ups, because it is their autonomous nature that is significant. The body fragments are subhuman, that is, they express sub-voluntary reactions and thus flaunt how different parts of the body may have a relative autonomy. This is the opposite of portraying a body that is fully controlled by the conscious will, or, expressed in more religious terms, a material body controlled by the spirit. These aroused vibrations of skin in an anxious arousal are even metaphorically projected on nature that in this early phase of the film is depicted as demonic and 'alive'. By means of a camera technique christened by von Trier as The Baby Lens, special lenses are mounted in front of the major camera lens, causing the image of the woods in the film's opening to vibrate in a demonic bodily arousal.

'She's breathing problems, that 'He' tries to get under control by telling her to count, to do the breathing in a controlled way, and the centrality of the vibrating flesh around the neck may also point to suffocation anxiety. As if her heavy breathing is caused by a fear of suffocation; suffocation problems points forward to 'She's death by strangulation. Some of the ultra-close-ups in the panic scene are repeated in connection with the way in which he kills her: by using his hands around her neck so that she asphyxiates. In the original manuscript 'She' asks him to kill her[2] as if his act could be regarded as helping her to commit a kind of suicide to get relief from her painful arousal. To some extent it is therefore a parallel to previous suffocations in von Trier's films. Medea's boys are hanged by their mother; one of the sons even requests it. The mother in *Dancer in the Dark* sacrifices her own life and agrees to be hanged in order to safeguard the money that will guarantee her son's eye-operation and thus give her peace from her strong care-based arousal. Death is of course a relief from arousal, just as orgasm is often called 'la petite morte', the little death. Men that are hanged will mostly die with a large erection,[3] and during female orgasm the frontal parts of the brain have strongly diminished blood flow (Georgiadas et al., 2006). The use of suffocation as a booster of sexual orgasm is called erotic asphyxiation and is for instance exemplified in Oshima's *In the Realm of the Senses*, and low oxygen levels in the brain may emit dopamine and endorphins, desire and pleasure neurotransmitters (Lloyd, 1986). But we need not presuppose that von Trier intended a fully sexual orgasm-framework for the scene, only a framework that sees death as an exit strategy for levels of arousal that are too high to bear (nearly all main characters in von Trier's oeuvre die and find peace).

The dominant reason for panic is, as mentioned, separation anxiety, and the main remedy for this is closeness and care. However, anxious fear may lose clear relations to concrete fear-evoking situations. Fear proper is directed at specific dangers, so when these dangers are removed or you have moved away from the fear-evoking situation, the fear stops. But chronic anxiety is not defined in relation to some specific phenomena or situations. The anxiety becomes a general state of anxious alertness and arousal. Therefore, there are no precise shutdown conditions or shutdown actions, and the anxious person may perform ritualistic obsessive-compulsive actions, checking, washing, hoarding, or whatever (Woody and Szechtman, 2011). Nightmares are episodes of extreme high arousal in a situation where the action outlet is blocked by the sleep atonia of the muscles.

In *Antichrist* 'She' uses sex, violent sex, as a means of transforming the anxious arousal to an arousal that seems to have a mechanism for shutting down the arousal and re-labelling the negative feelings linked to the arousal to positive erotic feelings. In the beginning of her anxiety she just wants violent sex without foreplay. Later, to boost arousal and maybe to boost orgasm she tries to solicit a sadomasochistic relation by appealing to 'He' to hit her. She also transforms her anxiety to anger and rage, first by molesting him and later by trying to kill him.

EROTIC AROUSAL, BODY DISGUST AND LYRICAL TONING

The emotional impact of the film has two or three intertwined but different layers: the level of the psychological motivations of the characters as portrayed in the film, the level of the impact of the film and its elements on the viewers, and additionally, the motivations of the director, Lars von Trier for doing the film. Because of the prominence of his oeuvre and because of the way in which he is marketing his own life as part of his films, this angle is certainly a valid aspect of an understanding of his film. The film has been described as being misogynistic; however it is important to emphasize that 'She' in most respects is von Trier's alter ego. She, like von Trier, suffers from a serious anxiety disorder, she has trouble finishing her important work, and like von Trier she feels herself threatened by those firm, rationalist doctors that according to her have no real understanding of her problems (cf. the polemics in *Riget / The Kingdom* against science and reason – as opposed to occult knowledge). In his first real fiction film, the 'The Orchid Gardener' (not accessible for public screening) in which Trier himself acts as the main character, he parades as a naked, miserable young man that flashes his own frontal nudity in front of women that are not turned on by his flesh. He has several dreams of empowerment. For instance he dresses himself as a Nazi officer in an effort to imagine a major archetype of empowerment, or dresses himself in women's clothes. His basic self-understanding is that of being a victim, even using his supposedly Jewish background to imagine being a concentration camp victim (also inspired by the film *The Night Porter* (cf. Björkman, 2003). However, a background fantasy of the experiences of being a victim is to get control by 'turning evil' and assume a Nazi role to obtain empowerment. The double sadomasochistic identity as victim and torturer is visible even in his name: his real name is Lars

Trier, Trier being a Jewish name, whereas the 'Nazi' middle name 'von' is an artistic add-on to the Jewish family name, made to provoke and to flash a kind of demonic masculinity, with the 'He' in *Antichrist* being a watered down version of masculine power, whereas 'She' may be seen as trying to achieve empowerment by 'turning evil' in the middle of the film by becoming an antichrist, a Satan. She starts out having a bad conscience because she feels that the death of her son is due to her negligence, but she ends up performing violent acts against her husband (and further it is implied that her interest in the history of witches may not only be innocent and scholarly).

The question of provoking, of being an exhibitionist that flashes his own naked body, of flirting with 'turning evil' and taking full control over other people's bodies brings us back to the question of arousal control that takes place as well at the level of von Trier's relation to the viewers and at the level of 'She's emotional state. In the diegesis 'She' takes control and tries to manage her arousal by violence. And von Trier produces exhibitionist scenes that insist on inducing arousal in the viewers by means of a penis that ejaculates blood and a clitoris that is cut off, both acts that create strong arousal in the viewers even if the arousal is based on strong disgust.

The scenes are exhibitionist in the sense that they force experiences on others, on viewers, even if these experiences are unwanted. What exhibitionists crave is that the(ir) naked bodies create arousal in the bodies and faces of the onlookers; not necessarily a positive lustful arousal: a reaction of disgust is better than no reaction. Even the disgust reaction is a sign of existence as an embodied person. When von Trier stages a scene in which the highly visible penis ejaculates blood it certainly creates arousal of disgust in the minds of the viewers, just as the close-up sight of a clitoris that is cut off and spurts blood is arousing. But the sexual part of the arousal is only a small part that reflects the transgression of modesty rules, the major part of the arousal stems from the disgust of viewing the painful and miserable physicality of the flesh, and the brutality by which the film-maker flaunts that physicality. The film 'turns evil' to create arousal, even by negative means.

However, the film is an art film. It wants to filter its emotional brutality. Important is the way in which the stylistic framing and the cultural associations of the imagery and narrative allow for an overall lyrical-poetic toning of the arousing events. This has already been introduced in the prologue, where the black-and-white slow motion images of intercourse blends with beautiful pictures of snow and a soft, 'pleasant' fall into death, it proceeds through lyrical portrayals of the woods and ends in mythical-lyrical scenes at the mountainside. As in paintings like those of Hieronymus Bosch, the crude physicality of the body in the film somehow becomes mental images by the very artfulness of their execution. By transforming physical photographic presence into mental images the film negates the full impact of their physicality. A similar movement from physical realism to symbolic presentation takes place when those animals that earlier in the film were bloody, like the deer in labour, suddenly at the end are transformed to a sweet iconicity just as the green grass gets a black-and-white abstract purity at the end of the film (colour is linked to the tactile and gustatory mechanisms in the brain and black-and-white photography therefore has a more abstract feel). The raw disgusting nature is not really raw after all when it has become humanized by von Trier's artistic efforts. Even if many viewers may reject this artistic, lyrical and mythical framing, and call his films trash, others may transform even the negatively toned arousal to lyrical feelings. After all, art is (also) emotion regulation.

ANXIETY AROUSAL AND THE URGE FOR CARE

The prologue's rendering of lust and of the death of the innocent child somehow appears as a pleasant, lyrical exploration of the world, and the death appears to be a playful jump into soft white snow that almost may be perceived as soft white pillows. The music expresses a controlled urge for bonding and care, a softened distress call (Grodal, 2012). The distress calls that are missing do however appear in the film. At around the midpoint and the turning point of the narrative we hear Nic crying on the soundtrack, about the same time as 'She' suddenly claims that she has become cured, and when her anxiety attacks are transformed to aggressive eroticism. Nic's distress calls are perhaps non-diegetic and seem in supernatural fashion to come from the wood, from nature, but may also be hallucinations, expressions of 'She's guilt, in parallel to her guilt at having caused his death by neglect and perhaps for damaging his feet by transposing his left and right shoes. So, the 'healing' and the aggressive sexuality seem to be linked to a suppression of care and tenderness.

The film also at that point perhaps makes an allusion to the story of Oedipus; 'She' states ironically in her discussion with 'He' about his cognitive therapy of her that 'Freud is dead', although she herself perhaps has mutilated her son's feet. Oedipus means 'swollen feet' due to a molestation done to him as a child to prevent him from killing his father and marrying his mother, although in Nic's case it is the mother that does the mutilation. The short glance that Nic in the prologue directs at his copulating parents might seem as a casual reference to Freud's idea of the primal scene in which the child observes the parents' intercourse and interprets it as an expression of violence. The totality of the film, however, does not confirm an Oedipal reading of the film, on the contrary it confirms that 'Freud is dead', because the central problem is not an Oedipal story about sexual desire between son and mother. What 'She' wants is care, although when 'He' provides it she feels that it is an infringement of her autonomy. 'She' mutilates the feet of her husband by drilling a hole in one of his legs and attaches a heavy object to the leg to prevent him from running away. And when he later on nevertheless escapes, she emits angry distress calls: 'Don't you dare to leave me.' Thus, even if 'She' hungers for care, she mutilates and violates those that she cares for. The bottom line seems to be that due to deep-seated problems with care and playful intimacy, the primary model of how to relate to another body is that of violence and aggression.

CONCLUSION

Antichrist seems to be a tragedy of human embodiedness. The film does not portray the basic pleasure of human embodiedness, typical of the mainstream hard-core porn film. Neither is it a romantic worship of bonding and intimacy, based on embodiedness as playfulness and care. Even if the film's lyrical beginning and end might express a longing for a perceptual-lyrical disembodiedness, its main course is one of painful exhibitionism: see how our physical bodies are sources of pain and mutilation, even, or especially those aspects of the body that should provide intense pleasure. The film's strategy is, however, not that of traditional bourgeois-Christian negation of the body by denying it representation. On the contrary, it flaunts the body and the sexual act, and denies representation of intimacy and care. It wants to 'turn bad' and tell the true, anti-Christian story of human embodiedness that has sheer force as its inner core. In von Trier's *Breaking the Waves*, where the main character is forced to continuous sexual abuse that leads to her death, it nevertheless ends with a beatification: 'She' goes to heaven as a saint. In *Antichrist* the 'beatification' consists of an abstract, lyrical return to nature and solitude but with a background where possible new antichrists stream up a mountain, perhaps to perform dysfunctional fertility rituals.

NOTES

1 http://dysfunctionalliteracy.com/2011/06/29/sharapova-banned-from-grunting-moaning-in-women's-tennis/ (accessed 17 March 2013).
2 cf. p.71 in the third edition of the Danish version of the manuscript, provided to me by Peter Schepelern.
3 http://en.wikipedia.org/wiki/Erotic_asphyxiation (accessed 17 March 2013).

Chapter 10

EXPLICIT TEEN SEX AND UTOPIAN PROBLEM-SOLVING IN *KEN PARK*

CLAIRE HINES

Towards the end of *Ken Park* (Larry Clark and Ed Lachman, 2002) is a poignant four-minute long sex sequence involving three of the teenage characters in this controversial film about the dysfunctional home lives of some troubled youths, co-directed by Larry Clark and Ed Lachman and based on a screenplay by Harmony Korine. In contrast to the uncompromising approach to the portrayal of adolescent sexuality and social problems otherwise in evidence in this production, and indeed throughout his career as a visual artist, Clark says that the idea was that this scene is uplifting, and though clearly explicit, in many ways its tone differs markedly from the rest of the film. Though Clark is no stranger to censorship or media debate, *Ken Park* provokes some particularly powerful responses, including those of the Australian Classification Review Board which found that the film contained 'scenes which depict child sexual abuse and sexualized violence in a way which offends against the standards of morality, decency and propriety generally accepted by reasonable adults' (2003: 3). Nevertheless it is noteworthy that whereas complaints tend to emphasize the needless 'shock value' of some scenes and might label the film obscene or perhaps pornography, Lachman and Clark defend the importance of what is shown, and emphasize that the nudity and sex acts were integral to the bid to achieve emotional and visual honesty.

When Lachman and Clark have spoken about this sex sequence in interviews, they have stressed that the intention was to leave the viewer feeling optimistic and like the teens were able to meet their emotional needs in a way that the adults were not. As Clark so bluntly puts it: 'The thing I want everyone to come away from *Ken Park* with is that the kids are going to be all right, no matter how fucked up their parents are' (Reeves and Roman, 2002). Elsewhere he has said that 'the idea was to have these kids come together and maybe have sex in the best way and maybe have redemption or temporary salvation ... That was my idea to end the film, and the problem making it work' (Rozemeyer, 2008). Unlike the many scenes involving adults, which are generally emotionally painful and unsettling to watch, the scene seems idealized in its presentation of tender teen sex. The main aim of this chapter therefore is to analyse the wider narrative and aesthetic contexts for the surprisingly utopian final threesome, and I will consider to what extent *Ken Park* might push at longstanding social and cinematic boundaries, especially with regard to sex. It is often commented that context proves vital when attempting to either justify the inclusion or understand the 'meaning' of explicit sex in non-pornographic films. *Ken Park* is certainly no exception in this matter, and as such the analysis will also refer to a number of other contexts in order to examine some of the nuances of the explicit depictions of sexuality, including the earlier works of Clark, adolescence and the sexual representation of the male body.

Set in the suburbs of Visalia in California, the loosely plotted narrative of *Ken Park* focuses on five teenagers and pays particular attention to the uneasy relationships they have with the adult world. In the main it is the eponymous Ken Park who holds the episodes in the film together, since it is the story of his suicide which provides the graphic start and abrupt ending to the stories of four of his friends. The opening titles follow a teen boy as he skateboards through the streets of the sunny suburban neighbourhood of Visalia listening to the raw punk sound of The Bouncing Souls. Watching him speed effortlessly past family houses, shops and public service buildings to reach an outdoor skate park, his apparent energy (at one point he joins in with the song and hollers 'Oi! Oi! Oi! Oi!'), and that of the title sequence, means that the uninitiated might be forgiven for thinking that this film is going to concentrate wholly on the skateboarding lifestyle from the perspective of this particular teen. However, for those accustomed to Clark's work it should not come as a surprise that when the boy arrives at the skate park, he neither shows off his skills nor socializes with his fellow skaters, but rather sits down in the middle of the park and pulls a video camera out of his backpack which he sets up and with some adjustment points at his head. He also takes a gun out of his bag and as he clutches it in his hand there is a reverse shot from the point of view of the camera of him scanning those around him with a blank gaze. There is a further series of shots that switch between the movie camera and the diegetic video camera which films the boy as he breaks into a big, fixed grin, puts the gun to his temple, and shoots himself. Blood sprays across the frame and onto the lens of his video camera. A high angle shot looking down lingers on the image of the dead teenager with a pool of blood around his head, and other skaters looking at his inert body, whilst a boy's voiceover cuts in and finally gives him a name, Ken Park. The scene sets up the acute sense of alienation which *Ken Park* explores, though the fact that the suicide is staged in the middle of the busy skate park, witnessed by skateboarders and captured on video, means that it stands out as a very public incident in a film that otherwise foregrounds the intimate lives and relationships of its characters.

Interestingly, the start of the voiceover on top of the distant and dramatic high angle shot at the end of this opening suicide scene makes an unusually unemotional claim to intimacy. The voiceover matter-of-factly states that 'I used to be friends with this guy. His name was Ken Park. His name spelled backwards was Krap Nek, and I used to tease him. One day after school I heard he blew his brains out. I don't think I had anything to do with it, but I still feel guilty', and he repeats the nickname 'Krap Nek' to a video replay of the gunshot suicide. Two still photographs immediately follow on from this graphic video replay. The first of these documents the young and freckly Ken Park at age 11. The camera rests on his photograph whilst the voiceover remarks that Ken Park was buried in his 'lucky' motorcycle jacket, and adds that his mother claims she can still feel her son's spirit. For now though, the question of motivation that the voiceover raised remains conspicuously unanswered. Instead, the second photo introduces a small group of mostly carefree looking teens, identified from left to right as Claude, Peaches, Mike and Tate, with Shawn, who is presently doing the narrating, right on the end. It becomes clear in the scenes that follow that something Claude, Peaches, Tate and Shawn share in common other than mutual friendship (including Ken Park) are disturbed relationships with the adults in their lives: the largely good-natured Claude treats with careful indulgence his mother and is abused by his violent father; Peaches is living with her fanatically religious father who is obsessed with her sexuality and the memory of his dead wife; Tate is being raised by his grandparents whom he hates, and Shawn is having an illicit sexual relationship with his girlfriend's thirtysomething-year-old mother. By the end of the film each one of these teens is emotionally damaged in some way, however this casual snapshot freezes a private moment which captures an earlier time perfectly. Other than Tate, who is staring down the lens of the camera ominously, in the photo the teenagers exchange glances, and generally appear relaxed and animated. Having introduced himself and his friends by first name only, Shawn's voiceover identifies that 'We all live in a little town in California called Visalia.' In Shawn's view, 'It's pretty boring but sometimes when we get together we have fun.' In contrast to the threatening themes of violence and alienation signalled by the tragedy of Ken Park's apparently unmotivated suicide at the beginning, this snapshot and Shawn's salute to his peers foreshadows something of the sense of warmth and community of the last sex scene between Shawn, Peaches and Claude near the end of the film.

In *Ken Park* still photographs give the characters and stories context, and vice versa. Following the group snapshot, Claude, Peaches, Tate and Shawn are presented to the viewer individually via an intertitle, a voiceover (for instance, Claude presents Shawn, Peaches presents Claude, and Shawn presents Tate), and a portrait photograph. It is worth mentioning that whilst Claude, Peaches and Shawn's fresh-faced portrait photos appear candid, Tate's is a studio photograph which is less lively. Nevertheless, to some extent the youthful personalities and mood reflected by these still photographs are at odds with the scenarios the teens are placed in during the majority of the film, making them unsettling (and often ironic) because of the context. The still photo of Shawn, for example, shows him smiling widely at the camera, a smile that could of course be genuine or fake. Over the top of this photograph Claude gives some personal insight into Shawn's character, telling a story about how he had thrown a tennis ball at an old lady from a car, but had instantly got out and apologized. In Shawn's first scenes, having performed the roles of dominant older brother and not very loving son, he rides away from his home to another house which he enters and stops in the hallway to question a little girl (Zoe) on the whereabouts of her father (Bob) and mother (Rhonda). At this point the reason for Shawn's enquiry is unclear, but when this short exchange is considered in the knowledge that he is seeking Rhonda in order to have sex with her, the presentation of this sequence is perhaps suggestive. The sequence uses the standard shot / reverse shot pattern, but more striking than the dialogue are the elements of mise en scène, particularly in the eye level medium shots. Seen from Shawn's perspective, Zoe is holding a tea party at a low table with two dolls (in states of undress) right in front of the close-up soft-core images of thong bikini-clad women which play on the television screen. When the viewer sees Shawn from Zoe's perspective there are a number of framed photographs in the background. Most noticeably, the two photographs hanging on the wall are child and baby portraits of girls. In this way it appears that the mise en scène in this shot / reverse shot sequence creates a visual metaphor for the loss of (childhood) innocence, which Clark identifies as a key theme of his work.

Innocent family photos, portraits and photographs capturing a slice of the characters' lives often appear in key sequences in *Ken Park* that deal explicitly with sexuality and relationships. Rhonda's bedroom contains many framed photographs of herself, her husband, and family in happier times. When Shawn enters the bedroom to find Rhonda involved in the depressingly mundane domestic task of folding laundry, he props himself up on the marital bed and enquires 'Can I eat you out?' In this scene, visible just behind his head, located on the bedside table, is an archetypal affectionate mother and daughter photo. Presently, Shawn and Rhonda remove each others' clothing and Shawn goes to work performing oral sex on the woman who is later revealed to be his girlfriend's mother. He positions himself at the end of the bed and carefully follows the instructions given to him by Rhonda who lies back, such as 'nice and slow', 'just a little faster', 'move with my hips', and the command 'Put your head back down!', which she exclaims when he makes the rookie mistake of stopping to ask for reassurance about whether he is pleasing her. Yet this scene is one of the least visually explicit of the film's depictions of sex acts, since there are no close-ups of Rhonda's genitals, which remain obscured. Instead, what is arguably most important about the portrayal of this sex scene is how intently Shawn looks up at (and listens to) Rhonda from between her thighs, and the touching mixture of schoolboy obedience and intensity in his eyes whilst he performs oral sex is worth a thousand lines of dialogue about how he feels. But even though sex with an older, more experienced woman might well be some teenage boys' fantasy, in reality this sort of relationship is obviously taboo, and when mid-scene Rhonda praises the teenager's sexual performance with the encouraging but inappropriate groan of 'That's a good boy Shawn', she involuntarily calls attention to the fact that what they are doing is transgressive. After her orgasm, Rhonda gently takes Shawn in her arms and soothingly strokes his back.

When the film later returns to Rhonda and Shawn they remain in the bedroom, and having got out of the bath Rhonda joins Shawn on the bed and takes a drag on his post-sex cigarette. Shawn looks for further consolation about whether Rhonda liked what they just did, and asks 'How many times did you come?' Following Rhonda's patient reassurances that 'It was really good', the camera suddenly cuts downstairs to her younger daughter Zoe, who is still quietly playing with her dolls whilst being parented by the TV set and those soft-core depictions of women, and then cuts back to a close-up of Shawn and Rhonda on the bed holding hands, their fingers interlocked. Before long, Rhonda puts her hand down Shawn's boyish white briefs and starts to manually stimulate him. The integration of this implied sex act within the flow of the scene is significant and serves to comment on character and relationships. A theme in this case is lost youth and attractiveness. The handjob is preceded by some unusual pillow talk between Shawn and Rhonda, in which Shawn compares Rhonda to her teenage daughter Hannah, who he also knows intimately, noting similarities in what they do in bed and what they enjoy. Shawn's youthful opinion that her age and experience is an asset (because it makes her better in bed) generates unspoken emotion from Rhonda, and possibly some sympathy from the viewer, when for a few brief seconds her eyes fill with tears. Minutes earlier the camera has cut and then tracks slowly to closely show the many framed photographs, trophies and newspaper cuttings (also noticeable if blurred in the background of the oral sex scene earlier) prominently displayed in the bedroom, of a young-looking Rhonda and her now husband Bob back when they fitted the image of stereotypical all-American teens. Together, these old photographs, the age-gap relationship between Shawn and Rhonda, and the sex acts evoke a mood that shifts awkwardly between adolescent sexual arousal, and adult longing. In subsequent scenes in the film, when standing on the front porch waving side by side, or gathered smiling around the dinner table, though it might look like Bob, Rhonda, Zoe and Hannah make the perfect American family, because Shawn is also part of the picture the viewer is alert to the fact that beneath this ideal lies a complex and disturbing lived reality.

Still photographs are also important to some of Peaches' scenes in *Ken Park*, and they highlight the extent to which her father has created overly idealized images of both his teenage daughter and his late wife. In one early sequence, when a male friend (Curtis) from Peaches' Bible study class visits the house, they sit down to lunch prepared by her father. After some polite but rather odd small talk (about Curtis' teeth and Peaches' father's tongue) Peaches' father brings out a cherished family photo album which he proceeds to take Curtis through, noting angelic photos of Peaches as child, and the beauty of her mother. Later, Peaches' father is seen making his daily pilgrimage to his wife's grave, where he proudly reports his daughter's academic progress and proclaims her 'such

Figure 10.1. In the foreground, Shawn performs oral sex on Rhonda. In the background, framed photographs and trophies are on display.

a good girl', which presumably means passive and still a virgin. Leaving Peaches' father gazing devotedly at a gravestone portrait of his late wife, whom he says his daughter looks more like every day, the camera cuts away to the house interior, and via the next three successive shots of this scene his impossible ideal is acknowledged and undercut. The first shot is of another photograph of Peaches when she was a little girl, pointedly positioned right by a porcelain figure of a cherub. The second shot reflects her father's religious fanaticism, represented by the iconography on what looks like a bedside table. The third shot is rather unexpected given Peaches' 'good girl' image: in close-up she is observed tying one of Curtis' wrists to a bedpost. For just under two and a half minutes (intercut with Peaches' father's journey home from the cemetery), Peaches proceeds to playfully tease Curtis, arousing him by moving on top of his body, demonstrating that contrary to her fathers' belief, not only is she already sexually active, she is also sexually confident. When Peaches' unsuspecting father walks in on this scene his immediate response is to beat up her boyfriend, and afterwards to force his daughter to take part in a wedding ceremony with himself as the groom, in a bizarre and desperate attempt to reclaim and control her sexuality.

Perhaps the most unsettling juxtaposition between the idealized family photograph and the realities of life is made in telling the story of Claude. Prior to the sequence in question, Claude is repeatedly harassed

Figure 10.2. 'Good girl' Peaches teases Curtis tied-up.

by his father, who drinks solidly and constantly puts his son down. One night this aggression reaches a critical stage. When Claude's father comes home from a drunken night out cruising the streets searching for a female prostitute with his sexually-frustrated buddy, he pays a visit to the kitchen in order to take yet another beer from the refrigerator, stops off to look in at his wife in bed and sleeping soundly, and then goes into the bathroom where in a medium shot he is seen pulling down his pants, showing his flaccid penis. Whilst chugging his beer he begins urinating. There is a cut to a close-up of his face, and as the sound of uninterrupted urine flow is heard the camera pans slowly down his body to once again show the stream. There is a lingering shot of his penis, after which the camera pans back upwards, and he lets out a resounding belch. Finally, the camera frames part of his face reflected in the bathroom mirror, whilst out of shot he finishes relieving himself and pulls up his pants. That this is non-simulated urination in real time does not stop the scene feeling uncomfortably prolonged and almost absurd, but importantly it also conveys effectively the animalisitic quality of his character. Furthermore the scene invites the viewer to contemplate what Claude's father might be thinking or feeling as he empties his bladder, not only by using the conventional technique of searching his face and reflection in the mirror, but also the unorthodox focus on his penis.

Just as interesting is the relationship between this private scene and what follows next. When Claude's father staggers toward the narrow hallway the

Figure 10.3. Real-time urination adds to the animalistic behaviour of Claude's father.

camera shifts to show his point of view, and pauses to look at the gallery of framed family photos that decorate the walls. What catches the eye is that many of these photographs are of his son at different ages. Moving on, Claude's father halts briefly outside a closed door at the end of the hallway, which plastered with stickers, is clearly his son's bedroom. Having opened the door he stops in the doorway, before advancing and curling up next to his son who is asleep on his bed. But what initially appears to be an expression of latent paternal affection turns out to be a manifest act of incestuous intrusion, when Claude's father attempts to perform oral sex on his sleeping son. Significantly, it is the in-between space of the photo-lined hallway that connects these two uncomfortable domestic scenes of brooding reflection and thwarted sexual abuse. Whereas the display of photos is typically used to maintain a sense of family and add warmth to the home, the sight of Claude's father urinating and the scene in which he attempts to force himself on his son frankly expose some undisclosed truths, such as self-hatred, shame and repression.

In terms of the wider context of *Ken Park*, photography is also relevant. Before moving into film-making Clark developed a reputation as a provocative documentary-style photographer whose early photographic works, including *Tulsa* (1971), *Teenage Lust* (1983) and *The Perfect Childhood* (1993), reveal some hard to take teen realities, such as sex, violence and drug abuse, to which he has repeatedly returned. Taken between 1963 and 1971, the black-and-white pictures in *Tulsa* established

Clark's distinctive visual style and themes, recording his own gritty and intense experiences of the teen subculture of drug abuse and crime. His second book, *Teenage Lust*, is similar and contains self-portraits and graphic images that depict adolescent sexuality. Also focused on teens, in *The Perfect Childhood*, Clark further combines his own photographs with newspaper clippings, handwritten letters, TV stills and teen poster boys, to examine media and youth culture. As a result, criticism and commentary on Clark's films typically refer to his background in still photography, and in interviews he has often talked about how by the same token his aspiration to be a film-maker influenced his approach to storytelling and the still image. In one infamous sequence of photographs in *Tulsa* for instance, there is a hauntingly beautiful photo of a young, pregnant woman shooting up in front of a window, bathed in light. The next two photographs unsentimentally approach the ugly consequences of this image, documenting the baby's funeral, including a picture of the dead infant in an open coffin. Clark has explained that he got his first experiences of photography working with his mother, who was a local photographer in Tulsa, and during his youth he used the skills he had learned to take photos, albeit of a very different style, of his teenage friends (Gibson, 2010). That his mother specialized in baby portraiture is fascinating given Clark's lasting interest in teenage life, and as described above, the challenge that his stark and uncompromising portrayals of adolescent lives and dysfunctional relationships present to the myth of the ideal American family which traditional posed photographs are a means of preserving, is made particularly evident in *Ken Park*. The film is difficult to watch for many reasons, but one of the most important is perhaps that it reveals how dominant constructions of children, parents and family might be powerful and dangerously deceptive.

It is reasonable, given the script for *Ken Park* was based on Clark's journals and stories, that the aesthetic and some of the scenes in the film should strongly resemble his books of photographs. Indeed, as Clark's most visually explicit film to date, the uninhibited portrayal of teen sex in *Ken Park* is close to the depictions of adolescent sexuality in his photography, where there is also a kind of graphic sensuality to some of his pictures. In one particularly iconic photograph in *Tulsa* three teenagers, two boys and a girl, take drugs in what appears to be one of their bedrooms: the boy who sits to the right has an erection, to the left the other boy who is flaccid leans over, and in the middle of them is the young woman shooting up. Here, nude adolescent bodies and drug abuse share the frame in a composition which creates an intense impression of intimacy, not that dissimilar from the threesome featured in *Ken Park*. Later, in *The Perfect Childhood*, an intimate rites-of-passage scene involving a young male and an older woman, previously included in *Teenage Lust* and entitled 'Prostitute Gives Teenager His First Blowjob, 1974', is memorialized via 30 photographs (over 27 pages) in which the vulnerability of the boy's skinny adolescent body and the nuances in his facial expressions prove as oddly memorable as the repeated image of his erect penis. Moreover, the episodic structure and intercutting of stories in *Ken Park* recalls Clark's collage work collected in *The Perfect Childhood*. In these collages newspaper clippings of the sensational stories of teen killers are displayed next to popular magazine pin-ups of once popular teen idols like River Phoenix and Corey Haim, and Clark's own images of youth, which are more explicitly portrayed. The book also contains imagery from clips of *The Phil Donahue Show* used by Clark in an art exhibition. The spectacle of the television talk show is referenced in *Ken Park* too, in a scene when Claude's abusive father and exhausted mother watch *The Jerry Springer Show*. More general connections can likewise be made between Clark's self-styled 'tell it like it is' approach to photography and his film-making, evident from his first film *Kids* (1995) onwards (O'Hagan, 2008). Most obviously, in *Kids*, *Bully* (2001), *Ken Park* and *Wassup Rockers* (2005) he uses real locations, non-professional teen actors and gives the films a vérité feel, to further blur the line between fiction and reality. After all, to a degree the photographs and feature films of Clark both capture and create paradoxical tensions between distance and proximity, hope and despair, and artifice and authenticity.

There is however one crucial difference between Clark's photographs taken in the 1970s and his later projects, including his films, which greatly impacts on the reception of his recent work. When *Tulsa* made Clark famous, he was involved in the subcultural scene he was photographing. The opening lines of *Tulsa* personalize the collection:

> i was born in tulsa oklahoma in 1943. when i was sixteen i started shooting amphetamine. i shot with my friends everyday for three years and then left town but i've gone back through the years. once the needle goes in it never comes out. L.C. (Clark, 1971: 1)

On the one hand, over the years, Clark's autobiographical impulse remains unchanged, as has his commitment to portraying troubled teens. But on the other hand his relationship to the youths he is shooting has inevitably shifted, not least of all because he has got older, and when he made *Kids* and *Ken Park*, both films about adolescent characters who are part of contemporary skateboard subculture, Clark was in his fifties and himself a parent. Predictably, this widening generation gap that separates the middle-aged director from his teen actors, who often play underage characters, is picked up on as an issue by many critics and commentators. At best, the gap is used as a basis to infer a kind of nostalgic empathy with the issues and experience of adolescence (e.g. Jones, 2005). At worst, it is used to support charges of voyeuristic teensploitation and amorality.

Tom Doherty's review of *Kids* is a good example of a negative critical response that invokes Clark's age. For Doherty, in the context of 1990s film and the teenpic, Clark's directorial debut was highly transgressive. His concluding paragraph includes the deeply disapproving remark that:

> this isn't kiddie porn, but *Kids* comes too close to the line for comfort, skating up to the very edge of acceptability, toying with the last imagistic taboo in American culture. To put it bluntly, Clark shouldn't be hanging around this particular playground if he's only there to scope out the young stuff. What *Kids* needs is adult supervision – a mature perspective, a moral vision. (Doherty, 1995: 16)

When Clark made *Kids* he wanted to show the 'secret world' of contemporary teens (Clark in Smith, 2008). *Ken Park* is widely considered the companion film to *Kids* because though it also looks at the lives of teenagers, in addition it enters the world of the parents. Interestingly, Clark was originally going to make *Ken Park* first, which might raise the question of how graphically the sex scenes would be presented if it was made rather than *Kids* in 1995, prior to the recent trend toward explicit sex in art films. Though in appearance *Kids* is a lot less explicit than *Ken Park*, in other ways it is no less confrontational or uncompromising. At the time of release *Kids* attracted a great deal of attention for its naturalistic depiction of the speech and attitudes of the teen characters who roam the streets of Manhattan in search of alcohol, drugs and sex. The film's extended opening sequence observes 16-year-old Telly expertly coaxing an underage girl into having sex with him. Afterwards, Telly boasts about his first sexual conquest of the day to his sidekick Casper, and describes his obsession with seducing virgins who he uses and quickly abandons. That the personalities and behaviour of Telly and his group of adolescent friends appear both engagingly charismatic and frighteningly sinister is part of how Clark wished to counter mass-mediated images of the teenager and 'make the teenage movie that America never made'

(Schrader, 1995: 74). To reflect on Clark and Lachman's images in relation to commercialized forms of teen culture and the male body is therefore enlightening, especially when it comes to his often brutally frank portrayal of adolescent male sexuality.

Without a doubt the single most confronting image in *Ken Park* is that of Tate's penis and the long, thick semen trail that he has just ejaculated. This hard-core image is part of the climax to a two-minute long sexually explicit scene in which he is shown in his bedroom engaging in the practice of auto-erotic asphyxiation whilst masturbating to the point of orgasm, something not much seen on film. But putting the scene in such simple terms disguises its complexity, including how this scene illustrates Tate's character and relationships, and how the scene continues the exploration of the main themes in the film. When the camera cuts to Tate's bedroom it would seem that his teen libido has been awakened by the women's tennis match he is watching on television, from the cocoon of his boyhood race car bed. After a moment he gets up, and the camera accompanies him into the bathroom, where he removes a belt from a bathrobe in much the same automatic way that he fully shuts off a faucet to stop the flow of water from one of the taps on the 'his and hers' sinks. When Tate returns to his bedroom there is one continuous shot that records his ritualistic preparations for masturbation; he loops the bathrobe belt around the doorknob, collects a pillow from his bed and puts it on the floor, takes off his underpants to reveal his limp penis, leans back against the door, and wraps the belt around his neck. Subsequent shots document the process of Tate's arousal and climax. The shots of Tate consist mainly of close-ups on his face and penis whilst he masturbates, and medium shots of his body, including his ejaculation and the lingering cum image that concludes the episode. In particular, the camera repeatedly tracks up and down his body, focusing attention on his penis which becomes engorged, and his face as his mouth froths and the vein in his forehead bulges. Like the later scene that shows Shawn's father urinating, Tate's masturbation scene is obviously unsimulated, and it is hard to regard the act as erotic or fun. Rather, this solitary act of sexual self-stimulation seems to highlight Tate's alienation and the loneliness and frustration that he feels in a house seemingly full of warmth and affection. Furthermore, there is a vulnerability to Tate as he engages in this private and potentially harmful form of sexual expression. The vulnerability is intensified by the awareness that the masturbatory act being performed is genuine, meaning that actor James Ransone did it for real in front of the camera. Indeed, Clark has spoken of the bravery, trust and willingness to be exposed that agreeing to film this one-take, two-camera scene needed on the part of Ransone and, in Clark's words, Ransone 'paid a tremendous emotional price' for doing it, 'When the scene was over he was shattered, he was a mess – he just, like, collapsed' (Cuir, 2007).

There might be an underlying problem though, with Tate's image as a lonely teen masturbator. Critical discussions about male masturbation in film identify that representations of the adolescent male masturbator tend to have overtones of 'disgust, horror, and, above all humour' (Schneider, 2005: 377), arguably present, to varying degrees, in the story of Tate. Notably, the masturbation scene in *Ken Park* is a tipping point between the sequences that portray Tate's mounting rage at his grandparents, and his dramatic transformation into a killer teen not unlike those that Clark documents in his photo books. (In fact, *The Perfect Childhood* includes newspaper cuttings on real-life cases of parricide, and a report on the social problem of auto-erotic asphyxiation in teens.) Of Tate's masturbation scene Tom Austin O'Connor comments that 'This scene [...] is vital to the logic of the film since it foreshadows Tate's psychotic break-down, i.e. Tate views sexuality as destructive – not healing. Tate's only desires in life at this point are oneiric and solipsistic' (2009: 6–7). In other words, Tate's auto-erotic practices may warn of his perverse impulses and the dangerousness later evidenced when his story is brought to an unpleasant end in a murderous act of revenge against his grandparents, and narratively there is a disturbing link made between sex and violence.

Tate is naked when he stabs his grandparents in bed with the very same knife that he used to cut himself a slice of cake, and he describes the feeling of killing them detachedly, adding in voiceover 'When I saw them there like that, I started to get an erection.' He recounts the night's events into a Dictaphone having got back into his race car bed, and completes the self-conscious process of mythologization by laying back relaxedly, eyes closed and hands folded behind his head, blood splattered across his body, wearing nothing but his grandfather's ill-fitting dentures locked in a creepy grin. A certain amount of dark humour is then also apparent in this and other scenes. Though Tate doesn't have to go through the shame and embarrassment of *'jerkus interruptus'*, suffered by the frustrated adolescent male masturbators examined by Steven Jay Schneider (2005) in popular Hollywood teen sex comedies such as *Fast Times at Ridgemont High* (1982) and *American Pie* (1999), he does get his privacy invaded by his well-meaning grandmother in an earlier sequence in the film. Later on, when Tate masturbates to the women's tennis on television, the loud grunts of the players provide a humorous soundtrack to accompany his naturalistic solo performance. Whilst humour is certainly not confined to the scenes in *Ken Park* that involve Tate (among many others, there is for instance a clear irony to the shots that linger on family photographs, and to the scene in which Claude's parents watch an episode of *The Jerry Springer Show*), in his story the humour seems especially dark. Yet the last of Tate's scenes is tragic, not funny. Having killed his grandparents, Tate is in the back of a police car in the rain, and in another voiceover he states that 'in my whole life, I've never had one true girlfriend'. That this atmospheric night-time scene, and Tate's lost and lonely confession, is directly juxtaposed to the utopian threesome involving Shawn, Peaches and Claude, vividly emphasizes how important it might be for his friends to find ways to give one another much needed emotional support.

As Peter Lehman has pointed out, showing the penis is perhaps the last 'great taboo' in Western culture, and with the exception of pornography, has long remained hidden in cinema and other media (2001: 28). Due to this taboo, 'the easiest thing to do is not represent the penis but, if the penis must be shown or even spoken about, its representation must carefully be regulated' (Lehman, 2001: 27). 'The media', he says:

> typically maintain a tense contradictory relationship with such taboos: on the one hand there are cultural imperatives for respecting the taboo and, on the other hand, there are the journalistic and artistic motives for breaking the taboos by creating new images which bring attention to themselves, sometimes in a shocking manner. (Lehman, 2001: 28)

Prior to making *Ken Park*, Clark had already broken the taboo in his photographic works, where the penis is essential to the authenticity of male adolescent sexuality. In these photographs, as in *Ken Park*, some of the penises shown are bigger than others, a number of them are erect, and some are flaccid, creating a range of images that visibly challenge the 'large, ever-present, long-lasting erection[s]' typically favoured by hard-core porn (Lehman, 2001: 27). At the same time, however, visibility is precisely the issue, and some might see no distinction between showing Tate's real-time masturbation and climax in *Ken Park*, and some of the iconography of hard-core porn. In particular, no matter how sad and lonely Tate's ejaculation may be, its spectacular visibility serves as a signal of the end of the (solitary) sexual act and a marker of authenticity, akin to the 'money shot' of hard-core pornography. For Clark, the pornographic associations of such images would seem to provide part of the motivation for using them, because he refutes the idea that showing certain imagery automatically creates porn. In his opinion, 'If it's in the story and it makes sense and if it's part of life and it's done right you know that it won't be pornography' (*Pataphysics*, 2003), and this is what he claims to have done in *Ken Park*, though the shock that these scenes cause, and the film's very limited release, indicates that not everyone feels the same.

In addition *Ken Park* demonstrates how particular images of teenage sexuality and the adolescent male body are also considered something of a taboo. Clark is especially renowned for his eroticized portrayals of teenage boys. Though what he shows is not the sanitized young male body of commercial advertising, or the stereotypical teen pin-up, this does not mean that the imperfect teenage bodies he depicts lack visual appeal and a certain kind of glamour. For example, in the sequence running up to the near-incest drama, there is captured a particularly stunning image of Claude. Alone in the privacy of his bedroom, Claude has removed his T-shirt and socks and casually wriggled his hips out of the baggy skater pants criticized by his father in an earlier scene in the film, and he has stretched out on his single bed wearing only a pair of white boxer shorts. When his father stops to look in on him, the camera cuts to a reverse shot which dwells on Claude sleeping, and on his pale, skinny, half-naked adolescent form. Claude's pose resembles that of a classical art nude, an association that brings to mind Amy Taubin's remark about a similar scene in *Kids* which 'tries to aestheticize the kids, panning over sprawled sleeping bodies as if they were Botticelli angels' (1995: 19). In Taubin's (ibid.) opinion, the observational scene she is writing about in Clark's first film 'is glaringly wrong'. The same might clearly be said of the shot of Claude sleeping in *Ken Park*, not because the young, beautiful and vulnerable image is from the point of view of an observational camera (or the middle-aged male film-makers), but because what the viewer sees is a result of the erotic gaze of his father, who having hesitated in the doorway proceeds to enter the bedroom and attempts to perform oral sex on his sleeping son.

It must be said that because Clark likes to show the male body in intimate detail many commentators and scholars find a homoerotic dimension to his work. For obvious reasons this suggests that Clark's images are in dangerous territory, though on record he tends to shrug off such claims. 'I saw that some people [...] just can't get past the fact that it's teenage boys,' Clark said on the topic of homoeroticism in his work in 1992, 'what can I do about that?' (Kelley, 1992: 85). Ten years later, asked

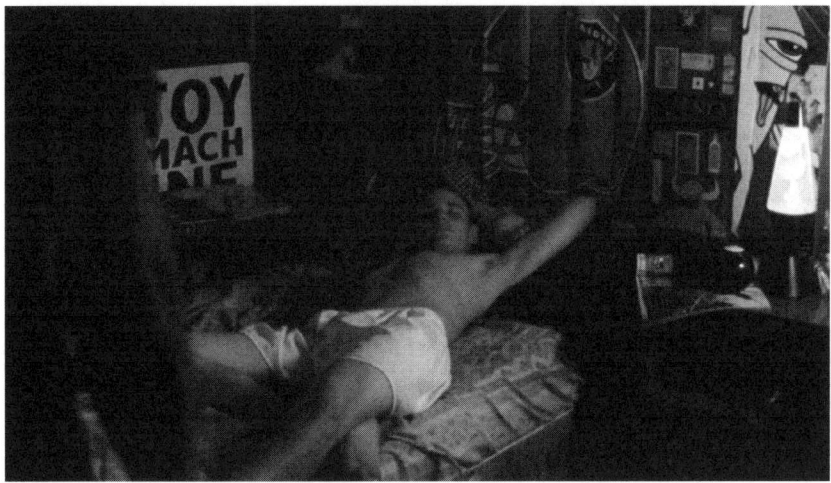

Figure 10.4. Claude appears angelic when he is observed sleeping by his father.

about his approach to filming nudity in *Ken Park*, Clark did not discuss this homoerotic tension; rather he talked about how he was driven by the urge to use full frontal male nudity as a cinematic provocation:

> In my other films, I show full frontal female nudity, and you can still get an R rating [...] But as soon as you have full frontal male nudity, forget it. You're never going to get the film shown widely, and you're not going to get a rating. And women I know have said, 'You know, that's sexist – we want to see penises. You show women naked, why can't you show men?' And they have a point. So in this movie, I'm showing everything. For every vagina, there's a penis. (Gurley, 2002)

Leaving aside whether *Ken Park* can conceivably be thought to do anything to undercut the prevailing sexual double standard, certainly there are more than enough shows of full frontal male nudity for every show of full frontal female nudity in the film. The most explicit display of female nudity in *Ken Park* occurs in the final sex scenes between Peaches, Shawn and Claude, though even in this sequence, nude boys outnumber the nude girl by two to one. In particular, there is a shot between Peaches' thighs and a close-up on Claude masturbating her with his hand. Inevitably there are many sights of the two boys' penises in the same sequence, which depicts the teens engaged in a variety of (heterosexual) sex acts, including oral, anal and vaginal sex, and in the scene where Peaches is shown fellating Claude, when she lifts her head up from his erect penis, a slow motion shot also captures a clear glimpse of a bodily fluid associated with sex. Superficially at least, this is another part of the film that offers portrayals of unrestrained sexuality which might be considered reminiscent of pornography (minus the graphic 'meat shots' of genital or anal penetration), and similar to Tate's explicit masturbation scene, in this threesome sequence the partner swapping, the variety of sexual positions, and the oral and anal sex, are standard pornographic tropes.

Yet the portrayal of sex during the extended teen threesome stands out from the rest of the film in a number of respects. Like the earlier scene between Peaches and Curtis, the sex between Shawn, Peaches and Claude is playful and relaxed, though with no disturbing end where the sex is cut short and the scene interrupted. In this sequence the teens have uninterrupted sex in what looks like the master bedroom and kitchen-living area of a family home. That no photographs are displayed on the walls or surfaces is especially noticeable considering most of the characters' homes are packed with portraits, and as such the sequence is without (ironic) commentary from family pictures. Compared to the other sex scenes in the film the sex in this sequence looks less spontaneous and perhaps somewhat choreographed, not because the actors' performances appear non-naturalistic or the film-makers change shooting or framing style, but because the sex acts are edited into a montage, which differs from the real-time presentation of other scenes. Also, the sex scenes are intercut with scenes where the naked threesome reflect on their dreams and play games, including being tickled, pillow fighting, and 'Guess who I am'. The frequent cuts from explicit sex acts to these scenes give the sequence a fun and almost innocent feel, where mutual intimacy appears to offer some means of salvation. As such not only is this one of the few sequences where adults are not present, it also seems to lack the potential for danger or abuse that dominates the film and the relationships between characters, pointing instead to the possibility of the power of expressions of teen sexuality.

The use of music further separates this sequence from the others. In contrast to either the punk or rap played by the characters when they listen to music, the unaccompanied sound of kissing, or sex, or the orgasmic grunts of the female tennis players that provide the background to Tate's masturbation scene, the Gary Stewart song 'Shady Streets' played over the threesome gives a soft and dreamy effect. The lighting of the threesome sequence is the final element that adds to the meditative and idyllic atmosphere. The setting means that scenes throughout the film are bathed in California light, and lighting is used to give sequences a blue or greenish cast or warmer tones of yellows and reds. The threesome is shot in a golden light which illuminates the teens and their surroundings with a soft glow, suggesting associations with romance. Moreover the lighting and mood of this sequence directly contrasts with the scene that immediately precedes it in which, having killed his grandparents, Tate is shown in the back seat of a police car at night. The colour of the scene is deep blue, giving Tate and his situation a distinctly cold and bleak appearance. There is therefore an overwhelming sense of hopefulness to the threesome absent from most of the film's other episodes. If the visual and music cues were not enough to signal that the sequence presents a utopian vision of sex, during their post-coital games and reflections, Claude asks Shawn whether he has read a book called *Island of Paradise*, and makes reference to the concept of utopia. He explains that the book is about:

> this island where the whole philosophy of the world is set up around having sex [...] It's like the best society, nobody ever fights, everybody gets along. All they do is fuck all day long, just fuck, fuck, fuck, that's all they ever do. It's supposed to be some kind of utopian society or something, I don't know.

This explanation moves into a voiceover that overlays several of the scenes in which Claude, Peaches and Shawn are themselves shown having sex and getting along with each other, thereby making a utopia, and it is a description which would seem to leave no room for doubt about the positivity or idealism of the sequence, and the hope that it represents. Nevertheless the utopian function of this episode is worth some consideration within the overall context of the film.

According to Linda Williams (1990) the fantasy of a sexual utopia is often found in hard-core film pornography. In different forms of feature-length hard-core, Williams says, sexual performance provides the 'utopian solutions to problems introduced in the narrative' (1990: 160), and she uses examples such as *Behind the Green Door* (1972), *The Resurrection of Eve* (1976) and *Insatiable* (1980) to illustrate the claim. To make this argument about the utopian sensibility at work in much of hard-core porn, Williams calls on Richard Dyer (1981), who writes about the utopian fantasy of the musical film genre (and mass entertainment in general), and Williams observes that 'Movie musicals and feature-length hard-core films are [...]

alike in offering escape from the problems of ordinary life' (1990: 160). In fact, a similar argument might be made about the threesome in *Ken Park*. Like the musical numbers in musicals and the sex in hard-core, the threesome in *Ken Park* appears to relate to many of the characteristics that Dyer says make up the utopian sensibility, such as energy, intensity, transparency, abundance and community. Furthermore these utopian solutions counteract the negative characteristics of exhaustion, dreariness, manipulation, scarcity, and fragmentation introduced by many of the other sequences in the film which observe the teens trying to find ways to live within the adult world.

It is interesting that, as mentioned at the beginning of this chapter, Clark talks about this feel-good threesome as if it were the end of the film. Understood in this way, the explicit sex in this sequence is nothing if not *eucatastrophic*, a term used by J. R. R. Tolkien in his essay 'On Fairy-stories' to refer to 'the sudden joyous "turn"' (1966: 86) in a story, which miraculously leads to a happy ending. Though it might seem somewhat strange to invoke this notion of fantasy with regard to a film that is in the main quite obviously concerned with depicting the 'real', the utopian sensibility of the final sex sequence would appear to invite the association, turning tragedy and sadness into joy and hopefulness to suddenly make some form of redemptive happy ending, which is in many ways unexpected. In the utopian society that Claude has read about he marvels that 'they came up with a way through like hundreds of years of practice where they can have sex and not make babies'. Of course the idea that teen sex might be a source of utopian escapism is far from unproblematic from a wider social perspective, and debates regarding teen sex often bring up the associated issues of teen pregnancy, HIV and other STDs. Yet these dystopian risks are somehow not significant in this particular episode, which is optimistic and dreamlike in its utopian feel. Nonetheless, however upbeat this extended *eucatastrophic* sequence, it is only temporary because in actual fact the film closes, as it began, on the character of Ken Park. In the game at the end of the threesome scenes, Shawn makes his friends guess who he is. In response to his clues, including 'I'm no longer here', Peaches incorrectly guesses Tate and then admits defeat, after which the camera cuts to the intertitle 'Ken Park'. At the very end it is thus revealed that Ken Park accidentally got his girlfriend pregnant, and whilst the couple discuss what they should do about the baby, the film finishes on her asking him the question 'Do you wish your parents had aborted you?'. In retrospect, Ken Park's suicide at the film's opening gives his definitive reply. Though the threesome may well show that some of the kids are going to be all right, the fact that Tate's story ends in double-murder and Ken Park's in suicide, means that not all of them will, and perhaps leaves a stronger sense of the social problems associated with teen life and feelings of despair.

In many ways it is the troublesome contradictions of a film like *Ken Park* that make up its challenge and its power. It is relatively easy and fairly tempting to label the style and sexual content amoral, sleazy or pornographic, and blame Clark in particular for gratuitously fetishizing teens. Another reasonable, almost oppositional, possibility is to brand Clark a reactionary (or even a moralist) for his bleak depictions of disenfranchised youth. It is perhaps far riskier to conclude that a film like *Ken Park* may expose the threshold of what is currently considered acceptable, including our conflicted attitudes toward adolescent sexuality, artistic freedom and questions about what is shown on screen.

Chapter 11

WITNESS TO THE PAIN

HOW EXPLICIT SEX SCENES IN MICHAEL ROWE'S *LEAP YEAR* DEMONSTRATE VISION BEYOND VISIBILITY

TAINE DUNCAN

It is the gaze which creates fiction.
Godard, quoted by Pascal Bonitzer, *Hitchcockian Suspense* (Žižek, 1992: 19)

Vision is the result of a process of relationships between bodies in the world, between images, traditions, institutions, laws, myths. What we see is the product of the process of coming to vision that is invisible yet can be interpreted and elaborated in its performance and effects. Vision is the result of the circulation of biosocial energy.
Kelly Oliver, *Witnessing: Beyond Recognition* (2001: 222)

Kelly Oliver explains in her book *Witnessing: Beyond Recognition* that feminist and psychoanalytic theorists have put too much stake in the concept of recognition. According to these more conventional theories, marginalized persons simply need to find a way to be recognized by the dominant persons and groups. Sexism, by this account, occurs largely because women are passed-over, forgotten, ignored. Similarly, racism and ethnocentrism occur because of a lack of identification with other types of bodies – differences crystallize others into objects, rather than analogous subjects. If only they were seen as 'like me', then everyone would easily get along. Oliver argues alternatively that visibility is not sufficient for subjectification, or the process of subject creation. In other words, women and minorities are not simply oppressed because they are unseen, but because of the continued separation of self and other, of subject and object, that surpasses mere recognition. In fact, far from overcoming oppression, increased visibility alone can contribute to the alienation, judgement and control necessary for perpetuating sexism, racism, and ethnocentrism.

In a chapter on the film *Leaving Las Vegas* (Mike Figgis, 1995) in her book *Reel to Real: Race, Sex, and Class at the Movies*, bell hooks challenges the conventional feminist argument that sexual vulnerability and interdependencies of desire are disempowering. Appropriating arguments from Georges Bataille's work on the erotic in his book *Erotism*, hooks argues instead that transgression of norms and transformation can radically occur precisely through the 'surrender' to love, and specifically via women surrendering to love with a man (2012). Using the example of the main character Sera in Mike Figgis' film *Leaving Las Vegas*, hooks contends that the familiar sexist and misogynist tropes of redeemed prostitute and salvation through love are flipped on their heads. Sera is not redeemed from her career in prostitution; she does not act as though this career is demeaning or dehumanizing for her in any way. Instead, hooks writes: 'In fact, the film disturbs many feminist viewers precisely because Sera is not presented as a victim' (1996: 22) Rather than being vulnerable because of her identity as a sex worker, hooks argues that Sera's vulnerability stems from her frustration with only being seen as a prostitute, with being objectified as her job.

Bell hooks sees interactions with others, and specifically sex and love with others, as necessary and foundational for subjectivity. This conception of love / sex and intersubjectivity correlates with the model of witnessing from Kelly Oliver. In this chapter, I align closely with hooks, seeing the importance of ambiguity, vulnerability, and authenticity as empowering to dissident feminist voices. *Leap Year*, like *Leaving Las Vegas* does not moralize or judge the main character. Instead, keeping in mind hooks and Oliver's theories, we viewers are invited to ask the following questions: What, then, does witnessing do that extends beyond mere spectatorship? What is vision beyond visibility? In this chapter, I argue that Michael Rowe's raw and emotional film *Leap Year* (2010) invites us to participate in exactly this process, calling viewers of the film to bear witness to Mónica del Carmen's portrayal of the protagonist Laura. In this way the film challenges expectations for identity, decency, and social norms, providing a model for explicit narrative film-making as liberatory, not simply for the character Laura, but for our own processes of subjectification.

SEEING *LEAP YEAR*

Leap Year (*Año Bisiesto*, in the original Spanish-language release) received an ample amount of critical praise when it was released in 2010, and won first-time director Michael Rowe a Cannes Festival *Caméra d'Or* award for Best First Feature in 2010. This is a Spanish-language film starring Mexican actors, but was co-written and directed by an Australian expatriate, a testament to the increasingly globalized world of film-making and storytelling. The film revolves primarily around a depressed protagonist named Laura, played by the relatively unknown actress Mónica del Carmen. Laura is a *mestiza* woman who recently relocated to the city, where she lives alone in an apartment and struggles to maintain an online writing job. Her past is vaguely sketched out in cryptic phone calls to her mother and brother, as well as by the ominous calendar counting down to an anniversary of sorts on 29 February. This date bears significance in relation to her father, and we know that her father passed away on that date, but whether that date is important as the anniversary of his passing or as a marker of traumatic event is unclear. Laura's behaviours and limited conversations also hint at past abuse at the hands of her father, and due to the nature of her increasingly masochistic behaviour it seems as though her father sexually assaulted her. However, these ideas are presented to the audience only obliquely, and much is left open to interpretation. In fact, the film has very little exposition or dialogue of any sort, and the movie takes place almost wholly within the confines of Laura's small apartment. These minimalist and delicate direction choices may have been borne of necessity – Rowe has explained in interviews that he had such a low budget, the production team stole their electricity – but they also add an additional element of realism and claustrophobia to the film.

The combination of low-budget, minimalist script, and fearless acting establishes a unique aesthetic for this film. One reviewer aptly called the film a 'chamber piece in the strictest sense of the word' (Senjanovic, 2010: 1). Character presence, minute detail, and explicit sexual activity take the place of traditional exposition and denouement in the film. The intimacy and physicality of explicit sex scenes throughout the film emphasize the importance of an intimacy and materiality in understanding complex subjectivity; the film's simultaneous explicitness and minimalism highlights elements of embodied reality and subjectivity that exceeds the simplified recognition of difference, and elevates the film to a model of witnessing and identifying with Laura's sexuality as a marker of complexity and liminality, philosophical concepts I will explore in detail in what follows.

The plot of the film centres on Laura's simultaneous descent into depression and her increasingly dangerous appetite for sadomasochistic sexual fulfilment. Her depression seems to be a causal factor in her sadomasochistic activities, but there is also an implication that her depression may stem from a previous sexual trauma. Therefore the explicit sex and her psychological state are not easily given sequential ordering, but instead seem to feed mutually off of one another. This is clear from the outset of the film with Laura settling in to her new apartment; almost immediately it is clear that Laura is not going to feel at home there. She wistfully and voyeuristically watches her neighbours through the window, but does not engage them. She masturbates to their lives and lies to her mother in phone conversations about entertaining her neighbours as close friends. Soon it becomes apparent that Laura's behaviour is not simply a passing phase of loneliness, but a destructive depression. She begins to leave home only to pick up unidentified men for one-night stands, and although she repeats this behaviour, it does not appear enjoyable or to alleviate her loneliness. She loses her freelance writing job, and struggles with finding a new one. She stops washing her sheets, eats food directly from the can, and stops working entirely. But all of this present pain apparent in the development of the plot seems tertiary to a past trauma and to the leap year's reminder of that trauma. Laura spirals into isolation and depression until she meets Arturo, played by Gustavo Sánchez Parra. Arturo seems, at first, to simply be another example of sexual diversion for a night. He, like the other men, is handsome by European standards of beauty: he's tall, athletically built, with an aquiline nose and lighter skin.

Arturo, however, proves to be quite a different partner for Laura. In their first encounter, he slaps her and pulls her hair. When they are finished, Arturo is the first of her partners to engage in pillow talk, and the first of her partners to return. Arturo and Laura engage in a relationship of sorts, one in which they both seem to feel affection and in which their sexual acts are interspersed with tender moments. As their relationship develops, Laura regains some engagement with the world and displays a wider emotional range. At the same time, their sexual relationship quickly develops into increasing violence – Arturo not only slaps, but chokes, burns, and even urinates on Laura. Throughout these acts, it is clear that both Laura and Arturo are consenting. As 29 February approaches, Laura becomes increasingly interested in life-threatening sex play and pushes Arturo to go further. She asks Arturo to end her life for her on Leap Day. However, Arturo does not come to kill her. Instead, Laura's younger brother comes to stay because of a recent heartbreak. The film ends with Laura sobbing and changing her calendar to March. Simply seeing the film, and recalling the basic plot, however, is not enough for exploring the potential witnessing power of *Leap Year*.

SEPARATING SUBJECT FROM OBJECT, OR, INTERPRETATION

In Alan Sheridan's introduction to Jacques Lacan's *Écrits: A Selection*, he defines the role of imagining: 'The imaginary was then the world, the register, the dimension of images, conscious or unconscious, perceived or imagined' (2001: ix). The role of the imaginary in this analysis then becomes an active mechanism for interpreting our perceptions of subjects and objects into our experiential reality. The subject / object dualism can be recognized in two distinct ways: the traditional distinction between person and thing, and the more complex relationship between self and other. Narrative film offers unique potential for exploring psychoanalytic theories of subjectivity and the imaginary – the image of film is simultaneously an object, and calls to mind another subject (the subjective Other) through the fantasy represented in character study.

Lacan identifies a mirror stage in every psychological being as a means for establishing a relationship between the subject and the world around her. He writes, 'the function of the *imago* [mirror image] [...] is to establish a relation between the organism and its reality' (2001: 4). Sometimes art can function as a reflecting glass for such an imago. As Milan Kundera describes in *The Art of the Novel*, the draw of a good novel is based on a psychological need: 'It is the need to gaze into the mirror of the beautifying lie and to be moved to tears of gratification by one's own reflection' (2005: 134). Narrative cinema reflects the same truth in fiction that Kundera describes for novels. In fact, director Michael Rowe describes his own intentions in a similar way:

I'm just sick of watching lies in the movies. I make films for the audience, to elicit an emotional response, not to safeguard the vanity of actors and sidestep classification boards. This story needed to be told in this way in order to be effective, and so that's the way I did it. To have watered down the images would be to show a lack of respect for the characters and their emotions. At the end of the day, I believe that in order to create the best film possible I should be answerable only to my characters. (Stafford, 2010)

In staging *Leap Year*, Laura is often positioned near a mirror. In other scenes, the camera functions as a sort of mirror for the activity on screen; rather than employing close-up shots in many of the sex scenes, as is often done in erotic cinema, the cinematographer uses wider shots.[1] These wider shots reflect the activity of the characters, rather than focusing on facial expressions or body parts. This filmic reflection serves to simultaneously distance the audience from the erotic situation, and to identify with the activity as a whole. In her discussion of director Mira Nair's ambitious and visceral film-making, Alpana Sharma argues that it is a conscious decision on the part of a director to open a film in such a way. Discussing Nair, she writes: 'Her camera opens both ways; it asks us to look at its subject just as frankly as we look at ourselves looking, in the process breaking down the dialectic of inside and outside, subject and object, viewer and viewee' (Sharma, 2007: 182). This evaluation of Nair's films emphasizes both the importance of physical presence of bodies in films addressing subjective existence, and the deconstructed role of viewer and portrayal that can happen in films that challenge the audience. Rather than depersonalizing the scene by creating a filmic distance on screen, Rowe's audience is similarly invited into the reflection, by making these sex scenes more visceral, more real, more intersubjective.

In his book *Cinematic Howling: Women's Films, Women's Film Theory*, Hoi F. Cheu explains an activity he uses to teach the impact of culture and context on filmic interpretation. He begins with a close-up image of female genitalia from pornography, and compares it to the highly suggestive plates of Judy Chicago's installation art piece *The Dinner Party*. He writes about how students feel that the common trope of close-ups in pornographic film serves to objectify the women, while Chicago intends to liberate, but Cheu questions the simplicity of this assessment. He argues that a pornographic still might also be intended to challenge normative gender constraints (2007). Cheu is implicitly arguing for a notion of intersubjective and contextual analysis of film.

It is not simply the appearance of directorial and cinematic choices that matter, but how these choices reflect the film's message, narrative, and audience in a reflexive activity of creation and interpretation. In *Leap Year*, mirroring Laura's own quest for self-identification, Rowe struggles with his role in synthesizing a complete, multi-dimensional personality; however, the director's struggle is not an internal struggle for his own realization, but a struggle for accurate representation of an imagined other. The director, therefore, performs the role suggested by the Lacanian imaginary. He creates the world represented on film, and, in so doing, shapes the imagination of the audience. For the cinematic auteur, then, a strict economy is placed on the (re)presentation of his characters; only those qualities that the director believes to be original, meaningful, or insightful are included in the depictions of his characters. Although the director does not gaze at his own reflection in the mirror, he does gaze at the reflection of his characters, in each shot, in each scene. This reflective process never gives the director a complete perception. Each reflection is particular to the current scene, and no evaluation attains finitude. The writer / director relies on the audience's external gaze to create the overall evaluation. In the next section, I argue that Rowe does in fact explore true complexity in subjectivity, particularly through the exploration of the intersubjective relationship of Laura and Arturo.

LAURA, ARTURO, AND AMBIGUITY

This exploration, I argue, occurs via careful representation of embodied characters. By this term of art, I mean that the characters are written, portrayed, and filmed in such a way as to emphasize the relationship between mind, body, and world, adding a sense of authenticity to the portrayal of complex subjectivity. This ability to represent a material and bodily presence to complex characters on screen is laudable. Sharma argues that complexity and ambiguity are often underrepresented in film, and misunderstood by film critics (2007: 180–2). This is especially true when such complexity has a material presence manifest in shots of bodies, body parts, bodily acts. Writing about Nair's films, but in a way that could be applied directly to Rowe's *Leap Year*, Sharma draws a parallel between Judith Butler's philosophy and representations of material bodies in movies. She writes:

> But there is something compelling about the idea that both philosopher and filmmaker seem agreed that the materiality of the body cannot be thought away; according to both, the gendered body is formed along the axis of a multitude of competing drives and power relations; and, for both, the overriding possibility of the body's mattering is one that coalesces performativity and political critique. (Sharma, 2007: 184)

Thinking in terms of Rowe's *Leap Year*, a particular scene comes to mind: the scene where Laura uses her hand to bring Arturo to orgasm while erotically whispering the increasingly violent acts she wishes him to perform on her own body. The simultaneity of seeing his bodily pleasure, while hearing about her bodily desires creates a material dialogue between two explicitly and realistically portrayed sexual bodies. Additionally, in this scene, the ambiguity of Arturo's comfort with Laura's escalating desire for violence becomes clear. Although his penis responds to her touch, culminating in a simulated orgasm, Arturo's face belies this pleasure, by showing concern over her request for extreme masochistic desire to die during their lovemaking, in fact to be killed violently by Arturo. The framing of the shots in this sequence is remarkable. In the beginning of this scene, we see a tight frame on Laura's and Arturo's upper bodies – we see the two of them lying close together on the bed, but unlike many of the other scenes of nudity in the film, we cannot see any genitalia. The framing is intimate and emphasizes the developing relationship between them. It also allows us to see Laura's obvious pleasure with her fantasy. Her face appears ecstatic, orgasmic, even though she is masturbating Arturo, and apparently not receiving any physical stimulation herself. It also allows us to see the changing expressions on Arturo's face, oscillating between obvious physical pleasure, and a halting concern over the fantasy. As the scene progresses, Laura's hand and the head of Arturo's penis slowly come into view at the lower edges of the screen. We can then see the material presence of both Arturo's pleasure (we see more of his penis, as his arousal increases), and the energy of Laura's desperate fantasy (her hand quickens as she escalates her explanation of her desire to die). The physicality of this scene underscores the tension between material bodies that Sharma explicates, but it also introduces the audience to the complexity of the politics of desire. The relative power between Laura and Arturo shifts throughout this sequence. Where a facile depiction of a handjob might emphasize the one-sided pleasure and therefore hierarchical power of such a sex act, this scene demonstrates that sexual power dynamics are fluid, fungible and complex.

Through the isolation of her life, the overpowering presence of the memory of her father, and her own inability to understand reality, Laura is unable to construct a permanent and meaningful personal identity, so she creates a world of sexual fantasy. Although we are never given clarity as to what the source of Laura's psychic pain truly is, it is clear that this pain is so unbearable that Laura's primary motivation is escape from the Real. At first, Laura determines reality externally, but lives in a dream world of isolation and sexual fantasy. The clearest example of this is the sequence in which Laura watches her neighbours through the edge of her curtain while masturbating. Although it would be easy to feel sorry for Laura, her character challenges any simple feelings of pity. Despite living in the shadow of death and trauma, she appears sexually animate, intellectually competent, and able to provide love and affection to others. Her seemingly inevitable progression towards an assisted suicidal death paradoxically frees her from her own emotional depression. She seems to actually enjoy looking for new jobs, engaging in sadomasochism, and in helping her brother in those last few days of February. This psychic resistance extends to her social behaviours as well. She lives duplicitously and dually, but not in a way intended to harm herself or others. She lies to her family, her lovers, and her employers, but she cares for them all, and, in fact, provides a care to them that they cannot or do not provide for themselves. She takes the fall for her employer when he fails to fact-check; she allows her mother to sell property left to her on her father's death; and, she takes her brother to a college fair and comforts him in his heartbreak. Each of these care acts is performed despite her seemingly debilitating and demoralizing depression. In an especially poignant gesture of personal affection, Laura buys and serves whiskey to Arturo, despite her own acknowledged dislike of it. These gentle and caring actions are performed alongside her sadomasochistic and self-destructive behaviours, providing tremendous moral and psychological ambiguity to the film.

The characters Laura and Arturo represent sex and gender dynamics in *Leap Year*, but they also represent dynamics of class and ethnicity. There is a similar ambiguity in the portrayal of her body. Del Carmen's Laura is not simply *mestiza*, her body is the paradigmatic *mestiza*. As dark-skinned, curvy, short, with a flat nose, Laura's body marks her as an outsider from urban Mexico. This contrast is only made more apparent through her selection of sexual partners, who all have bodies marking European descent. However, she seems unabashed by her own othered body, not only during sexual acts, but also when alone. There are many shots of Laura's nude or partially nude body throughout the film. These shots often challenge titillation – many involve mundane activities, like shaving legs or talking on the phone – and seem, instead, to highlight her embodied self-assuredness. However, her body also bears the signifiers of her sexual desires and erotic needs. She desires violence done to her neck, to her breasts, and to her buttocks – with her short neck and curves as primary signifiers of her *mestiza* bodily identity. The choice to make Laura a *mestiza* character, and to hire a *mestiza* actress, reinforces an interpretation of Rowe's film as intentionally supporting visionary ambiguity. In philosopher Gloria Anzaldúa's essay 'La Conciencia de la Mestiza / Towards a New Consciousness' she writes:

> The work of Mestiza consciousness is to break down the subject-object duality that keeps her a prisoner and to show in the flesh and through the images of her work how duality is transcended. The answer to the problem between the white and the coloured, between males and females, lies in healing the split that originates in the very foundation of our lives, our culture, our languages, our thoughts. (2003: 286)

Laura's body, psyche, and relationships all support an interpretation of complex subjective duality and tension.

Reinforcing this ambiguity is Arturo's relationship to Laura. Arturo relishes his sadistic treatment of Laura's body. In the scene I described above, Laura masturbates Arturo to ejaculation while describing increasingly violent fantasies of him murdering her. Despite his obvious enjoyment and arousal over such fantasies, Arturo does not kill Laura when she asks him, establishing separation between fantasy and sexual activity. Additionally, although he clearly enjoys the escalation of their sexual violence – up to the point of mortal danger – Arturo also seems to increasingly enjoy their post-coital tendernesses. In another scene in the film, the two of them sit on the couch, watching television and drinking, seemingly belying their transgressive sexual acts with mundane relationship behaviours. The scene is framed as a wide shot; viewers see the whole of the living room, the couch, and the lovers. There is an intimacy in this expansive framing, however. These wider shots function as a sort of inverse to Gilles Deleuze's interpretation of close-ups in *Cinema 1: The Movement Image*. He writes:

Ordinarily, three roles of the face are recognizable: it is individuating (it distinguishes or characterizes each person); it is socializing (it manifests a social role); it is relational or communicating (it ensures not only communication between two people, but also, in a single person, the internal agreement between his character and his role). Now the face, which effectively presents these aspects in the cinema as elsewhere, loses all three in the case of the close-up. (Deleuze, 1983: 101)

Deleuze is indicating that the close-up denudes the face in such a severe way as to remove its individuality. The face becomes bare – simply a face. The decision to employ a wide shot when many films would use a close-up turns this formula on its head. Additionally, the narrative oscillation between extreme sex and caring tenderness characterizes Arturo as another ambiguous character. Rowe's film appears to relish in the development of narrative ambiguity, the morally ambiguous characters, and filmic techniques that are inverted. This confluence of ambiguity destabilizes the viewer, making it impossible to simply watch and judge the film.

Film theorist M. Hunter Vaughan calls this ambiguity a form of seduction. He claims that the film industry is often trapped in a paradox between capitalizing on fantasy and seducing audiences with challenging ambiguities. He contrasts the theories of seduction with psychoanalytic models of desire, which he accuses of supporting exploitation and commodification (Vaughan, 2010). I agree with Vaughan that conventional desire, like conventional models of subjectivity, is essentially exploitative and marginalizing. However, I contend that a model of witnessing, in particular of witnessing marginalized identities, breaks through such a paradox rather than necessarily reinforcing a binary opposition at its core.

LAURA'S LIMINAL SUBJECTIVITY

Identifying with a liminal subject – a person, like Laura or Arturo, full of complexity and ambiguity that remains unresolved – occurs through a visionary process. Most philosophy defines identity formation in one of two ways: recognition or performativity. Those thinkers influenced by Hegel and the Enlightenment emphasize recognition, whereby subjects self-determine identity in relation to the respect and dignity afforded them by other subjects. Perhaps the most well-known formulation of such a theory of identity is in Hegel's Master / Slave dialectic in *The Phenomenology of Spirit* (1977). In this formulation, Hegel emphasizes that the master is only able to achieve self-consciousness through objectifying the slave, his identity is made possible through seeing his own reflection through the servitude of the other. Recognition, then, is an asymmetrical act of mirroring – the master and slave are not equals, but both are only aware of one another through their dependencies and relationships to each other.

Alternative theories of identity emerged in the twentieth and twenty-first century as ways of challenging the idea that subject-formation depends so entirely on another. Acknowledging the continued impact of Hegelian recognition theory, Butler argues that while we are undeniably constructed in relation to others, we can also adapt or change our 'performances' thereby changing what others expect of us. In her book, *Giving an Account of Oneself*, Butler explains that our performative accounts of self-identity occur in a larger context of history, language, and interpretation: 'The account is an act – situated within a larger practice of acts – that one performs for, to, even *on* another, an allocutory deed, an acting for, and in the face of, the other and sometimes by virtue of the language provided by the other' (2005: 130). For Butler, then, the process of seeing yourself through the eyes of another person also entails being located in a shared history, a shared understanding. But even more importantly, this act of subjectivity is a series of acts that are interpreted, changed, and mutable.

Both of these theories are often used in interpreting sexualized acts. Butler's own work often focuses on queer theory and feminist thought. She uses examples of transgendered identity as forms of performative resistance of restrictive social and sexual norms (2005). Following Rowe's directorial vision of challenging viewers to face the honest experience of human sexuality, then such an account seems helpful. Butler offers a way of understanding Laura as actively resisting the unfulfilling life of domesticity and neighbourliness that she pretends to have. Her resistance of this life is empowering in its authenticity, and in its ability to challenge the status quo. Hegel's Master / Slave dialectic is often used to argue for the potential empowerment in masochism, a likely way of interpreting Laura's character and experience in *Leap Year*. By this account, Laura's identity is even more fully realized than Arturo's, because Arturo needs Laura's submission and recognition to feel fulfilled, whereas Laura can feed off of his needs. However, in each of these interpretations, Laura's sexual behaviour is entirely determined

– as an act of resistance, or as an act of self-consciousness – and the ambiguity of her character diminishes.

In distinction to both the Hegelian dialectic and Butlerian performativity, I follow Kelly Oliver's theory of visionary identity. Oliver's model shares the importance of exchange with Hegel's formula, and it shares the importance of interpretation with Butler's, but it differs in ways that are meaningful for interpreting *Leap Year*. First, a visionary model of witnessing, requires exchange and interpretation that go beyond seeing or speech. Both visibility and comprehension limit the potential for marginalized and liminal identities because they reinscribe the identification of outsiders by requiring a normative framework for interpretation: the master, in the case of Hegel, or the Master's discourse, in the case of Butler. However, Laura's liminal and ambiguous identity is largely constructed by her invisibility to others. Her neighbours do not know her, her bosses communicate only over the phone or online, even her first few lovers do not seem to see *her* once they have achieved sexual fulfilment. Many marginal and liminal identities would be invisible, so how are we called upon to envision those outsiders – the *mestiza*, homebody, deviant, and vulnerable persons that Laura clearly embodies?

Laura's story forces the audience to confront the film beyond spectatorship, beyond simple seeing. The challenging themes the film explores paired with the fearless and raw acting, expose the film not as a mere mirror for creating an imago of the subject, which could be crystallized and objectified, but as a complex prism, reflecting facets of identity and relationality. The German phenomenologist Edmund Husserl argued that the visual gaze is limited in understanding embodiment in the intersubjective world – sight alone does not give us the ability to empathize and share with another subject. In his work *Ideas II* Husserl states: 'It is only with empathy and the constant orientation of empirical reflection onto the psychic life which is appresented along with the other's Body and which is continually taken Objectively, together with the Body, that the closed unity, man, is constituted, and I transfer this unity subsequently to myself' (1989: 175). Husserl claims that the other must be understood both objectively and as a Body with consciousness. The other's Body, like our own Bodies, cannot be understood visually – the visual merely makes a physical object of the body, not a Body-as-such. Empathy, and therefore, intersubjectivity are also limited by the visual sense, or the gaze. An understanding of the body, therefore, cannot be achieved through sight alone; it is not in the visible aspects, but the *touchable* aspects of objects that make an understanding of the body and its relation to the world possible.

The explicit and painfully real sex scenes of *Leap Year* offer movie viewers the opportunity of envisioning the bodies of Laura and Arturo as touchable. Touchable bodies are capable of pleasure and pain, often simultaneously; they are fraught with aesthetic variations like short legs and brown skin; they are felt in and through contact with other bodies. In this way, explicit and realistic sex scenes in narrative film might be uniquely helpful in creating alternative models of empathy and understanding. Additionally, a hybrid concept of visionary touch may offer a third way of understanding identity formation, granting narrative film the power of an imaginary domain, but one that highlights liberation, possibility, and self-identification at the boundaries of social norms and the status quo. Laura not only becomes a realistic character to be interpreted in the film, but an active interlocutor in helping viewers to imagine and construct their own subjectivities.

WITNESSING LEAP YEAR

As audience to a film, we automatically *see* the film just by watching; however, envisioning is a relational process. In the case of narrative films with the power to illuminate something about marginal identities, there are several possible interlocutors to participate with. The directors, the writers, the actors, even the characters and the scenes they are performing are all available to us for engaging in an envisioning process. In fact, in the best narrative films, a mutable and ever-changing locus of engagement forces viewers to experience beyond the visible alone.

In the end, it is not dreaming, gazing into a mirror, or creating art that gives the ultimate solution for solving the tension between being an object and being a subject. Instead, it is the realization that the tension exists, and a realization that that tension is neither meaningless nor all-powerful. It is the realization that something can be *both* subject *and* object, same *and* different. Rowe's Laura proves herself to be a psychologically and philosophically complex woman, not confined by a Panopticon gaze after all, but free from totalitarianism entirely. By transversing the boundaries of identity, decency, and social norms, Laura calls to us to bear witness. It is through the explicit sex scenes, in the low-budget film-making, and in the character's *mestiza* embodiment that this transversal is made possible. Witnessing is not an ethical good in and for itself, but is instead desirable as a liberatory model for creating subjectivity open to intersubjectivity: 'Only by witnessing the process of witnessing itself, the unseen in vision, the unsaid in language, can we begin to reconstruct our relationships by imagining ourselves together' (Oliver, 2001: 223).

NOTE

1 For more on the use of close-ups to sexualize and objectify see Laura Mulvey, 'Visual Pleasure and Narrative Cinema', *Screen, 16.3* (Autumn 1975), pp. 6–18.

Bibliography

Alfonso, Rita (2009). 'Permeability and Impermeability in John Cameron Mitchell's *Shortbus*', *Radical Philosophy Review*, 12, 1-2, pp. 121-36.
Altman, Rick (2001). 'Cinema and Popular Song', in Arthur Knight and Pamela Robertson Wojcik, (eds), *Soundtrack Available: Essays on Film and Popular Music* (Durham and London: Duke University Press), pp. 19-30.
American Booksellers Association, Inc. v. William H. Hudnut, Mayor, City of Indianapolis, 771 F.2d 323, 324 (7th Circuit, 1985).
Andrews, David (2006). *Soft in the Middle: The Contemporary Softcore Feature in its Contexts* (Columbus, OH: Ohio State University Press).
—— (2012). 'Toward a More Valid Definition of 'Pornography', *The Journal of Popular Culture*, 45, 3, pp. 457-77.
—— unpub. 'Rape as a Tool of Female Characterization in Peckinpah'.
Angelo, Adrienne (2010). 'Sexual Cartographies: Mapping Subjectivity in the Cinema of Catherine Breillat', *Journal for Cultural Research*, 14. 1, pp. 43-55.
Anon. (2002). 'Cannes film sickens audience', *BBC News*, 26 May. Available at http://news.bbc.co.uk/2/hi/entertainment/2008796.stm (accessed 15 August 2013).
—— (2007). 'ANG LEE Directs LUST, CAUTION', *Close-Up Film*. Available at http://www.close-upfilm.com/features/Interviews/anglee_lust_caution.html (accessed 6 April 2012).
Anzaldúa, Glória (2003). 'La Conciencia de la Mestiza: Towards a New Consciousness', in Carole R. McCann and Seung-Kyung Kim (eds), *Feminist Theory Reader: Local and Global Perspectives* (New York, NY: Routledge), p. 286.
Archer, Neil (2011). 'Beyond Anti-Americanism, Beyond Eurocentrism: Locating Bruno Dumont's *Twentynine Palms* in the Context of European Extremism', in Tina Kendall and Tanya Horeck, (eds), *The New Extremism in Cinema: from France to Europe* (Edinburgh: Edinburgh University Press), pp. 55-65.
Armengou, Frank García-Castrillón (2009). 'The death drive: Conceptual analysis and relevance in the Spanish psychoanalytic community', *International Journal of Psychoanalysis*, 90, 2, pp. 263-89. Available at http://ezproxy.auckland.ac.nz/login?url=http://search.proquest.com/docview/203961509?accountid=8424 (accessed 13 July 2013).

Australian Classification Review Board (2003). '*Ken Park* Refused Classification'. Available at http://www.classification.gov.au/About/Documents/230%20-%20Classificatoin%20Review%20Board%206%20June%202003.pdf (accessed 5 August 2012).

Barbey d'Aurevilly, J., and Jacques Petit (1964). *Oeuvres romanesques completes* (Paris: Gallimard), p.184.

Barthes, Roland (1977). 'The Death of the Author', *Image-Music-Text*. Trans. Stephen Heath (New York, NY: Hill and Wang), pp. 142–8.

Bataille, Georges (1929). 'Informe', Documents 1, Paris, 1929, (translated by Allan Stoekl with Carl R. Lovitt and Donald M. Leslie Jr), Georges Bataille. *Vision of Excess. Selected Writings, 1927–1939*, (Minneapolis: University of Minnesota Press), p. 328.

Bateman, Steve (2007). Interview with Black Rebel Motorcycle Club. Available at http://www.repeatfanzine.co.uk/interviews/brmc.htm (accessed 1 October 2013).

Bazin, Andre (2003). 'Death Every Afternoon', in Ivone Margulies (ed.), *Rites of Realism* (Durham, NC and London: Duke University Press), pp. 27–31.

Best, Victoria and Martin Crowley (2007). *The New Pornographies: Explicit Sex in Recent French Fiction and Film* (New York, NY and Manchester: Manchester University Press).

Beugnet, Martine (2007). *Cinema and Sensation: French Film and the Art of Transgression* (Edinburgh: Edinburgh University Press).

Beugnet, Martine (2007). *Cinema and Sensation: French Film and the Art of Transgression*. (Carbondale: Southern Illinois University Press).

Bitel, Anton (2012). 'Beauty Review', *Little White Lies*. 20 April. Available at http://www.littlewhitelies.co.uk/theatrical-reviews/beauty-18575 (accessed 17 November 2014).

Björkman, Stig (2003). *Trier on von Trier* (London: Faber & Faber).

Bombarda, Olivier (2011). 'Catherine Breillat à propos de son film "Une Veille maîtresse"'. Available at http://www.youtube.com/watch?v=4rChOG8vOuo (accessed 15 July 2013).

— (2012) 'Fu'ad Ait Aattou à propos de son rôle dans "Une Veille maîtresse" de Catherine Breillat'. Available at http://www.youtube.com/watch?v=4rChOG8vOuo (accessed 15 July 2013).

Bonitzer, Pascal (1992). 'Hitchcockian Suspense', in Slavoj Žižek (ed.), *Looking Awry: An Introduction to Jacques Lacan through Popular Culture* (London: Verso), p. 19.

Bradshaw, Peter (1999). 'Romance', the *Guardian*, 8 October. Available at http://www.guardian.co.uk/film/1999/oct/08/5 (accessed 1 October 2013).

— (2005) '9 Songs', the *Guardian*, 11 March. Available at http://film.guardian.co.uk/News_Story/Critic_Review/Guardian_Film_of_the_week/0,4267,1434764,00.html (accessed 1 October 2013).

Breillat, Catherine (2007). *Une vieille maitresse / The Last Mistress*. Perf. Asia Argento, Fu'ad Aït Aattou Roxane Mesquida. Videorecording. Artificial Eye, S.l.
Breillat, Catherine, and Claire Clouzot (2004). 'L'ABÉCDÉDAIRE de Catherine Breillat', *Catherine Breillat : indécence et pureté*. (Paris: Cahiers du cinéma), pp. 143–80.
Breillat, Catherine, Jean-Christophe Ferrari and Grégory Valens (2007). 'On doit brûler pour l'art: Entretien avec Catherine Breillat', *Positif*, pp. 21–5.
Brennan, Justice William. *Roth v. United States*, 354 U.S. 476 (1957).
Brevik-Zender, Heidi (2012). 'Undressing the Costume Drama: Catherine Breillat's *Une vieille maîtresse*', *Adaptation*, 5, 2, pp. 203–18. Available at http://adaptation.oxfordjournals.org/content/5/2/203.abstract (accessed 4 July 2013).
Brinkema, Eugenie (2005). 'Rape and the Rectum: Bersani, Deleuze, Noé', *Camera Obscura 58*, 20, 1, pp. 33–57.
—— (2006). 'Celluloid is Sticky: Sex, Death, Materiality, Metaphysics (in Some Films by Catherine Breillat)', *Women*, 17, 2, pp. 147–70. Available at http://ezproxy.auckland.ac.nz/login?url=http://search.ebscohost.com/login.aspx?direct=true&db=a2h&AN=21572286&site=ehost-live&scope=site (accessed 4 July 2013).
British Board of Film Classification. *9 Songs* 'Case Study'. Available at http://www.sbbfc.co.uk/CaseStudies/9_Songs (accessed 1 October 2013).
——. *Maitresse*, 'From the Archive'. Available at http://www.bbfc.co.uk/casestudies/maitresse. (accessed 2012).
Brooks, Libby (2001). 'The joy of sex', the *Guardian*, 22 November. Available at http://www.theguardian.com/film/2001/nov/23/filmcensorship.artsfeatures (accessed 4 July 2013).
Brooks, Xan (2009). '*Antichrist*: A work of genius or the sickest film in the history of cinema', the *Guardian*, 16 July. Available at http://www.guardian.co.uk/film/2009/jul/16/antichrist-lars-von-trier-feminism (accessed 16 July 2013).
Buch-Hansen, Gitte (2011). 'Lars von Trier's *Antichrist*, the Bible and Docetic Masculinity', *Relegere: Studies in Religion and Reception*, 1, 1, pp. 115–44.
Buck-Morss, Susan (1993). 'Aesthetics and Anaesthetics: Walter Benjamin's Artwork Essay Reconsidered', *New Formations*, 20, pp. 123–43.
Bunbury, Stephanie (2011). 'Ang Lee pushes his actors to the brink', *The Age*, 21 January. Available at http://www.theage.com.au/news/film/fang-lee-cruel-but-true/2008/01/10/1199554807538.html (accessed 6 April 2012).
Butler, Judith (2005). *Giving an Account of Oneself*. (New York, NY: Fordham University Press), p. 130.
Cameron, Allan (2006). 'Contingency, Order, and the Modular Narrative: *21 Grams* and *Irréversible*', *The Velvet Light Trap*, 58 (Fall), pp. 65–78.
Carroll, Noël (1996). *Theorizing the Moving Image* (Cambridge: Cambridge University Press).

Cheu, Hoi (2007). *Cinematic Howling: Women's Films, Women's Film Theories* (Vancouver, BC: UBC Press).

Chiesa, Lorenzo (2012). 'Of Bastard Man and Evil Woman, or, the Horror of Sex', *Film-Philosophy*, 16, 1.

Clark, Larry (1971). *Tulsa* (New York: Grove Press).

Clouzot, Claire (2004). *Catherine Breillat : indécence et pureté*. (Paris: Cahiers du cinéma).

Coates, Norma (1997). '(R)evolution Now? Rock and the Political Potential of Gender' in Sheila Whitely (ed.), *Sexing the Groove: Popular Music and Gender* (London and New York, NY: Routledge), pp. 50–64.

Cohen, Sara (1997). 'Men Making a Scene' in Shiela Whitely (ed.), *Sexing the Groove: Popular Music and Gender*. (London and New York, NY: Routledge), pp. 17–36.

Coulthard, Lisa (2010). 'Desublimating Desire: Courtly Love and Catherine Breillat', *Journal for Cultural Research*, 14, 1, pp. 57–69. Available at http://ezproxy.auckland.ac.nz/login?url=http://search.ebscohost.com/login.aspx?direct=true&db=aph&AN=47602961&site=ehost-live&scope=site (accessed 4 July 2013).

Crabbe, Anthony (1988). 'Feature-length Sex Films', in Gary Day and Clive Bloom (eds), *Perspectives on Pornography* (New York, NY: St. Martin's Press).

Creed, Barbara (1983). 'Pornography and Pleasure: The female spectator', *Australian Journal of Screen Studies*, 15/16, pp. 67–88.

Cuir, Raphaël (2007). 'Larry Clark interview', *Art Press*, August. Available at http://harmony-korine.com/text/int/lc/?p=137 (accessed 5 August 2012).

Damasio, Antonio (2012). *Self Comes to Mind* (New York, NY: Vintage).

Dargis, Manohla (2006). 'Naughty and Nice in Carnal Carnival', *New York Times*, 4 October. Available at http://movies.nytimes.com/2006/10/04/movies/04shor.html?_r=0 (accessed 30 November 2014).

Davis, Nick (2008). 'The View from the *Shortbus*, or All Those Fucking Movies', *GLQ: A Journal of Lesbian and Gay Studies*, 14, 4, pp. 623–37.

Deleuze, Gilles (1983). *L'image-mouvement* (Paris: Minuit).

Deleuze, Gilles and Félix Guattari (1980). *A Thousand Plateaus*. Trans. Brian Massumi (London and New York: Continuum).

Ding, Shaoyan (2011). 'Beyond language: The postmodern poetics of Ang Lee's adaptation of *Lust/Caution*', *Critical Arts: South-North Cultural and Media Studies*, 25, 1, pp. 88–101.

Doherty, Tom (1995). 'Clueless Kids', *Cineaste*, 21, 4, pp. 14–16.

Douglas, Justice William O. *Ginzburg v. United States*, 383 U.S. 463 (1966).

Downing, Lisa (2004). 'French Cinema's New 'Sexual Revolution': Postmodern porn and troubled genre', *French Cultural Studies*, 15, 3.

Dworkin, Andrea (1994). 'Where Do We Stand on Pornography?' (Roundtable) *Ms.*, January / February. Cited in Nadine Strossen (2000). *Defending*

Pornography: Free Speech, Sex, and the Fight for Women's Rights (New York, NY: New York University Press).

Dyer, Richard (1981). 'Entertainment and Utopia', in Rick Altman (ed.), *Genre: The Musical – A Reader* (London: Routledge).

—— (1992). *Only Entertainment* (New York, NY: Routledge), p. 18.

Eagleton, Terry (1990). *The Ideology of the Aesthetic* (Oxford: Blackwell).

Ebert, Roger (2005). '9 Songs'. Available at http://www.rogerebert.com/reviews/9-songs-2005 (accessed 1 October 2013).

Esch, Kevin and Vicki Mayer (2007). 'How Unprofessional: The Profitable Partnership of Amateur Porn and Celebrity Culture', in Susanna Paasonen, Kaarina Nikunen, and Laura Saarenmaa, (eds), *Pornification: Sex and Sexuality in Media Culture* (Oxford: Berg).

Fayard, Nicole (2006). 'The Rebellious Body as Parody: *Baise-moi* by Virginie Despentes', *French Studies: A Quarterly Review* 60, 1, pp. 63–77.

Fisher, Helen E. et al. (2002). 'Defining the Brain Systems of Lust, Romantic Attraction, and Attachment', *Archives of Sexual Behavior*, 31, 5, pp. 413–19.

Flambard-Weisbart, Véronique (2013). 'Prendre le désir par les cornes : De Leiris à Breillat', *Contemporary French & Francophone Studies*, 17, 3, pp. 338–46.

Foucault, Michel (1977a). *Discipline and Punish: The Birth of the Prison* (New York, NY: Pantheon).

—— (1977b) *Society Must Be Defended: Lectures at the Collège de France, 1975–1976* (New York, NY: St. Martin's Press). pp. 243–44.

Franco, Judith (2004). 'Gender, Genre and Female Pleasure in the Contemporary Revenge Narrative: *Baise-moi* and what it feels like for a girl', *Quarterly Review of Film and Video* 21, 1, pp. 1–10.

Freud, Sigmund (1991). 'Essay 1: The Sexual Aberrations', *On Sexuality: Three Essays on the Theory of Sexuality.* (Harmondsworth: Penguin Books).

Frith, Simon (1996). *Performing Rites: On the Value of Popular Music* (Cambridge, MA: Harvard University Press).

Gamman, Lorraine (1989). 'Watching the Detectives: The Enigma of the Female Gaze', in Lorraine Gamman and Margaret Marshment (eds), *The Female Gaze: Women as Viewers of Popular Culture* (Seattle: The Real Comet Press).

Gazzaniga, Michael S., Richard B. Ivry and George R. Mangun (2009). *Cognitive Neuroscience. The Biology of the Mind.* (New York, NY: Norton).

Georgiadis, Janniko R., Rudie Kortekaas, Rutger Kuipers, Arie Neuwenburg, Jan Pruim, A. A. T. Reinders and Gert Holstege (2006). 'Cerebral blood flow changes associated with clitorally induced orgasm in healthy women', *European Journal of Neuroscience*, 24, pp. 3305–16.

Gibbons, Fiachra and Stuart Jeffries (2001). 'Cannes audience left open-mouthed', the *Guardian*, 14 May. Available at http://www.theguardian.com/world/2001/may/14/cannes2001.cannesfilmfestival (accessed 15 August 2013).

Gibson, Ralph (2010). 'Larry Clark', *Interview Magazine*. Available at http://www.interviewmagazine.com/art/larry-clark/#/_ (accessed 5 August 2012).
Grodal, Torben (1997). *Moving Pictures. A New Theory of Film Genres, Feelings, and Cognition* (Oxford: Oxford University Press).
— (2008). 'Evolutionary Theory and the Naturalist Fallacy'. *Style*, 42, 2–3, pp. 192–6.
— (2009). *Embodied Visions. Evolution, Emotion, Culture and Film*. (New York, NY: Oxford University Press).
— (2012). 'Frozen style and strong emotions of panic and separation: Trier's prologues to *Antichrist* and *Melancholia*', *Journal of Scandinavian Cinema*, 2, 1, p. 47–53.
Guillen, Michael (2007). '2007 MVFF30: LUST, CAUTION – Interview With Ang Lee & Tang Wei', *Twitch*. Available at http://twitchfilm.com/2007/10/2007-mvff30-lust-cautioninterview-with-ang-lee-tang-wei.html (accessed 26 February 2013).
Gurley, George (2002). 'A Naked Star is Born', *New York Observer*, 22 July. Available at http://observer.com/2002/07/a-naked-star-is-born/ (accessed 5 August 2012).
Hammett, Jennifer (2003). 'The Ideological Impediment: Epistemology, Feminism, and Film Theory', in Richard Allen and Murray Smith, (eds), *Film Theory and Philosophy* (Oxford: Oxford University Press).
Hegel, Georg Wilhelm (1977). *The Phenomenology of Spirit*. Trans. Arnold Vincent Miller. (Oxford: Oxford University Press), p. 116.
Hennigan, Adrian (2005). 'Michael Winterbottom', *BBC*. Available at http://www.bbc.co.uk/films/2005/03/03/michael_winterbottom_9_songs_interview.shtml (accessed 1 October 2013).
Higgins, Charlotte (2004). 'Cannes screening for most sexually explicit British film', the *Guardian*, 17 May. Available at http://www.guardian.co.uk/uk/2004/may/17/cannes2004.film (accessed 1 October 2013).
hooks, bell (1996). *Reel to Real: Race, Sex, and Class at the Movies* (New York, NY: Routledge). http://www.amazon.com/Reel-Real-Movies-Routledge-Classics-ebook/dp/B00AZ4U7AO/ref=la_B000APGZIG_1_10?s=books&ie=UTF8&qid=1427484922&sr=1-10.
— (2012). *Reel to Real: Race, Sex and Class at the Movies* (Routledge, ebook, 6 December).
Horeck, Tanya and Tina Kendall (2011). 'Introduction', in Tanya Horeck and Tina Kendall, (eds), *The New Extremism in Cinema: From France to Europe* (Edinburgh: Edinburgh University Press).
Houellebecq, Michel (2001). *Platform* (London: Vintage).
Hsu, Hsuan L. (2006). 'Radical Privacy, the L.A. Ensemble Film, and Paul Haggis's *Crash*', *Film Criticism*, 31, 1–2, pp. 132–56.

Husserl, Edmund (1989). *Ideas Pertaining to a Pure Phenomenology and to a Phenomenological Philosophy – Second Book: Studies in the Phenomenology of Constitution*. Trans. Richard Rojcewicz and Andre Schuwer (Dordrecht: Kluwer).

Hutcheon, Linda (2002). *The Politics of Postmodernism* (Taylor & Francis). Available at http://lib.myilibrary.com.ezproxy.library.ubc.ca?ID=7453 (accessed 30 April 2013).

Jeremy, Ron with Eric Spitznagel (2007). *Ron Jeremy: The Hardest (Working) Man in Showbiz – Horny Women, Hollywood Nights, and the Rise of the Hedgehog* (New York, NY: HarperCollins Publishers).

Johnson, Eithne (1993). 'Excess and Ecstasy: Constructing Female Pleasure in Porn Movies', *The Velvet Light Trap*, 32, (Fall), pp. 30-49.

Jones, Kristin M. (2005). 'Larry Clark', *Frieze*, Issue 91. Available at http://www.frieze.com/issue/review/larry_clark1/ (accessed 5 August 2012).

Kaminsky, M. Sean (Dir.) (2007). 'Gifted and Challenged: The Making of *Shortbus*', *Shortbus* DVD Special Features documentary.

Keesey, Douglas (2009). *Catherine Breillat* (Manchester and New York, NY: Manchester University Press).

— (2010a). 'Neither a Wife nor a Whore: Deconstructing Feminine Icons in Catherine Breillat's *Une vieille maitresse*', *Journal for Cultural Research*, 14, 1, pp. 5-14. Available at http://ezproxy.auckland.ac.nz/login?url=http://search.ebscohost.com/login.aspx?direct=true&db=a2h&AN=47602954&site=ehost-live&scope=site (accessed 4 July 2013).

— (2010b), 'Split identification: Representations of rape in Gaspar Noé's *Irréversible* and Catherine Breillat's *À ma soeur! / Fat Girl*', *Studies in European Cinema*, 7, 2, pp. 95-107.

Kelley, Mike (1992). 'Larry Clark: In Youth is Pleasure', *Flash Art*, 25, 164, pp. 82-6.

Kendrick, Walter (1996). *The Secret Museum: Pornography in Modern Culture* (Berkeley: University of California Press).

Knight, Arthur and Pamela Robertson Wojcik (eds), (2001). *Soundtrack Available: Essays on Film and Popular Music* (Durham, NC and London: Duke University Press).

Koether, Jutta (1992). 'Larry Clark', *Journal of Contemporary Art*. Available at http://www.jca-online.com/clark.html (accessed 5 August 2012).

Konrad, Todd '9 Songs', *Independent Film Quarterly*. Available at http://independentfilmquarterly.com/index.php?option=com_content&task=view&id=295&Itemid=115 (accessed 1 October 2013).

Koschorke, Albrecht (2001). 'Mastery and Slavery: A Masochist Falls Asleep Reading Hegel', *MLN*, 116.3, pp. 551-63.

Krzywinska, Tanya (2006). *Sex and the Cinema* (London: Wallflower Press).

Kundera, Milan (2005). *The Art of the Novel* (London: Faber & Faber).

Lacan, Jacques (2001). *Écrits: A Selection*. Trans. Alan Sheridan (New York, NY: Routledge), p. ix.

Lachman, Ed (2002). 'Ed Lachman on *Ken Park*'. Online video available at http://www.youtube.com/watch?v=Qog9asJwwzw (accessed 5 August 2012).

Langton, Rae (2009). *Sexual Solipsism: Philosophical Essays on Pornography and Objectification* (Oxford: Oxford University Press).

Lanxon, Nate (2013). 'Hardcore sex in *Nymphomaniac* puts porn actor genitals on cast's bodies'. *Wired UK*. 22 May. Available at http://www.wired.co.uk/news/archive/2013-05/22/nymphomaniac (accessed 28 July 2013).

Lehman, Peter (2001). 'Crying Over the Melodramatic Penis: Melodrama and Male Nudity in Films of the 90s', in Peter Lehman (ed.), *Masculinity: Bodies, Movies, Culture* (London: Routledge), pp. 25–41.

— (2006). 'Revelations about Pornography', in Peter Lehman, (ed.), *Pornography: Film and Culture*. (Piscataway, NJ: Rutgers University Press).

Lehman, Peter and Susan Hunt (2009). 'Exposing the Body Guy: The Return of the Repressed in *Twentynine Palms*', in Santiago Fouz-Hernandez (ed.), *Mysterious Skin: Male Bodies in Contemporary Cinema* (London: I.B.Tauris), pp. 207–19.

Lenos, Melissa and Ryan, Michael (2012). *An Introduction to Film Analysis: Technique and Meaning in Narrative Film* (London and New York: Bloomsbury).

Light, Jonathan (2002). *The Art of Porn* (New York, NY: Light Publishing).

Lloyd, E. L. (1986). 'Points: Hallucinations, hypoxia, and neurotransmitters', *British Medical Journal*, 292, p. 903.

Lubecker, Nikolaj (2011). 'Bruno Dumont's *Twentynine Palms*: The avant-garde as tragedy?', *Studies in French Cinema*, 11, 3, pp. 235–47.

MacDowell, James (2010). 'Notes on Quirky', *Movie: A Journal of Film Criticism*, Issue 1. Available at http://www2.warwick.ac.uk/fac/arts/film/movie/contents/notes_on_quirky.pdf (accessed 7 May 2014).

MacKenzie, Scott (2002). '*Baise-moi*, feminist cinemas and the censorship controversy', *Screen: The Journal of the Society for Education in Film and Television*, 43, 3, pp. 315-24.

— (2010). 'On Watching and Turning Away: Ono's *Rape*, *Cinéma Direct* Aesthetics, and the Genealogy of *Cinéma Brut*', in Dominique Russell (ed.), *Rape in Art Cinema* (New York, NY: Continuum), pp. 159–70.

MacKinnon, Catharine A. (1995). 'Frances Biddle's Sister: Pornography, Civil Rights, and Speech', in Susan Dwyer (ed.), *The Problem of Pornography* (Belmont, CA: Wadsworth Publishing Company).

Mahadevan, Sudhir (2005). 'Perfect Childhoods: Larry Clark Puts Boys Onscreen', in Murray Pomerance and Frances Gatewood (eds), *Where the Boys Are: Cinemas of Masculinity and Youth* (Detroit, MI: Wayne State University Press), pp. 98–113.

Maitland, Sara (1993). 'Ecstasy', in Harriett Gilbert (ed.), *The Sexual Imagination* (London: Jonathan Cape), p. 78.

Manlove, Clifford T. (2007). 'Visual "Drive" and Cinematic Narrative: Reading Gaze Theory in Lacan, Hitchcock, and Mulvey', *Cinema Journal*, 46, 3, pp. 83-108.

Marks, Laura U. (2000). *The Skin of the Film: Intercultural Cinema, Embodiment, and the Senses* (Durham, NC: Duke University Press).

Mathews, Tom Dewe (1994). *Censored: The Story of Film Censorship in Britain* (London: Chatto & Windus).

McCarthy, Todd (2009). 'Review: *Antichrist*', *Variety*, 17 May. Available at http://variety.com/2009/film/reviews/antichrist-1200474819/ (accessed 15 Aug 2013).

McElroy, Wendy (1995). *XXX: A Woman's Right to Pornography* (New York: St. Martin's Press).

McKew, Maxine (2003). 'Director defends *Ken Park*'. Available at http://www.abc.net.au/7.30/content/2003/s896904.htm (accessed 5 August 2012).

Metz, Christian (1982). *The Imaginary Signifier: Psychoanalysis and the Cinema* (Bloomington, IN: Indiana University Press), p. 77.

Miller, Susan (2004). *Disgust: the Gatekeeper Emotion* (London: Routledge).

Miller v. California, 413 U.S. 15 (1973).

Mulvey, Laura (1975). 'Visual Pleasure and Narrative Cinema', *Screen: The Journal of the Society for Education in Film and Television* 16, 3, pp. 6-18.

Muñoz, José Esteban (1998). 'Rough boy trade: queer desire / straight identity in the photography of Larry Clark', in Deborah Bright (ed.), *The Passionate Camera: Photography and Bodies of Desire* (London: Routledge), pp. 167-77.

Nancy, Jean-Luc (2008). 'Icon of Fury: Claire Denis's *Trouble Every Day*', *Film-Philosophy* 12, 8. Available at http://www.film-philosophy.com/2008v12n1/nancy.pdf (accessed 1 May 2013).

Needham, Gary (2009). 'Closer Than Ever: Contemporary French Cinema and the Male Body in Close-Up', in Santiago Fouz-Hernandez (ed.), *Mysterious Skin: Male Bodies in Contemporary Cinema* (London: I.B.Tauris).

NME (2005). 'Arctic Monkeys – A Scummy Man and Mardy Bums: The ultimate Arctic Monkeys Album Guide', October. Available at http://www.nme.com/arcticmonkeys/albumguide (accessed 1 October 2013). (Link no longer working.)

Noys, Benjamin (2000). *Georges Bataille: A Critical Introduction* (London: Pluto Press).

O'Connor, Tom Austin (2009). 'Genre-%!$?Ing: Harmony Korine's Cinema Of Poetry', *Wide Screen*, 1, 1. Available at http://widescreenjournal.org/index.php/journal/article/view/62/103 (accessed 5 August 2012).

O'Hagan, Sean (2008). 'The kids stay in the picture', *The Observer*, 17 February. Available at http://www.guardian.co.uk/artanddesign/2008/feb/17/photography.exhibition1 (accessed 5 August 2012).

O'Sullivan, Simon (2001). 'The Aesthetics Of Affect: Thinking art beyond representation', *ANGELAKI journal of the theoretical humanities*, 6, 3, pp. 125-35.

Oliver, Kelly (2001). *Witnessing: Beyond Recognition* (Minneapolis, MN: University of Minnesota Press).

Oumano, Elena (2011). *Cinema Today a Conversation with Thirty-nine Filmmakers from around the World* (New Brunswick, NJ and Baltimore, MD: Rutgers University Press).

Paasonen, Susanna and Laura Saarenmaa (2007). 'The Golden Age of Porn: Nostalgia and History of Cinema', in Susanna Paasonen, Kaarina Nikunen and Laura Saarenmaa, (eds), *Pornification: Sex and Sexuality in Media Culture* (Oxford: Berg).

Palmer, Tim (2006). 'Style and Sensation in the Contemporary French Cinema of the Body', *Journal of Film and Video*, 58, 3, (Fall), pp. 22-32.

— (2011). *Brutal Intimacy: Analyzing Contemporary French Cinema* (Middletown, CT: Wesleyan University Press).

— (2013). *Directory of World Cinema: France: 15* (London: Intellect), p. 93.

Panksepp, Jaak (1998). *Affective Neuroscience* (New York, NY: Oxford University Press).

— (2005). 'Affective Consciousness: Core emotional feelings in animals and humans'. *Consciousness and Cognition* 14 (2005), pp. 30-80.

— and Lucy Biven (2012). *The Archeology of Mind* (New York, NY: Norton).

Papoulias, Tina (1993). 'Masochism', in Harriett Gilbert (ed.), *The Sexual Imagination* (London: Jonathan Cape), p. 165.

Pataphysics (2003). 'Pataphysics Magazine Interview with Larry Clark'. Available at http://www.yanniflorence.net/pataphysicsmagazine/clark_interview.html (accessed 5 August 2012).

Perkins, Claire (2012). *American Smart Cinema* (Edinburgh: Edinburgh University Press).

Phillips, Adam (1994). *On Flirtation* (London and Boston: Faber & Faber).

Phillips, John (2001). 'Catherine Breillat's Romance: Hard Core and the Female Gaze', *Studies in French Cinema*, 1, 3, p. 133.

Phipps, Keith (2006). 'Shortbus', *Onion AV Club*, 5 October. Available at http://www.avclub.com/articles/shortbus,3763/ (accessed 30 November 2014).

Piepenburg, Erik (2012). 'What Frightens Horror Directors?', Interview with John Carpenter, Tobe Hooper, James Wan and Adam Rehmeier, *New York Times*, 3 October. Available at http://www.nytimes.com/interactive/arts/art-shock.html (accessed 4 October 2012).

Pomerance, Murray (2013). *Alfred Hitchcock's America* (Cambridge: Polity Press).

Pomeranz, Margaret (2006). 'An Interview with Michael Winterbottom' for ABC. Available at http://www.abc.net.au/atthemovies/txt/s1358917.htm (accessed 1 October 2013).

Prince, Stephen (1998). *Savage Cinema: Sam Peckinpah and the Rise of Ultraviolent Movies* (Austin, TX: University of Texas Press).
Reeves, David and Shari Roman (2002). 'Larry's Kids', *The Face*, October. Available at http://harmony-korine.com/text/int/lc/?p=103 (accessed 5 August 2012).
Ridley, Jim (2006). 'The Harder They Come', *The Village Voice*, 26 September. Available at http://www.villagevoice.com/2006-09-26/film/the-harder-they-come/ (accessed 30 November 2014).
Romney, Jonathan (2008). 'Abominable Glory', *Sight & Sound*, 18, 5, pp. 34-8.
Rozemayer, Karl (2008). 'Sex on Film: Larry Clark', *Premiere*, April. Available at http://harmony-korine.com/text/int/lc/?p=147 (accessed 5 August 2012).
Rushton, Richard (2010). 'Acknowledgement and Unknown Women: The Films of Catherine Breillat', *Journal for Cultural Research*, 14, 1, pp. 85-101. Available at http://ezproxy.auckland.ac.nz/login?url=http://search.ebscohost.com/login.aspx?direct=true&db=a2h&AN=47602959&site=ehost-live&scope=site (accessed 4 July 2013).
Russell-Watts, Lynsey (2010). 'Marginalized Males? Men, Masculinity and Catherine Breillat', *Journal for Cultural Research*, 14, 1, pp. 71-84. Available at http://ezproxy.auckland.ac.nz/login?url=http://search.ebscohost.com/login.aspx?direct=true&db=a2h&AN=47602960&site=ehost-live&scope=site (accessed 4 July 2013).
Sank, Lawrence I. (1998). 'Traumatic Masturbatory Syndrome', *Journal of Sex and Marital Therapy*, 24, 1, pp. 37-42.
Scalia, Justice Antonin. *Pope v. Illinois*, 481 U.S. 497 (1987).
Schaefer, Eric (2002). 'Gauging a Revolution: 16mm Film and the Rise of the Pornographic Feature', *Cinema Journal*, 41, 3, pp. 3-26.
Schneider, Steven Jay (2005). '*Jerkus Interruptus*: The Terrible Trials of Masturbating Boys in Recent Hollywood Cinema', in Murray Pomerance and Frances Gatewood (eds), *Where the Boys Are: Cinemas of Masculinity and Youth* (Detroit, MI: Wayne State University Press), pp. 377-93.
Schrader, Paul (1995). 'Babes in the Hood', *Artforum International*, 23, 9, May, pp. 74-9.
Schuessler, Jennifer (2012). 'Maggie Nelson on the Limitations of Shock', *New York Times*, 3 October. Available at http://www.nytimes.com/interactive/arts/art-shock.html (accessed 4 October, 2012).
Sconce, Jeffrey (2006). 'Smart Cinema', in Linda Ruth Williams and Michael Hammond (eds), *Contemporary American Cinema* (Maidenhead: Open University Press/McGraw-Hill), pp. 429-39.
Segal, Lynne (1993). 'Pornography', in Harriett Gilbert (ed.), *The Sexual Imagination* (London: Jonathan Cape), pp. 207-8.

Senjanovic, Natasha (2010). '*Leap Year* has too much sex for moviegoers', 17 May. Available at http://www.reuters.com/article/2010/05/17/us-film-leapyear-idUSTRE64G6NI20100517 (accessed 20 March 2014).

Sharma, Alpana (2007). 'Body Matters: The Politics of Provocation in Mira Nair's Films', in Julie F. Codell (ed.), *Genre, Gender, Race, and World Cinema* (Malden, MA: Blackwell), p. 182.

Sharrett, Christopher. (2012). 'Woman Run Amok: Two Films by Lars von Trier', *Film International*, 10, 6, pp. 12-36.

Smith, Angela (2011). 'Femininity Repackaged: Postfeminism and *Ladette to Lady*' in Melanie Waters (ed.), *Women on Screen: Feminism and Femininity in Visual Culture* (London: Palgrave), pp. 153-66.

Smith, Damon (2008). 'The Kids Are Not All Right: Larry Clark on *Wassup Rockers* and More', *Bright Lights Film Journal*, August. Available at http://www.brightlightsfilm.com/61/61larryclarkiv.php (accessed 5 August 2012).

Smith, Gavin (1995). 'The Joyous Pessimism of Barbet Schroeder', Film Comment, Film Society of Lincoln Center, 2004, pp. 1-20. Available at http://www.barbetschroeder.com/ (accessed 22 December 2010).

Society for Promotion of Community Standards 2004, Press release, 8 November. Available at http://www.scoop.co.nz/stories/CU0411/S00064.htm (accessed 2 September, 2012).

Stafford, Mark (2010) '*Leap Year*: Interview with Michael Rowe', 21 November. Available at http://www.electricsheepmagazine.co.uk/features/2010/11/21/leap-year-interview-with-michael-rowe/ (accessed 1 April 2013).

Stein, Elliott (1977). 'Planetary Fantasies: Barbet Schroeder interviewed by Elliott Stein', *Film Comment*, 13, 1, pp. 52-7.

— (2004). 'Maîtresse', pp. 1-6. Available at http://www.criterion.com/current/posts/309 (accessed 14 February 2013).

Steinem, Gloria (1995). 'Erotica and Pornography: A Clear and Present Difference', in Susan Dwyer (ed.), *The Problem of Pornography* (Belmont, CA: Wadsworth Publishing Company).

Sterritt, David (2007). '"Time Destroys All Things": An Interview With Gaspar Noé', *Quarterly Review of Film and Video*, 24, 4, pp. 307-16.

Stewart, Justice Potter. Jacobellis v. Ohio, 378 U.S. 184 (1964).

Strossen, Nadine (2000). *Defending Pornography: Free Speech, Sex, and the Fight for Women's Rights* (New York, NY: New York University Press).

Taubin, Amy (1995). 'Chilling and Very Hot', *Sight and Sound*, 5, 11, p. 19.

— (2008). 'Carnal Extremes', *Film Comment*, 44, 3, pp. 26-9.

Tinkcom, Matthew (2011). '"You've got to get on to get off": *Shortbus* and the Circuits of the Erotic', *The South Atlantic Quarterly*, Summer, pp. 693-713.

Tolkien, J. R. R. (1966). 'On Fairy-stories', in *The Tolkien Reader* (New York, NY: Random House).

Travers, Peter (2006). 'Shortbus', *Rolling Stone*, 5 October. Available at http://www.rollingstone.com/movies/reviews/shortbus-20061005#ixzz2XAVdPF2T (accessed 30 November 2014).

Valdesolo, Piercarlo (2011). 'How our Brains Turn Women into Objects', *Scientific American*, 11 October. Available at http://www.scientificamerican.com/article.cfm?id=how-our-brains-turn-women-into-objects&WT.mc_id=SA_WR_20111013 (accessed 1 November 2012).

Vaughan, M. Hunter (2010). 'The Paradox of Film: An Industry of Sex, a Form of Seduction (on Jean Baudrillard's *Seduction* and the Cinema)', *Film-Philosophy*, 14.2, pp. 41–61.

Vignoles, Patrick (2011). *La perversité* (ed.) Laurence Hansen-Løve. Available at http://www.ac-grenoble.fr/PhiloSophie/file/vignoles_perversite.pdf (accessed 4 July 2013).

Waddell, Terrie (2012). '*Antichrist*: Lost Children, Love, and the Fear of Excess', in Karen Ritzenhoff and Karen Randell, (eds), *Screening the Dark Side of Love* (Basingstoke: Palgrave Macmillan).

Walker, Deborah (2007). 'Re-reading the Femme Fatale in Film Noir: an evolutionary perspective', *Journal of Moving Image Studies*, 4, p. 25. Available at http://www.avila.edu/journal/vol4/Fatale%20evolutionary%20reading%20DW%20final2.pdf (accessed 4 July 2013). (Link is no longer available.)

Walters, Natasha (2005). 'When Sex Got Boring', cited the *Guardian*, 9 March. Available at http://www.guardian.co.uk/film/2005/mar/09/comment.features (accessed 1 October 2013).

Wang, Xiaoping (2010). 'Making a Historical Fable: the narrative strategy of *Lust, Caution* and its social repercussions', *Journal of Contemporary China*, 19, 65, pp. 573–90.

Weatherwill, Rob (2006). 'Bataille and Levinas at the Limits of Psychoanalysis', pp. 1–6. Available at http://www.psychoanalysis.ie/index.php?id=87 (accessed 14 February 2013).

Weddle, David (1994). *The Life and Times of Sam Peckinpah* (New York, NY: Grove).

Whale, Chase (2014). 'Wet And Wild', *Central Track*. 10 September. Available at http://centraltrack.com/Film/5824/Wet-And-Wild-/Wetlands-Is-A-Filthy-And-Touching-Story-About-A-Girl-And-Her-Hemorrhoids- (accessed 17 November 2014).

Wicke, Peter (1990). *Rock Music: Culture, Aesthetics, and Sociology*. Translated by Rachel Fogg (Cambridge: Cambridge University Press).

Williams, Linda (1990). *Hard Core: Power, Pleasure, and the 'Frenzy of the Visible'* (London: Pandora Press).

— (1996). 'When the Woman Looks', in Barry Keith Grant (ed.), *The Dread of Difference* (Austin, TX: University of Texas Press), pp. 15–34.

— (1999). *Hard Core: Power, Pleasure, and the 'Frenzy of the Visible'* (Berkeley, CA: University of California Press).

— (2001). 'Cinema and the Sex Act', *Cineaste*, 27(1).
— (2001). 'Sick Sisters', *Sight & Sound*, 11, 7, pp. 28-9.
— (2004). *Porn Studies* (Durham and London: Duke University Press).
— (2008). *Screening Sex* (Durham and London: Duke University Press).
Williams, Linda Ruth (2005). 'The Girl Can't Help It', *Sight & Sound*. Available at http://old.bfi.org.uk/sightandsound/review/2297 (accessed 4 July 2013).
Williams, Melanie (2006). '9 Songs', *Film Quarterly*, 59, 3, pp. 59-63.
Wilson, Emma (2001). 'Deforming Femininity: Catherine Breillat's Romance', in Lucy Mazdon (ed.), *France on Film: Reflections on Popular French Cinema* (London: Wallflower Press), pp. 145-57.
Wood, Robin (2003). '*Irréversible*: Against and For', *Film International*, 5, 5, pp. 4-9.
Woody, Erik Z. and Henry Szechtman (2011). 'Adaptation to Potential Threat: The evolution, neurobiology and psychopathology of the security motivation system', *Neuroscience and Biobehavioral Reviews*, 36, pp. 1019-33.
Young, Elizabeth (1993). 'Georges Bataille', in Harriett Gilbert (ed.), *The Sexual Imagination* (London: Jonathan Cape), pp. 23-4.
Zillmann, Dolf (1998). *Connections Between Sexuality and Aggression*. 2nd edn (Mahwah, NJ: Lawrence Erlbaum).
Žižek, Slavoj (1991). *Looking Awry: An Introduction to Jacques Lacan Through Popular Culture* (Cambridge, MA: MIT Press).
— (1997a). *The Abyss of Freedom* (Michigan: University of Michigan Press).
— (1997b). *The Plague of Fantasies* (London: Verso).
— (2000a). *The Art of the Ridiculous Sublime: On David Lynch's Lost Highway* (Seattle, WA: University of Washington Press).
— (2000b). 'The Thing from Inner Space', in Renata Selecl (ed.), *Sexuation* (Durham, NC: Duke University Press), pp. 216-59.
Zuromskis, Catherine (2007). 'Prurient Pictures and Popular Film: The Crisis of Pornographic Representation', *The Velvet Light Trap*, 59 (Spring), pp. 4-14.

Index

À l'intérieur (2007) 72
Alfonso, Rita 106
Almendros, Nestor 13
Altman, Rick 156
Altman, Robert 101, 104, 105
   Nashville (1975) 101, 104
   Short Cuts (1993) 104, 105, 113
American Pie (1999) 208
Anderson, Rafaella 38
Andrews, David 6, 31
Aniston, Jennifer 104
Anthony, Andrew 150
Anzaldúa, Gloria 226
Ardrey, Robert 177
Argento, Asia 54-6, 59, 64
Art of the Ridiculous Sublime: On David Lynch's Lost Highway, The 74
Attou, Fu'ad Ait 57, 64
d'Aurevilly, Jules Amédée Barbey 5, 49, 51-7, 61, 64, 65, 67

Bach, Karen 38, 46
Barker, Raphael 96
Barthes, Roland 140
Bataille, Georges 15-17, 218
Bazin, Andre 19
Beamish, Lindsay 95
Beauty (2011) 1, 2
Behind the Green Door (1972) 32, 213
Belle de Jour (1967) 11
Bellucci, Monica 159, 161, 178
Best, Victoria and Martin Crowley 10

Beugnet, Martine 82
Birks, Chelsea 5
Black Rebel Motorcycle Club 139-42, 156
Blood of Beasts (1949) 18
Bonitzer, Pascal 217
Bosch, Hieronymus 182, 192
Bradshaw, Peter 149, 151
Brannan, Jay 95
Breillat, Catherine 49
   Anatomy of Hell (2004) 53, 60, 98
   Fat Girl (2001) 57, 60, 64, 68, 71
   Romance (1999) 23, 49, 52, 53
   Une vieille maîtresse (2007) 5, 49
Brennan, Justice William 26, 27
Brinkema, Eugenie 62, 178
British Board of Film Classification (BBFC) 10, 11, 22, 23, 96, 97, 137, 138, 144, 152
Buch-Hansen, Gitte 91
Buck-Morss, Susan 125
Butler, Judith 223, 228, 229

Calvaire (2004) 72
Canyon, Christy 32, 45, 46
Cassel, Vincent 161
Catherine of Siena 16
Chen, Joan 122
Chéreau, Patrice 64, 72, 142, 151
Chicago, Judy 222
Chiesa, Lorenzo 91

Cinematic Howling: Women's Films, Women's Film Theory 222
Clark, Larry 6, 7, 10
  Bully (2001) 205
  Ken Park (2002) 6, 195–215
  Kids (1995) 205–6, 210
  Perfect Childhood, The (1993) 203–5, 208
  Teenage Lust (1983) 203–5
  Tulsa (1971) 203–5
  Wassup Rockers (2006) 205
Coates, Norma 148
Cohen, Sara 141
Comstock Act, 17 Stat. 598 26
Coulthard, Lisa 5
Courbet, Gustave 32
Creed, Barbara 4, 6

Dafoe, Willem 87, 171
Dalle, Béatrice 76, 78
Dans ma peau (2002) 71, 72
Dargis, Manohla 112, 115
The Dark Knight XXX: A Porn Parody (2012) 36, 37
Darwin, Charles 180
  On the Origin of Species 180
Dawson, Paul 95
Days of Heaven (1978) 13
DeBoy, P. J. 95
Deen, James 32
Deep Throat (1972) 32–5
del Carmen, Mónica 218, 219, 225
Deleuze, Gilles 226, 227
Denis, Claire 74–80, 151
  Trouble Every Day (2001) 5, 71–3, 75–9, 92, 151
Depardieu, Gérard 9
Derrida, Jacques 16
Despentes, Virginie 5, 10, 25, 151, 178
  and Coralie Trinh Thi
  Baise-moi (2000) 5, 25, 71, 98, 151, 152, 178

Dewe Mathews, Tom 138
Ding, Shaoyan 124
Doherty, Tom 206
Ducey, Caroline 49, 52, 151
Dumont, Bruno 5, 71, 74, 81, 83–6
  Twentynine Palms (2003) 5, 71–3, 81–2, 85–7, 92, 93
Duncan, Taine 7
Dupontel, Albert 161
Dworkin, Andrea 28–30
Dyer, Richard 112, 126, 213, 214

Eagleton, Terry 125
Ebert, Roger 138
Ecstasy (1933) 169
Ecstasy of Saint Teresa 67
Emmanuelle (1974) 23, 33
The English Patient (1996) 145

Fast Times at Ridgemont High (1982) 208
Fox, Kerry 100, 142
Franju, Georges 18
Friends 104
Frith, Simon 156

Gainsbourg, Charlotte 87
Gallo, Vincent 75
George, Susan 171, 172
Golubeva, Katia 81
Grodal, Torben 3, 6, 7, 58

Handel, George Frideric 88, 91
Haneke, Michael 151
Hardman, Adam 96
Hegel, Georg Friedrich 228
Held, Jacob M. 4, 5
Hennigan, Adrian 137
Hines, Claire 6, 7
Hoffman, Dustin 172
Hollywood Production Code 169
hooks, bell 218

Horeck, Tanya and Tina Kendall 72
Houellebecq, Michel 146, 150, 152
Hsu, L. Hsuan 105, 113, 114
Husserl, Edmund 229

In the Realm of the Senses (1976) 189, 150
Intimacy (2001) 64

Jameson, Jenna 32
Jane, Jesse 32
Jara-Millo 161
Jeremy, Ron 32
The Jerry Springer Show 205, 209
Johnson, Beth 6
Juri, Carla 2

Keesey, Douglas 57
Konrad, Todd 138
Kristeva, Julia 16

L'Origine du Monde 32
LaBeouf, Shia 2
Lacan, Jacques 73, 79, 92, 221
Lachman, Ed 6, 195, 207
Lady Chatterley's Lover (1981) 33
The Last Metro (1981) 13
Leaving Las Vegas (1995) 218
Lee, Ang 119, 120, 128, 130, 135, 136
  Lust, Caution (2007) 5 119-35
Lee, Sook-Yin 95
Lehman, Peter 83, 86, 209
Leigh, Mike 101
Les amants (1958) 160, 169
Leung, Tony 120, 129
Lorna (1964) 160, 169, 171
Lotar, Eli 17
Lubecker, Nikolaj 82
Lynch David 73-5, 160, 171
  Wild at Heart (1990) 160, 169, 171

MacKinnon, Catherine 28-30
Magnolia (1999) 101

Malcolm, Derek 138
Malèna (2000) 159
Manet, Eduoard 55
Martyrs (2008) 72
McCarthy, Todd 95
McElroy, Wendy 26, 29-31
Mesquida, Roxanne 64, 68
Metz, Christian 4-6
Miller, Brendon 37
Miller v. California, 413 U.S. 15 (1973) 27
Minneapolis Civil Rights Ordinance, The 28
Mitchell, John Cameron 4, 98-100, 102, 104, 106-7, 112, 114-16
  Shortbus (2006) 4, 5, 95-117
Mulvey, Laura 39-41, 231

Nadine (1987) 13
Nahon, Philippe 163
Nair, Mira 222, 223
Nancy, Jean-Luc 78, 80
Needham, Gary 60
Never Mind the Bollocks: Here's the Sex Pistols 139
New Extremism 71-5, 77
New Pornographies: Explicit Sex in Recent French Fiction and Film, The 10
The Night Porter (1974) 11, 23, 190
Noé, Gaspar 6, 151, 159, 160, 164, 166, 172, 173-8
  Irreversible (2003) 6, 71, 72, 151, 152, 159, 161, 166, 169, 171, 173, 175, 177, 178
  Seul contre tous (1998) 163, 178
Nyman, Michael 144, 156

O'Brien, Kieran 100, 137, 150
O'Connor, Tom Austin 208
O'Day, Anita 101
O'Sullivan, Simon 125
Obscene Publications Act 96, 97

Olgier, Bulle 9
Oliver, Kelly 217, 218, 229
On-Scenity Network, The 97
Opening of Misty Beethoven, The (1976) 32, 33

Palme d'Or 51
Palmer, Tim 71, 72, 151, 152
Paou, Christophe 2
Papoulis, Tina 16
Paris Adult Theatre I v. Slayton, 413 U.S. 49 (1973) 27
Pax, Penny 37
Peckinpah, Sam 6, 160, 172, 173, 177, 178
　Straw Dogs (1971) 6, 160, 169, 171, 177
Phillips, Adam 147
Phipps, Keith 99
Pirates (2005) 32
Playboy 98
Pollock, Jackson 102, 107, 108
Pomeranz, Margaret 155
The Pornographer (2001) 97
pornography 2, 4, 5, 10, 11, 20, 25–40, 43, 46, 53, 60, 71, 74, 78, 84, 96, 98–100, 108, 109, 111, 137, 138, 143, 144, 148, 152–5, 195, 209, 210, 212, 213, 222
Prestia, Jo 159

Quandt, James 71, 72

Ramsay, Jamie 1
Ransone, James 207, 208
Redford, Robert 74
Reel to Real: Race, Sex, and Class at the Movies 218
Ridley, Jim 98, 99, 116, 117
Roth v. United States, 354 U.S. 476 (1957) 26, 27
Rowe, Michael 7, 218, 219, 221–4, 226–30

Leap Year (2010) 7, 218–25, 229, 230
The Royal Tenenbaums (2001) 105
Rylance, Mark 100, 142

S/M sex acts 11
Sánchez Parra, Gustavo 220
Savage Fury (1985) 45
Schneider, Steven Jay 208
Schroeder, Barbet 4, 9, 11–20, 22, 23
　Maîtresse (1976) 4, 9–11, 13–15, 18–23
Sconce, Jeffrey 99–102, 104, 115
Segal, Lynne 10
Seventh Circuit Court of Appeals 29
Sharma, Alpana 222–4
Sharrett, Christopher 91
Sheridan, Alan 221
Siffredi, Rocco 151
Smart Cinema 5, 99–102, 104, 115
Smith, Angela 146
Smith, Carrie 147
Sombre (1998) 71
Spider-Man XXX: A Porn Parody (2011) 36
Star Wars XXX: A Porn Parody (2012) 36
Stein, Elliott 13
Steinem, Gloria 30
Sterritt, David 159, 163, 168, 175–8
Stewart, Justice Potter 32
Stickles, Peter 95, 107
Stilley, Margo 137, 139, 150
The Story of O (1975) 11, 23
Stranger by the Lake (2013) 1, 2
Streep, Meryl 74

Taboo (1980) 32
Taubin, Amy 56 210
Theresa of Avila 16
Tolkien, J. R. R. 214
Travers, Peter 98

Vaughan, M. Hunter 227
Vessey, Tricia 75
von Trier, Lars 1, 2, 4, 6, 10, 71, 74, 98, 179, 181, 184, 186, 188–93
  Antichrist (2009) 4–6, 71–3, 87–9, 92, 93, 98, 181–6, 188, 190, 191, 193, 194
  Breaking the Waves (1996) 181, 184, 193
  Dancer in the Dark (2000) 189
  Dogville (2003) 181
  Nymphomaniac (2013) 1, 2

Waddell, Terrie 91
Walker, Deborah 5
Walter, Natasha 144
Wang, Leehom 123
Weatherill, Rob 17
Wei, Tang 120, 129

West, Mae 54
Wetlands (2013) 1, 2
Whitely, Sheila 140
Wicke, Peter 142
Williams, Linda 3, 4, 31, 39, 63, 107, 116, 144, 145, 149, 150, 153–6
  Screening Sex 3, 149
Williams, Linda Ruth 5, 144
Williams, Melanie 138, 144, 149
Wilson, Emma 49, 50
Winterbottom, Michael 6, 137–9, 142, 143, 146, 150, 152, 155, 156
  9 Songs (2004) 6, 100, 137–9, 142, 144, 148–52, 154–7
Wissak, David 81

Young, Elizabeth 16

Žižek, Slavoj 73–5, 77, 78, 90, 217